Contemporary British Identity
English Language, Migrants and Public Discourse

CHRISTINA JULIOS

WITHDRAWI

ASHGATE

Published by
Ashgate Publishing Limited
Gower House
Croft Road
Aldershot
Hampshire GU11 3HR
England

Ashgate Publishing Company
Suite 420
101 Cherry Street
Burlington, VT 05401-4405
USA

Ashgate website: http://www.ashgate.com

British Library Cataloguing in Publication Data
Julios, Christina
    Contemporary British identity : English language, migrants
    and public discourse. - (Studies in migration and diaspora)
    1. Minorities - Great Britain - Language 2. Immigrants -
    Cultural assimilation - Great Britain 3. National
    characteristics, British 4. Sociolinguistics - Great
    Britain 5. Great Britain - Ethnic relations
    I. Title
    305.8'00941

Library of Congress Cataloging-in-Publication Data
Julios, Christina.
  Contemporary British identity : English language, migrants, and public discourse / by
Christina Julios.
    p. cm. -- (Studies in migration and diaspora)
  Includes bibliographical references and index.
  ISBN-13: 978-0-7546-7158-9
  ISBN-10: 0-7546-7158-5 (hbk.)
 1. National characteristics, British--History--20th century. 2. Group identity--Great
Britain--History--20th century. 3. Multiculturalism--Great Britain. 4. Ethnology--Great
Britain--History--20th century. 5. Great Britain--Civilization--20th century. 6. British--
Ethnic identity. I. Title.

  DA118.J78 2008
  305.0941--dc22

2007031232

ISBN 978-0-7546-7158-9

Printed and bound in Great Britain by TJ International Ltd, Padstow, Cornwall.

Contents

Foreword

At the same time as this book was going into print (autumn 2007) Prime Minister Gordon Brown announced that he intended to introduce more stringent linguistic requirements for skilled non-EU migrants wishing to enter the United Kingdom. Not only was this a signal that Britain was tightening immigration control but, in addition, of the centrality of the English language in the construction of British identity and in the acquisition of British citizenship. As the sociologist Robin Cohen stated some years ago, 'British identity is modelled on an English speaking white Anglo-Saxon Protestant ideal'. In this book, Christina Julios sets out, as she says, 'to shed some light' on the construct of modern British identity, of which the English language is a central constituent. By so doing she reminds us that, in spite of its nation building role, English is not just the preserve of the United Kingdom and its citizens. The legacy of Empire and the global use of the world wide web has made it one of the world's dominant languages in countries which span the continents and range in size from the vastness of the world's most powerful nation – the United States of America – to one which has only recently gained a degree of self-government, Wales. And, by exploring the way in which different governments have addressed the policy dilemma of mono or bilingualism, she reminds us that the construction of national identity is a complex fusion of culture, demographics, economics, politics and, lastly but significantly, mythology.

However, what Julios provides in this book is much more than a linguistic study. It is an exploration of the evolution of a nation and the way in which patterns and volumes of immigration have impacted on policy-makers and their perception of the place of language in that process. By so doing we are confronted by the contemporary dichotomy of multicultural versus multiculturalism. The former, being a legitimate description of British society in the first decade of the twenty-first century; the latter, the subject of continuing and contrasting policy deliberations. Yet we should not ignore the historical perspective, for the issues of today are part of the nation's immigration heritage and the variations of policy approach which tinted the last half of the twentieth century. As the author demonstrates, over the past 50 years governments have vacillated between supporting multiculturalism and bilingualism or signalling the supremacy of majority language and opting for an integrative approach.

It is clear is that there is no easy resolution. Irrespective of government policies or public sentiment, the majority language absorbs incomer characteristics: for example, the linguistic legacy of earlier Huguenot and Eastern European immigrants is clearly manifest in the pages of the *Shorter Oxford English Dictionary*. Is it in this way, through subtle absorption – one which evokes little negative reaction, indeed often goes unnoticed – that diversity and difference can peacefully and successfully contribute to the ever-evolving British identity? A reading of this volume goes a considerable way towards answering that question.

Anne J. Kershen
Queen Mary, University of London
Autumn 2007

Preface and Acknowledgements

The co-operation of many people has made it possible for me to complete this book, and I am indebted to them all. First and foremost, I should like to thank Dr Anne Kershen for her encouragement and support throughout. From my early years as an undergraduate student at Queen Mary, University of London to the present day as Third Sector practitioner, Anne has always been a source of inspiration and guidance. She was the driving force behind this project and it is to her credit that it has come to fruition.

I am most grateful to Krishna Sarda, Chief Executive of the Ethnic Minority Foundation (EMF), for his interest in the book and invaluable assistance. I should like to thank Lord Amir Bhatia, EMF's Chairman, for his genorous support. Thanks as well to the helpful staff both at the British Library (BL) and the British Library of Political and Economic Sciences (BLPES) for advising on locating relevant materials. Special thanks to Donna Elliot and the Editorial team at Ashgate for their kindness and professionalism. Finally, my greatest debt is to my dearest Nicholas for his patience, advice and love always.

Dr Christina Julios
June 2007

PART 1
Language and Identity

Chapter 1

Introduction

The British Citizenship Question

Defining British identity has long been the subject of much debate. Questions such as what does it mean to be British? Which values does Britishness enshrine? Is the English language an integral part of our national identity? Invariably generate strong views and lengthy academic discussions; but few satisfying answers. Writing in 1912, Sargant already mused that 'every schoolboy might be expected to know what is meant by British Citizenship. But the fact is that the answer to this seemingly elementary question is far from easy' (Sargant 1912, 7).[1] Nearly ten decades later, we are still struggling to pin down this elusive concept. Delivering a recent Millennium Lecture in 10 Downing Street on 'Britishness in the 21st Century', Professor Linda Colley, a leading British historian at Princeton University, reflected on the difficulties Britain continues to face when trying to define who we are as a nation:

> Politicians and pundits shape existing national identities. They rarely by themselves invent or sustain them. And while it may be valuable to try to identify core national values, it is in practice difficult to do so in a way that commands broad assent, unless you descend to uttering platitudes. This is particularly the case in a multi-national, multi-cultural, infinitely diverse polity like Britain (Colley 1999).[2]

Professor Sir Bernard Crick, former Chair of the government's Advisory Board on Naturalisation and Integration (ABNI) and the acknowledged architect of British nationality and citizenship policy, has similarly wrestled with the complexity of this concept:

> Britishness is, to me, an overarching political and legal concept: it signifies allegiance to the laws, government and broad moral and political concepts – like tolerance and freedom of expression – that hold the United Kingdom together. But there is no overall British culture, only a sharing of cultures. Britishness is a strong concept, but narrower than many suppose. Do we not speak of and recognise at once English, Irish, Scottish and Welsh novels, plays and poems? And whatever Fifa [International Federation of Association Football] may think, we see nothing odd in fielding four national football teams. And we

---

1   Sargant, E.B. (1912), *British Citizenship: A Discussion Initiated* (London: Longmas, Green and Co.) (reprint of discussion on citizenship 'United Empire' by the *Journal of the Royal Colonial Institute*), November 1912.

2   Colley, L. (1999), 'Britishness in the 21st Century', Millennium Lectures Series, 10 Downing Street, 8 December 1999 <http://www.number-10.gov.uk/output/Page3049.asp> (accessed 19 June 2007).

recognise an immigrant literature in English, though even the authors sometimes find it hard to name (Crick 2004).[3]

Among the countless attempts made at articulating the idea of Britishness over time, perhaps the basic definition offered by the *Collins Concise Dictionary of the English Language* succeeds in encapsulating the core of our national identity. The three main meanings thus attributed to the term 'British' include it relating either to 'Britain', her 'inhabitants' or 'the English language' as spoken and written in Britain (*Collins Concise* 1990, 137).[4] Significantly, it is the latter characteristic that has nowadays come to be perceived as a particularly crucial indicator of Britishness. Unlike their predecessors, our elected representatives have indeed gone further than ever before in spelling out the essence of British citizenship as an English-speaking model (Home Office 2004).[5] In 2006, as part of his 'Our Nation's Future' lecture series, Prime Minister Blair firmly placed the English language at the very heart of Britain's national identity:

> We should share a common language. Equal opportunity for all groups requires that they be conversant in that common language. It is a matter both of cohesion and of justice that we should set the use of English as a condition of citizenship. In addition, for those who wish to take up residence permanently in the UK, we will include a requirement to pass an English test before such permanent residency is granted (Blair 2006).[6]

Despite such efforts to delineate our national identity contour, the essence of Britishness continues to elude us. The reason being, Richardson reminds us, the very multifaceted nature of this notion:

> It is not easy to identify the values, processes and customs which are distinctly British; not easy, having identifying them, to be in all respects proud, grateful and loyal; not easy to be recognised and accepted fully by other people who are British; not easy to establish and protect public policies and laws which recognise and rejoice that there are many different ways of being British, with sources of strength in different continents, religions, histories, languages (Richardson 1992, xi).[7]

Since the 1970s, Ward argues, there has been a sense of crisis about Britain's national identity, 'being British is no longer seen as innate, static and permanent. Indeed, it

---

3   Crick, B. 'All this Talk of Britain is so … English', *The Guardian*, 12 April 2004 <http://society.guardian.co.uk/raceequality/comment/0,,1190252,00.html> (accessed 17 June 2007).

4   *The Collins Concise Dictionary of the English Language* (1990), (London: Collins).

5   Home Office (2004), *Life in the United Kingdom: A Journey to Citizenship*, (London: TSO); Home Office (2002), *Secure Borders, Safe Haven: Integration with Diversity in Modern Britain*, (London: TSO).

6   Blair, T., PM (2006), Speech by Prime Minister Tony Blair 'The Duty to Integrate: Shared British Values', 8 December 2006 <http://www.pm.gov.uk/output/Page10563.asp> (accessed 4 January 2007).

7   Richardson, R. (1992), 'Preface' in T. Modood, *Not Easy Being British: Colour, Culture and Citizenship*, (Stoke-on-Trent: Runnymede Trust and Trentham Books).

is seen as under threat' (Ward 2004, 1).[8] Part of the problem lays in the very fluid nature of national identity, which far from remaining constant – as often presumed – it has been recognised to be periodically constructed and deconstructed. Britain's collective identity comprises multiple layers of meaning as well as overlapping and often conflicting loyalties, while forever evolving in a relentlessly changing world.

British citizens come in all shapes, ages, genders and colours; they belong to various social strata and economic backgrounds; speak hundreds of different languages and self-ascribe to a wide spectrum of cultural and political traditions, faiths and religious beliefs. Yet, although powerful the forces that pull these individuals apart may be, they all share an even stronger communal bond that brings them together as one British nation. British citizens, Parekh points out, are not only private individuals, but 'members of particular religions, ethnic and cultural communities, which are comparatively stable as well as open and fluid. Britain is both a community of citizens and a community of communities' (Runnymede Trust 2000, ix).[9]

The key to resolving the national identity question ultimately lays in reconciling the always overlapping and sometimes incompatible values each of us abides by in our public and private lives; as Prime Minister Blair explains 'People want to make sense of two emotions: our recognition of what we legitimately hold in common and what we legitimately hold distinct' (Blair 2006).[10] Given the unfathomable complexity of our needs as private individuals, profound personal and cultural differences, beliefs and lifestyles; it seems that the only viable way for us to coexist and function at a public level – and thus as fully-fledged members of British society – is by 'integrating at the point of shared, common unifying British values' (Blair 2006).[11] In the end, the Prime Minister reasons, it is not what characterises us as 'people', but what defines us as 'citizens' that makes it possible for our British civil society to operate. It follows that the public sphere must inevitable take priority over the private one: our rights and responsibilities as British citizens and the common values, traditions and language we share as such ought to supersede any others. The question then becomes one of defining what those inalienable British values are.

The abiding product of our country's past, so-called 'British values' reflect the principles upon which our nation's social order has been built over centuries. As Gordon Brown, Chancellor of the Exchequer, has put it:

> What has emerged from the long tidal flows of British history – from the 2,000 years of successive waves of invasion, immigration, assimilation and trading partnerships; from the uniquely rich, open and outward looking culture – is a distinctive set of values which influence British institutions (Brown 2006). [12]

---

8   Ward, P. (2004), *Britishness Since 1870* (London: Routledge).

9   Runymede Trust (2000), *The Future of Multiethnic Britain – Report of the Commission on the Future of Multiethnic Britain (The Parekh Report)* (London: the Runnymede Trust).

10   Blair, T., PM (2006), Speech by Prime Minister Tony Blair 'The Duty to Integrate'.

11   Blair, T., PM (2006), Speech by Prime Minister Tony Blair, 'The Duty to Integrate'.

12   Brown, G., MP (2006), Keynote speech by Gordon Brown, Chancellor of the Exchequer, to the Fabian Society 'The Future of Britishness', 14 January 2006 < http://www. fabian-society.org.uk/press_office/news_latest_all.asp?pressid=520> (accessed 15 June 2007).

Having endured the test of time, such values are now well-established moral, ethical and civil standards against which all others are measured, namely: a belief in universal Human Rights, equality and democracy, respect for Britain's heritage and traditions as well as compliance with the ever supreme rule of law. In the words of the Chancellor, these are 'the values of liberty, responsibility and fairness – shared civic values which are not only the ties that bind us, but also give us patriotic purpose as a nation and sense of direction and destiny' (Brown 2006). Under the banner of 'Citizenship Studies' such principles are now officially inculcated to school children across the country, as part of the National Curriculum. From an early age, pupils are taught a variety of civic disciplines such as Human Rights, diversity, government and democracy, the role of the media in society and globalisation (Curriculumonline 2002).[13] The aim is to encourage children to relate and engage with each other, their immediate community and British society at large; ultimately becoming informed active citizens, guided by sound principles of freedom, equality and social justice. By instilling in the younger generation the need to focus on our common values, rights and responsibilities as British citizens, as opposed to our personal differences as individuals, Citizenship Studies only reinforce the pre-eminence of the public sphere over the private one. After all, the Prime Minister reminds us, it is our public persona that makes British citizens out of otherwise nondescript individuals:

> when it comes to our essential values – belief in democracy, the rule of law, tolerance, equal treatment for all, respect for this country and its shared heritage – then that is where we come together, it is what we hold in common; it is what gives us the right to call ourselves British. At that point no distinctive culture or religion supercedes our duty to be part of an integrated United Kingdom (Blair 2006).[14]

Nowhere has this conflict between the private and the public realms, between our personal individual choices and our overriding collective responsibilities been more apparent that in the recent controversy over 'gay adoptions'. Faced with impending antidiscrimination legislation allowing same-sex couples to adopt children, the Catholic Church has argued for Christians' moral objections to such practice to take preference over the rule of law. In a letter to the Prime Minister, Cardinal Cormac Murphy-O'Connor, Archbishop of Westminster, stated the case for Catholic adoption agencies to be exempt from equality legislation, which at the time had not been yet enforced:

> The Catholic Church utterly condemns all forms of unjust discrimination, violence, harassment or abuse directed against people who are homosexual. Indeed the Church teaches that they must be accepted with respect, compassion and sensitivity. We, therefore, recognise many elements of recent legislation – including much in the Northern Ireland Regulations – that takes steps to ensure that no such discrimination takes place. What, then, is the problem? It is that to oblige our agencies in law to consider adoption applications from homosexual couples as potential adoptive parents would require them

---

13 Curriculumonline (2002), 'Citizenship – Overview' <http://www.curriculumonline. gov.uk/Subjects/Ci/Resource.htm?oid=2947&taxonid=&hid=1002081&navid=&b=1&vl=1 &SortPrice=3&page=&recreturned=> (accessed 13 February 2007).

14 Blair, T., PM (2006), Speech by Prime Minister Tony Blair, 'The Duty to Integrate'.

to act against the principles of Catholic teaching ... We believe it would be unreasonable, unnecessary and unjust discrimination against Catholics for the Government to insist that if they wish to continue to work with local authorities, Catholic adoption agencies must act against the teaching of the Church and their own consciences by being obliged in law to provide such a service (Murphy-O'Connor 2007).[15]

Echoing this sentiment, the Archbishop of Canterbury, Dr Rowan Williams, and the Archbishop of York, Most Rev John Sentamu, wrote in turn a joint letter to the Prime Minister warning him of the dangers of pressing ahead with gay rights legislation at the expense of people's religious convictions:

Many in the voluntary sector are dedicated to public service because of the dictates of their conscience. In legislating to protect and promote the rights of particular groups the government is faced with the delicate but important challenge of not thereby creating the conditions within which others feel their rights to have been ignored or sacrificed, or in which the dictates of personal conscience are put at risk. The rights of conscience cannot be made subject to legislation, however well meaning (Church of England 2007).[16]

In a similar vein, the Anglican Bishop of Durham, Dr Tom Wright, went as far as to say that the government's proposed legislation on same-sex adoptions 'completely fails to take into account the views and beliefs of all those involved ... the idea that new Labour can come up with a new morality which it forces on the Catholic Church after 2,000 years; I am sorry, this is amazing arrogance on the part of the government' (Gledhill 2007).[17]

Predictably, such strong views provoked a backlash from secularists, gay and lesbian lobby groups as well as likeminded Parliamentarians. The Lesbian and Gay Christian Movement (LGCM)'s Chief Executive, the Reverend Richard Kirker, for instance, called for Cardinal's Murphy O'Connor's pleas 'to be rejected, and for one, non-discriminatory set of rules to be approved which – as in Northern Ireland – assure equality to suitable gay or lesbian couples seeking to adopt children, where this is in the child's best interests' (Kirker 2007a).[18] As he put it:

There is no doubt that the Catholic hierarchy are themselves uncomfortable with their stance which is demonstrably inconsistent in that they are happy to allow single gay

---

15 Murphy-O'Connor, C., Cardinal (2007), 'Cardinal asks Prime Minister and Cabinet to exempt Adoption Agencies from Equalities Act', Diocese of Westminster, <http://www.rcdow.org.uk/cardinal/default.asp?library_ref=&content_ref=1179> (accessed 17 February 2007).

16 Church of England (2007), 'Letter from the Archbishops of Canterbury and York to the Prime Minister', The Church of England, 23 January 2007 <http://www.cofe.anglican.org/news/pr0107lb.html> (accessed 18 February 2007); 'Anglican Leaders Support Right to keep Ban on Gay Adoptions', *Independent Catholic News*, 24 January 2007 <http://www.indcatholicnews.com/rightadopt329.html> (accessed 18 February 2007).

17 Gledhill, R. 'Bishop scorns 'Arrogance''', *The Times*, 30 January 2007 <http://www.timesonline.co.uk/tol/news/uk/article1299064.ece> (accessed 13 February 2007).

18 Kirker, R., The Reverend (2007a), 'Equality (Sexual Orientation) Regulations Great Britain 2007 – Religious Adoption Agencies', Lesbian and Gay Christian Movement (LGCM) <http://www.lgcm.org.uk/> (accessed 17 February 2007).

people to adopt or an unmarried atheist heterosexual couple, while rejecting same-sex families bringing up their children in the Catholic faith. But it is understood they have been pushed to this point by Rome (Kirker 2007b).[19]

Several Cabinet Ministers publicly expressed their rejection of any exemptions under the law; with Harriet Harman, Solicitor General, having gone on record as saying 'We will stay true to our commitment in tackling sexual discrimination in terms of sexual orientation ... You can either be against discrimination or you can allow for it. You can't be a little bit against discrimination' (Bright and Kampfner 2007).[20]

In the event, the pleas of the Catholic Church's leadership failed to sway the government's position, as media headlines such as 'Cabinet rejects Exemption on Gay Adoptions', 'Blair caves in over Adoption Laws' and 'Catholic Agencies given Deadline to comply on Same-sex Adoptions' reflect (Woodward and Carrell 2007; Chapman 2007; Wintour *et al.* 2007).[21] By rejecting the argument that rights of conscience cannot be made subject to legislation, the government not only reasserted the fundamental right to equal treatment for all under British law; but resolved the conflict between the public and the private spheres of our lives in favour of the former. Despite such an apparent firm stand on the matter, divisions in the Cabinet at the time and a polarised public opinion only served to highlight the difficulties involved in reconciling the personal beliefs of private individuals and the shared common values they must abide by as fully-fledged members of British society (Porter 2007; Elliot 2007; Byers 2007; Hurst 2007; Hall 2007).[22] Debate over the British citizenship question is certainly set to continue.

---

19 Kirker, R., The Reverend (2007b), LGCM Press Release 'Archbishops comment on Gay Adoption Debate', Lesbian and Gay Christian Movement (LGCM) <http://www.lgcm. org.uk/> (accessed 17 February 2007).

20 Bright, M. and J. Kampfner 'Interview – Harriet Harman: the Constitutional Affairs Minister warns Colleagues that They can't be "A Little Bit against Discrimination"', *New Statesman*, 29 January 2007 <http://www.newstatesman.com/200701290028> (accessed 18 February 2007).

21 Woodward, W. and S. Carrell 'Cabinet rejects Exceptions on Gay Adoptions', *The Guardian*, 25 January 2007 <http://www.guardian.co.uk/frontpage/story/0,,1998016,00.html> (accessed 15 February 2007); Chapman, J. 'Blair caves in over Adoption Laws', *Daily Mail*, 25 January 2007 <http://www.dailymail.co.uk/pages/live/articles/news/news.html?in_article_ id=431248&in_page_id=1770> (accessed 15 February 2007); Wintour, P., W. Woodward and S. Bates 'Catholic Agencies given Deadline to comply on Same-sex Adoptions', *The Guardian*, 30 January 2007 <http://www.guardian.co.uk/frontpage/story/0,,2001834,00. html>(accessed 15 February 2007).

22 Porter, A. 'Labour Gay Adoption Row', *The Sun*, 25 January 2007 <http://www. thesun.co.uk/article/0,,2-2007040156,00.html> (accessed 15 February 2007); Elliot, F. 'Gay Adoption Row: Kelly puts Faith in Catholic Opt-out', *The Independent*, 28 January 2007 <http://news.independent.co.uk/uk/politics/article2192968.ece> (accessed 15 February 2007); Byers, D. 'Ministers defy Downing Street in Gay Adoption Row', *The Times*, 25 January 2007 <http://www.timesonline.co.uk/tol/newspapers/sunday_times/britain/article1296042.ece> (accessed 15 February 2007); Hurst, G. ' Catholics get Time to adapt to Gay Rights', *The Times*, 25 January 2007 <http://www.timesonline.co.uk/tol/newspapers/sunday_times/britain/ article1295991.ece> (accessed 18 February 2007); Hall, M. 'Lame Duck Blair caves in on

During the past hundred years, British citizens' shared sense of identity has been shaped and reshaped by a combination of geo-political developments, demographic and migration trends, racial and cultural conflict and the advent of English language globalisation. Ascertaining what modern British identity amounts to, however, continues to yield plentiful searching questions, but few discernable answers. By tracing the evolution of our national identity over time, this book aims to shed some light on such an intricate and fascinating conundrum.

Perceptions of Identity

Whether private or public, minority ethnic or mainstream, monolingual or multilingual, the notion of identity is essentially defined as 'self-ascription' to a particular group.[23] In other words, our sense of identity ultimately depends on the meanings attached to it by us and those around us. Perceptions are indeed a fundamental factor in determining how individuals view themselves, how, in turn, they view others, and how others eventually look upon them. A second-generation English-speaking Bangladeshi child brought up in the East End of London, for example, may see themselves as being wholly British; however it is unlikely that the rest of the indigenous white British population may regard them as being 'one of them'. Similarly, a Mexican-American child born and raised in the United States, may consider themselves to be a fully-fledged US citizen; however they will hardly be regarded in the same fashion by members of the dominant white North American Anglo-Saxon society. In unravelling the complexities of British identity, attention must be paid to the various interpretations vested upon it as well as the social, cultural and political drivers behind such classifications. Stephens reminds us that although the language used to articulate identity is in itself 'neutral', the many ways in which it may be deployed carry social as well as political implications.[24]

It is through different 'narratives' that individual and national identities can be said to be constructed and re-constructed in relation to each other.[25] In the course of Britain's history, different public discourses of 'Britishness' have played an important role in shaping both a private citizen's sense of themselves and their wider British collective identity. Key socio-political developments have often heightened such perceptions. Post-War historians, for instance, have come to see the Second World War as a defining moment in the development of British identity. Faced with

---

Gay Adoptions', *Sunday Express*, 25 January 2007 <http://express.lineone.net/news_detail. html?sku=1106> (accessed 18 February 2007).

23 Coleman, D. and J. Salt (eds) (1996), *Ethnicity in the Census 1991: Demographic Characteristics of the Ethnic Minority Populations*, Office of Population Censuses and Surveys (OPCS), vol. 1, (London: HMSO), 9.

24 Stephens, T.M. (1989), 'The Language of Ethnicity and Self-identity in American Spanish and Brazilian Portuguese', *Ethnic and Racial Studies,* (London: Routledge), 138.

25 Baxendale, J. (1998), 'Mentioning the War: the Second War and Post-war National Identity', in U. Borgman, *From Empire to Multicultural Society: Cultural and Institutional Changes in Britain*, Proceedings of the Ninth British Cultural Studies Conference, (Würzburg: WVT Wissenschaftlicher Verlag Trier), 9.

arguably the greatest threat of invasion in the country's modern history, Churchill's government knew it had to foster 'a robust popular sense of Britishness' in order to maintain public morale.[26] It did so by reaffirming a consensual shared identity through the evocation of a 'timeless national history, in language which referred back to Shakespeare, the authorised version of the Bible and the Book of Common Prayer'.[27] At the time, the British nation became refocused not just as a historic, but linguistic community. As Baxendale has put it, this was a time 'when at least we knew who we were'.[28] Wartime mythology has subsequently being used to influence changing views of British national identity as well as strengthening our collective bond during challenging times. It has also been deployed to reassert the *status quo* enjoyed by the country's dominant white citizenry.

The accelerated transformation of Britain into a multiethnic society, in the second half of the twentieth century, has seen the intensification of this trend; with mass media's nationalistic prose accompanying derogative depictions of minority ethnic communities and faith groups. Pandering to deep-seated fears of cultural and linguistic fragmentation, unfavourable images of non-white British citizens have strengthened the already growing social divide between 'us' – the UK's white indigenous population – and 'them' – the non-white newcomers. Negative images, stereotypical and pejorative public representations of minority ethnic groups are known to contribute to a sense of alienation and low self-esteem among members of these communities. Zentella, for example, has long maintained that the 'racial' manner in which the dominant English-speaking white North American society defines minority ethnic communities determines to a large extent the way in which these groups come to see themselves. Accordingly, many US-Puerto Ricans' experiences of rejection and social exclusion by mainstream North American society often find them embracing their 'ethnic' roots. As a result, they choose to associate themselves with a somehow distant 'Puerto Rican' tradition, as opposed to their adopted 'North American' culture, which forms an integral part of their everyday lives.[29]

Unedifying treatment by the British media of some of the country's minority ethnic communities has time and again contributed to marginalise these vulnerable groups further. During the 1980s, for example, as urban riots erupted in various towns and cities across England, the Afro-Caribbean community was singled out as the underlying source of conflict. Coverage of the so-called 'race riots' was characterised by sensationalist headlines such as 'Violence on England's Streets', 'Liverpool: the Threat of Disaster' and 'Brixton could become like a Harlem, Police Chief says', which undoubtedly played a part in exacerbating already strained community

---

26 Weight, R. (2002), *Patriots: National Identity in Britain 1940–2000*, (London: Macmillan), 23.

27 Baxendale, J. (1998), 'Mentioning the War', 12.

28 Baxendale, J. (1998), 'Mentioning the War', 10.

29 Zentella, A.C. (1997), *Growing Up Bilingual: Puerto Rican Children in New York City,* (New York: Blackwell Publishers).

relations.[30] At the time, newspaper editors' reactions to the disturbances were accompanied by similarly provocative pronouncements from government officials and public figures. In the aftermath of the first wave of disturbances, for instance, Douglas Hurd, Home Secretary, went as far to warn of 'young black tinder' which could be sparked into further rioting.[31] Over two decades later, the public spotlight turned to the refugee and asylum-seeking community. In 2002, a well-publicised wave of asylum seekers crossing the Channel Tunnel from a French refugee camp based near Calais triggered a media frenzy with nationalistic overtones. At the time, broadcast comments by David Blunkett, Home Secretary, regarding refugee children 'swamping' Britain's schools were universally criticised for stigmatising this exiled community.[32] In 2006, it was the British Muslim community which came under scrutiny, after the publication of a series of controversial Dutch cartoons depicting the Prophet Muhammad sparked international protests by Muslim groups. Already heightened Islamophobic sentiment following the New York City's World Trade Centre atrocities in 2001, and the bombings in London by home-grown Islamic terrorists four years later was compounded by the Muslim world's virulent reaction to the cartoons. Press coverage often portrayed the so-called 'cartoon row' as a 'clash of civilisations' and a conflict between the right to 'freedom of expression' on the one hand, and 'religious intolerance' on the other.[33]

Most recently, BBC's Channel Four became embroiled in an extraordinary controversy over the airing of its reality television show Celebrity Big Brother's latest series. On this occasion, the seemingly racist bullying of an Indian contestant at the hands of three white British participants was allowed to go unchecked. The broadcasting, which was overwhelmingly deemed offensive and damaging to Britain's credentials as a tolerant, multicultural society, attracted an unprecedented over 44,500 complaints from the public and triggered an investigation from the broadcasting regulator, Ofcom. Despite a protracted attempt by Channel Four's Chief

---

30 'Violence on England's Streets', *The Times*, 6 July 1981, 13; Hodge, L. 'Brixton could become like Harlem, Police Chief says', *The Times*, 19 June 1981, 3; Charters, J. 'Liverpool: the Threat of Disaster', *The Times*, 6 July 1981, 2; Waller, P. 'Liverpool: Why the Clue to Violence is Economic not Racial', *The Times*, 7 July 1981, 12.

31 Bevins, A. 'Warning by Hurd of 'Black Tinder'', *The Times*, 19 October 1985, 23.

32 'Row erupts over Blunkett's 'swamped' Comment', *The Guardian,* 24 April 2002 <http://www.politics.guardian.co.uk/homeaffairs/stry/0,11026,689919,00.html> (accessed 9 June 2002).

33 Williams, D. and M. Born 'Islam Cartoons spark Worldwide Protests', *Daily Mail*, 3 February 2006 <http://www.dailymail.co.uk/pages/live/articles/news/news.html?in_article_id=375997&in_page_id=1770> (accessed 31 March 2006); Moore, M. 'Muslims outraged by new Cartoon of Prophet in Hell', *The Daily Telegraph*, 17 April 2006 <http://www.telegraph.co.uk/news/main.jhtml?xml=/news/2006/04/17/wcart17.xml> (accessed 17 April 2006); McVeigh, K. 'BNP publishes Danish Cartoon', *Times Online*, 23 February 2006 <http://www.timesonline.co.uk/article/0,,2-2053659.html> (accessed 31 March 2006); Asthana, A. 'Muslims fly Flag for Peaceful Protest against Cartoons', *The Observer,* 12 February 2006 <http://observer.guardian.co.uk/uk_news/story/0,,1708001,00.html> (accessed 31 March 2006); Hardy, R. 'Healing the Cartoon Row Wounds', *BBC* News, 11 May 2006 <http://news.bbc.co.uk/2/hi/europe/4759187.stm> (accessed 11 May 2006).

Executive to justify the programme's actions; unrelenting national and international headlines saw the programme discussed in Parliament, with prominent public figures such as the Prime Minister, the Chancellor of the Exchequer (who coincidentally was on an official visit to India at the time), the Leader of the Opposition, the London Mayor, the Chair of the Commission for Equality and Human Rights (CEHR) and even the former Chair of Channel Four openly acknowledging the damage caused by the broadcasting (Graef 2007; Hastings and Harper 2007; Robinson and Hinsliff 2007; Verkaik et al. 2007; BBC News 2007).[34] In the event, the expulsion, by public vote, of the 'Big Brother bigots' from the programme and the eventual winning of the competition by Shilpa Shetty, the Indian contestant, was overwhelmingly applauded as a reflection of modern British society's tolerant attitudes to diversity and multiculturalism (Wilson and Davies 2007; Phillips 2007; Kent 2007; Brown and Verkaik 2007; Hattersley 2007).[35] While the controversy served to highlight underlying deep-seated racist attitudes within our midst, it can also be said to have illustrated public rejection of such prejudices. On the whole, however, it provided the latest example in a long list of media-fuelled stereotypical depictions of minority ethnic individuals and marginalised groups in Britain.

Dual and Virtual Identities

Among members of the British nation, it is perhaps the second-generation UK-born immigrants that best exemplify the complexities of constructing a modern British identity. Tensions created by the inherently multiethnic nature of British society today pose fundamental challenges to these second generation migrant-citizens, who must affirm their unique dual identity within an English-speaking environment. For young

---

34 Graef, R. 'A Vote of No Confidence', *The Guardian*, 23 January 2007 <http://www. guardian.co.uk/comment/story/0,,1996482,00.html> (accessed 1 March 2007); Hastings, C. and T. Harper 'Axe Big Brother says Ex-Channel 4 Boss', *Telegraph*, 21 January 2007 <http://www.telegraph.co.uk/news/main.jhtml?xml=/news/2007/01/21/nbb21.xml> (accessed 1 March 2007); Robinson, J. and G. Hinsliff 'C4 Boss faces Big Brother Backlash', *The Observer*, 21 January 2007 <http://www.guardian.co.uk/race/story/0,,1995420,00.html> (accessed 1 March 2007); Verkaik, R., B. Russell and J. Huggler 'Racism gets a Reality Check', *The Independent*, 18 January 2007 <http://news.independent.co.uk/media/article2162868.ece> (accessed 1 March 2007); BBC News (2007), 'Brown seeks to calm TV show row' <http:// news.bbc.co.uk/1/hi/uk_politics/6273803.stm> (accessed 1 March 2007).

35 Wilson, G. and C. Davies 'CBB's Goody evicted after Public Anger', *Telegraph*, 21 January 2007 <http://www.telegraph.co.uk/news/main.jhtml?xml=/news/2007/01/20/ nbbro20.xml> (accessed 1 March 2007); Phillips, T. 'Hooray for Shilpa, Hooray for Britain, Hooray for the Sun', Commission for Equality and Human Rights (CEHR), 30 January 2007 <http://www.cehr.org.uk/content/stories/sun20070130.rhtm> (accessed 1 March 2007); Kent, M. 'Shilpa wins the CBB Crown', *The Sun*, 28 January 2007 <http://www.thesun.co.uk/ article/0,,11049-2007040583,00.html> (accessed 1 March 2007); Brown, J. and R. Verkaik 'Shilpa tours the Media with Message of Peace, Love and Self-promotion', *The Independent*, 2 February 2007 <http://news.independent.co.uk/media/article2208276.ece> (accessed 1 March 2007); Hattersley, G. 'Interview – You have to be Hard to be a Princess', *The Sunday Times*, 18 February 2007 <http://entertainment.timesonline.co.uk/tol/arts_and_entertainment/ film/bollywood/article1400117.ece> (accessed 1 March 2007).

members of minority ethnic groups, such struggles begin earlier in life. At home, their parents will typically display a strong sense of ethnic identity, including use of mother-tongue and often strict observance of their cultural traditions and religious practices – frequently advocating gender differentials. At school, minority ethnic children will instead be taught in the English language, immersed in the Anglo-Saxon culture and expected to conform to the Euro-centric, liberal values of British society. Faced with fundamental conflicts between home and school, their community's non-western outlook and that of the wider western society, their own expectations and those of their parents; these youngsters' attitudes towards their dual identity invariably differ from that of their forebears. Consider, for instance, the Chinese child who discovers that the language of their parents is neither understood nor appreciated by their fellow classmates; or the Indian youngster who is constantly bombarded by mainstream television, advertising and mass media with the message that all successful, powerful and beautiful people are white. From these children's perspectives, becoming adults in a society that devalues their minority status increasingly makes them question who they are and who they would like to be (Zentella 1997). Second generation UK-born immigrants thus display inherently contradictory attitudes towards language and identity. On the one hand, few seem happy to see their mother tongues disappear, because they consider them an important part of their cultural heritage. On the other hand, achieving English language proficiency is paramount to them, for most of these individuals aspire to succeed in their adopted English-dominant nation. As time passes, the gap between their cultural expectations and the realisation of such wants invariably widens. Eventually, hardly any of them will realistically be able to hand down their native language skills to their offspring. By being brought up in a bicultural and bilingual environment, second generation UK-born immigrants are torn apart between simultaneous but incompatible desires, realities and drives.

While the process of cultural and linguistic assimilation into mainstream society is estimated to take as little as a single generation, the identity of successive cohorts of home-grown immigrants is in no way devoid of all ethnic traits (Zentella 1997). On the contrary, many of these individuals manage to retain a virtual, if not actual, connection with their increasingly distant roots. By way of introspection, these full-fledged citizens go on to develop a unique individual self-image, which rather than relying on tangible characteristics – such as phenotype, language and religion – is instead based on a very personal, and somewhat idealised, belief about one's character. The Puerto Rican community in Hawaii provides a case in point (Watson-Gegeo 1994, 101–20). Established at the turn of the twentieth century, this population group firmly considers itself to be Puerto Rican. They have however maintained an existence entirely detached from Puerto Rico. In their present form, Puerto Rican-Hawaiians neither speak Spanish nor consume Puerto Rican goods, and their customs and habits are not those of mainland Puerto Ricans. Puerto Rican-Hawaiians' social networks do not resemble those of their forebears either, for they have intermarried with Hawaiians, Filipinos and the Japanese. Even the music they listen to cannot strictly be described as Latino. How can these people then claim to be Puerto Ricans? How can they maintain a Puerto Rican identity? And more importantly, what does it mean to them? Puerto Rican-Hawaiians' self-image can be said to simply reflect an external manifestation of their own personalised views of themselves. In other words, it does not matter that Puerto Rican-Hawaiians do not look, speak or behave like 'genuine' Puerto Ricans; they *feel* Puerto Ricans, and therefore they *are* Puerto Ricans. Within this context, the question of British identity can be ultimately said to relate to a 'state of mind', mainly determined by deeply personal and abstract considerations rather than tangible external factors. I *consider* myself to be British; ergo I *am* British.

English Language Colonisation, De-colonisation and Globalisation

Linguistic heritage has long been regarded a key feature of ethnicity as well as a central element of nationhood (Glazer 1997; Smith 1991; Yinger 1994). In exploring the nature of British national identity, we are therefore compelled to consider its relationship with the English language.

Demographic and linguistic estimates suggest that the English language is spoken by nearly a quarter of the world's population (UNESCO 1995; *Encyclopedia Britannica 1996*; Grimes 1992). Whether completely fluent or merely competent, being native speakers or having acquired the necessary linguistic knowledge, between 1.2 billion and 1.5 billion people regularly communicate in English. Of the approximately 5,000 tongues spoken worldwide, no other language can match this growth. Even, Chinese – arguably the language spoken by more speakers than any other – is known only to some 1.1 billion people; but it lacks the universality of English as is spoken by few individuals not of Chinese origin (Katzner 2002, 205). The spectacular advance of English across the face of the globe, Katzner notes, is indeed 'a phenomenon without parallel' in the history of humanity (Katzner 2002, 39).

The present dominance of the English language is primarily the result of two factors. On the one hand, the expansionism of the British Empire towards the end of the nineteenth century effectively put this language on the international map, bringing English into the United States, Canada, Australia and New Zealand, the Caribbean, South East Asia, the South Pacific and Colonial Africa.[36] On the other hand, the emergence of the United States as the leading economic and political power of the twentieth century further catapulted the English language into a global dimension. While the end of the Cold War and the collapse of Communism consolidated the cultural predominance of the United States; subsequent geopolitical developments, together with the unprecedented technological explosion of the US-led Internet, have ultimately cemented the now unchallenged supremacy of English as 'the' universal language. With 70 per cent of all English mother-tongue speakers worldwide (excluding Creole varieties) living on US territory, North Americans are undoubtedly afforded a controlling power over the way the English language is universally developed (Crystal 1997, 53).

The transformation of English into a global linguistic phenomenon has contributed to heighten the value attached to this tongue as a key feature of British national

---

36 Note: the term 'Colonial Africa' refers to the following states: South Africa, Sierra Leone, Ghana, Gambia, Nigeria, Cameroon, Liberia, Kenya, Tanzania, Uganda, Malawi, Zambia and Zimbabwe.

identity. It has also ensured that when in contact with other languages, English invariably acquires a premium value. This reality is reflected in the overwhelming emphasis on 'English language teaching' that the educational policies of successive UK governments have consistently advocated over time.

The Educational Needs of Non-English-speaking Immigrants

The increasingly large presence of ethnic linguistic minorities in Britain presents the country with the challenge of incorporating these groups into mainstream society, while catering for their socio-cultural and linguistic needs. In doing so, policy-makers are faced with the difficult task of designing and implementing second language programmes, which adequately respond to the complex educational requirements of Britain's sizeable non-English-speaking school population.

The second half of the twentieth century saw unprecedented mass influxes of non-English-speaking immigrants of non-European descent into UK territory. While in 1948, one of the first cohorts of West Indians sailed into Britain on board of the celebrated Empire Windrush; mass entries of natives from New Commonwealth countries during the 1960s and 1970s swiftly followed. Throughout the 1990s, New Commonwealth migration was increasingly accompanied by a steady growth in refugee and asylum-seeking arrivals, mostly fleeing war-torn countries in Africa, South East Asia as well as the Middle and Far East regions. The early years of the twentieth first century have seen a return to European migration in the shape of Eastern European 'migrant workers' from the new European Union Accession States, notably Poland, Hungary, the Czech Republic, Latvia, Estonia, Lithuania, Slovakia and Slovenia as well as Cyprus and Malta.

Such population movements into the UK have resulted in the development of large enclaves of minority ethnic linguistic settlements in certain urban and metropolitan areas across the country. London, for instance, has become home to the largest concentration of Sylheti-speaking Bangladeshis in the United Kingdom and anywhere outside Bangladesh; while cities such as Leicester and Birmingham are set to be become 'minority majority cities' over the next two decades. Lack of English proficiency coupled with an array of socio-economic factors such as poverty, illiteracy and racism, have given way to successive generations of UK-born migrant children experiencing high rates of academic underachievement and school dropouts. Exploring how British society has dealt – and continues to deal – with such a challenge will afford us an insight into the values underlying our national identity as well as its relationship with the English language.

Migrants and the Public Discourse

Over the past hundred years, the construction of British identity has been shaped by a variety of public narratives that have come to articulate the essence of Britain's collective through different perspectives.

1900s–1950s: A Discourse of Laissez-Faire

During the period of 1900s to 1950s, a predominantly white Anglo-Saxon British society was dominated by a discourse of *laissez-faire* that sought the preservation of the *status quo*. In demographic terms, Britain remained a somehow homogenous white Christian nation throughout this time, with an immigrant population largely featuring communities of European stock. Given that nationalistic sentiment was running high after the Second World War and the subsequent reconstruction years, the dominant English language, Anglo-Saxon traditions and the state institutions of monarchy, Parliament and the Church of England were deemed to convey the very essence of Britishness. Migrants coming into the UK were simply expected to learn the English language and become absorbed within the country's British culture. As Lord Tebbit, former Conservative Party Chairman, has pointed out, 'Nobody used to talk about Britishness in the 1940s and 1950s, it is a phenomenon of large numbers of non-British people coming into the country' (BBC News 2002).[37] This was arguably the case and perhaps not surprising given the makeup of the country's population at the time. It was not until the late 1940s that non-white post-war migration to Britain began.

On 22 June 1948, the troop ship SS Empire Windrush arrived at Tilbury Dock in England carrying 492 passengers, mostly ex-servicemen from the Caribbean who have fought for Britain during the Second World War. This seemingly innocuous incident marked a turning point in the nation's journey towards diversity and multiculturalism; for these newcomers comprised one of the first cohorts of coloured New Commonwealth immigrants to enter Britain following the conflict. They set a historic precedent that, over the years, was to be replicated by other Diaspora communities in far greater numbers. At the time of their arrival, hostile reaction to their presence saw the government preside over a series of discriminatory legislative measures aimed at curbing their entry, while progressively eroding their rights of abode. Those who were allowed to settle in Britain were largely expected to learn the English language, adapt to the country's customs and become part of British society's everyday life. Civic society nevertheless proved largely unable to provide them with adequate educational and social support. As a result, their educational and linguistic needs went for the most part unchecked.

1960s–1980s: A Discourse of Multiculturalism

Following the arrival of the first West Indian cohorts into Britain, significant numbers of South East Asians, Africans and peoples originating from New Commonwealth countries were to follow in quick succession. During the ensuing two decades, as the numbers of newcomers swelled and minority ethnic settlements within inner-city conurbations grew, attention inevitably focused on these migrant communities. One of the earliest signs of their impact on the host society was the unavoidable strain put on Britain's welfare system; whether housing, employment, health or education

---

37 BBC News (2002), 'What is Britishness Anyway?' <http://news.bbc.co.uk/1/hi/uk_politics/1701843.stm> (accessed 17 June 2007).

services, the continuous influx of immigrant families saw them competing with their fellow British counterparts for the allocation of scarce resources. Feelings of resentment and hostility towards these 'foreigners' were, as a result, never far from the surface. This was the time when Enoch Powell, Conservative Shadow Defence Spokesman, delivered his controversial 'rivers of blood' speech, in which he used apocalyptic language to warn a Conservative Association meeting in Birmingham of the potential consequences of continuous immigration to Britain from New Commonwealth countries. Powell said that Britain would be mad to allow in 50,000 dependants of immigrants every year, and compared enacting the *Race Relations Bill* – at the time going through Parliament – to 'throwing a match on to gunpowder'(BBC News 2007).[38] Successive government's attempts to appease public opinion saw them simultaneously enacting legislation aimed at tightening border controls, while at the same time implementing measures to promote good community relations and equal opportunities at home. Such muddled approach to diversity only betrayed their continuing struggle to adequately deal with it.

Against this background, a particularly problematic by-product of immigration was the enrolment of unprecedented numbers of non-English-speaking children in British schools. As migration continued to gather pace, Local Education Authorities across the country progressively struggled to cope with their ever growing non-English-speaking school populations. By the mid-1960s, the situation had already become serious enough for it to be discussed in Parliament. Recognising that the problem could no longer be ignored, the government went on to provide a remedy of sorts by enacting the *Local Government Act 1966*. This piece of legislation afforded Local Education Authorities with financial assistance to cover the extra costs incurred in catering for the needs of their non-English-speaking pupils. The significance of the so-called 'Section 11 grant' laid in it signalling a public attitudinal change regarding Britain's minority ethnic communities. Although still largely perceived as placing a 'burden' on the country's labour market, welfare and educational system, migrants were also viewed as part of the wider British society. Their needs were consequently no longer being overlooked.

During the 1970s, as knowledge of these communities developed, public awareness of their circumstances slowly surfaced. A growing body of scholarly and research work contributed to highlight the extent of the adverse circumstances affecting members of these groups including, poverty, unemployment as well as lack of education and English language skills. As time went by, British society's enhanced understanding and acceptance of migrants was aided by further parliamentary and legislative work. This process culminated with the landmark *Race Relations Act 1976*, which enshrined into law the principle of protection against discrimination, while at the same time promoting equality of opportunity.

Despite progress, the challenges of living with diversity in an increasingly multiethnic and multicultural British society that featured marked wealth differentials along socio-economic and ethnic lines, led to sporadic tensions at the grassroots

---

38 BBC News (2007), '1968: Powell slates Immigration Policy', On This Day' – 20 April 1968 <http://news.bbc.co.uk/onthisday/hi/dates/stories/april/20/newsid_2489000/2489357.stm> (accessed 19 June 2007).

level. In the early and mid-1980s however, a spate of extraordinary race-related urban disturbances across English towns and cities focused the public mind firmly on the minority ethnic question. These unexpected 'race riots' mostly involved confrontations between the Police and groups of disaffected Afro-Caribbean youth. The virulent outbreak of the disturbances and the extent of the resulting destruction shocked the nation and prompted swift action from government. In the aftermath of the riots, the *Scarman Report* into the events identified a combination of adverse socio-economic conditions disproportionally affecting certain minority ethnic groups as the root of the problem. A cocktail of poverty, unemployment and isolation, the report concluded, was conducive to the flaring up of angry, violent community reactions. In order to prevent the latter from happening again, further legislative measures as well as social and educational policy initiatives were to follow; broadly aimed at tackling inequality, restoring good community relations as well as nurturing social harmony. A belief in the intrinsic value of diversity as a core component of Britain's social makeup was to underline this package of measures. One of such interventions was the setting up of a Committee of Inquiry into the Education of Children from Minority Ethnic Groups. The resulting *Education for All* report, so-called *Swann Report* after its chairman, provided a comprehensive analysis of the multiplicity of factors influencing non-English-speaking children's academic performance within a diverse British society as well as the measures needed to address barriers to progress. Here, cultural and linguistic diversity were seen as positive assets to be celebrated by civic society and nurtured by the country's school system; with multiculturalism being understood as an intrinsic part of the British nation. At the time, the report was hailed as 'a landmark in pluralism'.

Over three decades after the first cohorts of Caribbean migrants had sailed on to British shores, the country's demographic and socio-cultural landscape had changed beyond recognition. Not only had its collective understanding of and approach to diversity been altered in fundamental ways; public perceptions of our now diverse nation and multi-layered national identity had also undergone a startling metamorphosis. As Britain approached the new millennium, her public discourse's transition from *laissez-faireism* to multiculturalism was all but complete.

1990s–2000s: A Discourse of Integration

In the late 1990s, a rise in the country's overseas illegal immigrant and refugee intake together with persistent social inequalities and perceived fears of cultural and linguistic fragmentation resulted in increased unease about the state of multiculturalism in Britain. Over three decades of equality and diversity legislation and social policy initiatives had not produced a tolerant British nation that provides opportunity for all. On the contrary, the considerable body of evidence now available seemed to suggest that we lived in the midst of a deeply unequal society, where a minority ethnic underclass remained firmly stranded at the margins. Where did we go wrong? Questions indeed started to be asked regarding the effectiveness and desirability of our particular brand of multiculturalism, the government's approach to diversity and ultimately the kind of society we would like to live in.

At the turn of the twentieth first century, this emerging ideological process went into overdrive partly as a result of a series of seemingly coordinated terrorist attacks perpetrated by Islamic terrorists against three main western metropolises, namely: New York City (11 September 2001), Madrid (11 March 2004) and London (7 July 2005). Political considerations aside, in addition to the human cost and devastation caused, the atrocities had the effect of thrusting the Muslim community into the spotlight. A long-established settlement in Britain, Muslims nevertheless continued to experience high levels of unemployment, reported ill-health, economic inactivity – particularly among women, and educational underachievement. Their distinct culture and religious traditions had moreover often seemed at odds with the modern liberal values upon which the British secular state is based. Given that the perpetrators of the London attacks were home-grown British Muslims, a heighten sense of antagonism towards this community inevitably emerged. A national Populus survey carried out among Muslims a year after the London attacks showed this certainly to be the case. According to the 'Muslim 7/7 Poll', four out of five British Muslims (79 per cent) said their community had experienced increased hostility since the July bombings, and three quarters (74 per cent) felt that Muslims were viewed with suspicion by their fellow citizens (Populus 2006, 1).[39]

At the time, one particular aspect of the Muslim community that came under increased criticism from some quarters was their apparent inability and/or unwillingness to integrate into mainstream British society. Their Islamic beliefs and practices were seen as incompatible with those of Britain's liberal democracy, in particular, their views on sexuality and the treatment of women. Such sentiments were exacerbated by the so-called 'veil row': a well-documented national debate over the appropriateness of Muslim women wearing the Islamic niqab or veil in modern day society. What started as a rather innocuous observation by Jack Straw, Leader of the House of Commons, to one of his Muslim female constituents, transmuted into a full-blown public test on integration for the whole British Muslim community. The veil ultimately came to be perceived as synonymous with separation and separateness; an anachronistic reminder of an Islamic culture out of step with the modern world. The earlier Populus poll had already shown how Muslim respondents identified both the wearing of Islamic dress in schools and the role of women as the two most significant indicators of social difference between their Islamic culture and Britain's liberal tradition. Three quarters of Muslims (76 per cent) thought that pupils should be free to wear religious dress whatever the school's uniform policy; by contrast only two fifths of the general public (42 per cent) believed the same. With regard to the role of women, half of the population at large (51 per cent) said that Islam treats women as inferior to men and one third (31 per cent) thought that it promoted more violence than other religions (Populus 2006, 2). At the same time, more than a third of Muslims (36 per cent) claimed that the values of British society degrade women. The same proportion (36 per cent) felt that British values are a threat to the Islamic way of life; in comparison a quarter (25 per cent) of the general public believed that Islam is a threat to the British way of life (Populus 2006, 2).

---

39 Populus (2006), 'Muslim 7/7 Poll', 4–5 July 2006 <http://www.populuslimited.com/> (accessed 20 June 2007).

Against a backdrop of various similar media-fuelled controversies regarding deep-seated racism, increased migration and strained community relations in Britain, debate over the state of multiculturalism finally erupted in the national political arena. Controversial at the best of times, it featured a wide range of contrasting views that often polarised public opinion. On the whole, however, the debate over multiculturalism laid open the perceived failures of an ideology which had ultimately not delivered on the ground. It also signalled a paradigm shift in Britain's public discourse towards integration.

In 2001, in the wake of further urban disturbances in a number of English northern towns and cities, mostly involving clashes between the Police and groups of disaffected Asian youth, the government embarked on a programme of significant social and education policy initiatives as well as legislative reforms. Here, state intervention was overwhelming aimed at promoting the integration of migrants into British society while fostering social cohesion through a strengthened sense of national identity and citizenship. Following the *Cantle Report* into the disturbances, the government produced a White Paper titled *Secure Borders, Safe Haven: Integration with Diversity in Modern Britain*, specifically aimed at ensuring 'social integration and cohesion in the UK'. The precursor of the *Nationality, Immigration and Asylum Act, 2002*, the White Paper dealt with a wide range of social policy issues relating to nationality and citizenship, migration and asylum seeking. In line with the Paper, the ensuing Act considered every aspect of a migrant's entry and life in Britain. Just as the education-based *Swann Report* had been hailed 'a landmark in pluralism' over a decade earlier, the *Nationality, Immigration and Asylum Act, 2002* could now be said to represent a landmark in integration. In laying down the criteria for obtaining British citizenship, the Act for the first time required would-be immigrants to comply with the following requisites: firstly, showing sufficient knowledge of a language (i.e. English, Welsh or Scottish Gaelic) for the purpose of naturalisation; secondly, showing sufficient knowledge of life in the United Kingdom; and thirdly, taking up a Citizenship Oath and a Pledge of allegiance at a civil ceremony. Given the new language and civic structures now envisaged by the Act, the Home Office set up an independent Advisory Board on Naturalisation and Integration (ABNI) chaired by Professor Sir Bernard Crick to advice on assessment processes. After an initial report by the Board, a handbook for prospective British citizens titled *Life in the United Kingdom – A Journey to Citizenship* was first produced in 2004 (Home Office 2004).[40] Now in its second edition, this publication has become the official guide of study for those taking British citizenship tests (Home Office 2007).[41] Reflecting on the changes introduced at the time, John Reid, Home Secretary, indicated:

> Those [citizenship] tests, together with the new citizenship ceremonies which celebrate the achievement of new Britons in becoming citizens, have bee a real success. They have encouraged people who have decided to make their lives in Britain to learn more about our culture and institutions, and in many cases to improve their knowledge of our language.

---

40 Home Office (2004), *Life in the United Kingdom – A Journey to Citizenship*, published on behalf of the Life in the United Kingdom Advisory Group (Norwich: TSO).

41 Home Office (2007), *Life in the United Kingdom – A Journey to Citizenship* (Norwich: TSO).

We think that the benefits of this approach in creating strong and cohesive communities are clear (Home Office 2007, foreword).

In addition to its far-reaching citizenship strategy, the government has presided over a series of Anglo-centric language education policy reforms arguably aimed at prioritising the learning of English at the expense of Foreign Modern Languages. Whether the *14–19: Extending Opportunities, Raising Standards* Green Paper in 2002, its ensuing White Paper or the national language strategy document, *Languages for All: Languages for Life*; the past five years have witnessed a concerted governmental effort to sideline Foreign Modern Languages learning from the school curriculum. As a result, the discipline has gone from a position of strength as a mandatory subject at Key Stage 4, to one of relegation as a discretionary statutory entitlement; which to all purposes has amounted to dropping the subject from the National Curriculum. The learning of Foreign Modern Languages has now become an elective choice for students who operate in an English-dominated curriculum and live within an English-dominated world. This monolingual Anglo-centric approach, doggedly pursued by the government against overwhelming evidence to the contrary, has predictably resulted in a serious and sustained loss of multilingual skills among the country's school population. Such course of action has been in stark contrast to the overtly multilingual educational strategy of our European counterparts, which continues to produce highly skilled, multilingual and multicultural European citizens.

The British government, now faced with the prospect of a linguistically challenged workforce struggling to compete with their far better equipped European and global partners has recently performed a U-turn of sorts. Its latest *Languages Review* has sought to achieve a 'renaissance' of Foreign Modern Language learning in schools. To this end, a combination of early years' education and compensatory measures, including specialist language colleges, are meant to redress the balance. Within the school curriculum, however, there has been no return to the original mandatory requirement for Modern Foreign Languages at Key Stage 4.

Conclusion

Over the past hundred years, Britain's citizens' perceptions of themselves and their national identity have undergone a considerable metamorphosis. The process of defining and redefining what it means to be 'British' has been shaped by a combination of key demographic factors as well as socio-economic and cultural developments that have seen the country transformed in unexpected and fundamental ways. Underlying them all, shifting public narratives have come to articulate the changing meanings attributed to 'Britishness' by successive generations of UK citizens, living within the confines of specific ideological circumstances at particular points in time. In the course of a century, we have seen our public discourse fluctuating from a rather hostile attitude to migrants, to one of rapprochement with our nation's multiethnic roots, to the current somewhat nationalistic reaffirmation of our Anglo-Saxon, English-speaking British identity. Despite the time elapsed, countless debates on the subject and attempts to resolve the Britishness question, the indefinable essence of our national identity continues to elude us; just as it did our ancestors.

Chapter 2

English Language Colonisation, De-Colonisation and Globalisation

The English Language

During the reign of Queen Elizabeth I (1558–1603), the number of English speakers in the world is thought to have been between five and seven million. At the beginning of Queen Elizabeth II's tenure, over three centuries later, this amount had increased almost fifty-fold. By 1952, 250 million people were estimated to speak English as a mother tongue and a further 100 million or so had learned it as a foreign language (Graddol et al. 1996, 29).[1] The 1980s witnessed the continuation of this trend. Throughout this period, the number of native English speakers reached over 300 million, while the amount of people who spoke English as a foreign language numbered well over one billion (Graddol et al. 1996, 29). The English-speaking countries of Britain, the United States (with 70 per cent of all English mother tongue speakers worldwide), Canada, Australia and New Zealand can easily account for the bulk of the indigenous English-speaking population. In contrast, the spread and influence of English in non-English-speaking countries can only be understood by analysing wider socio-economic and political factors that have catapulted the English language onto a global dimension. Within this context, the role played both by Britain as the original Mother Country of English, and the USA as the world's current English-speaking leading nation are particularly significant. As Crystal has indicated, 'why a language becomes a global language has little to do with the number of people who speak it. It has much more to do with who those speakers are' (Crystal 1997, 5).[2]

The magnitude of the English language's global expansion, Katzner argues, is reflected in its unique position as the world's most widely spoken tongue:

> It [English] is the official language of dozens of countries in which only a small per centage of the population actually speaks it. It is the working language of a number of international organisations (the European Free Trade Association for one) whose membership does not include a single English-speaking nation. In many countries, a knowledge of English is helpful – and in some cases essential – for obtaining a certain job

---

1   Graddol, D., D. Leith and J. Swann (eds) (1996), *English: History, Diversity and Change,* The Open University (London: Routledge).

2   Crystal, D. (1997), *English as a Global Language* (Cambridge: Cambridge University Press).

or pursuing a certain career. No one can ever guess the number of people in the world who are currently studying English as a Second Language (Katzner 2002, 39).[3]

While Chinese is considered to be spoken by more people than any other language in the world, it is used by a particular ethnic group within a vast, yet limited, territory. In contrast, English is the most extensively used language on Earth, with peoples from every continent daily communicating through this ubiquitous linguistic code.

UK-led English Language Colonisation

The historical process by which English has become the world's most prominent language can be traced back to Britain's imperial times. In the first instance, the spread of the English language within the British Isles was a direct consequence of a colonial process that would culminate in the formation of the United Kingdom (Brutt-Griffler, 2002).[4] Following the conquest of England in 1066, the Norman monarchs incorporated the various existing Celtic territories by awarding land to their knights in return for subduing the indigenous population. It is in this manner that English came to be widely used in Ireland, Scotland and Wales, where previously Celtic languages had been spoken at length. As colonies developed and became of greater strategic importance to England, the English government took larger responsibility for their administration. The Celtic territories were the first to experience 'political incorporation' in this way (Graddol et al. 1996, 182). By 1536, the English nation included Wales within its territory. In 1707, Scotland joined the so-called Great Britain, with Ireland being finally incorporated in 1800, as part of the United Kingdom. Throughout the nineteenth century these territories constituted the original Mother Country and many British nationals from Ireland, Scotland and Wales actively contributed to the subsequent establishment of a British Empire abroad. Being subjects of the British monarchy, the original colonists were placed under the political and economic control of the Mother Country. With English now firmly established as 'the language of the state', these British settlers went on to deploy it as a powerful tool of acculturation (Graddol et al. 1996, 183).

Beyond the British Isles, colonies were first established at the end of the sixteenth century. With the process of overseas colonisation lasting over 300 years and affecting four continents, it is very difficult to make generalisations about its nature. It can nevertheless be argued that many of the foreign colonies where English emerged as the main language shared two common traits: firstly, they were populated by English-speaking settlers; and secondly, they had become politically and culturally incorporated into the wider British imperial state (Graddol et al. 1996, 182). The combined ethno-linguistic and political implications of such circumstances help to explain the accelerated spread of the English language overseas. The establishment of English-speaking colonies in North America at the beginning of the seventeenth

---

3   Katzner, K. (2002), *The Languages of the World*, third edn. (London: Routledge).

4   Brutt-Griffler, J. (2002), *World English – A Study of its Development* (Clevendon: Multilingual Matters).

century illustrates this process. Here, large scale immigration of English speakers and other European settlers rapidly displaced the existing indigenous population. The ensuing socio-economic, political and linguistic dominance of the former gave way to a dominant Anglo-Saxon cultural model whose collective *lingua franca* was English.

One of the defining characteristics of the English language, which has allowed it to spread quickly and to co-exist with other tongues, is its innate 'hybridity and permeability' (Graddol 1997, 6).[5] As a language, English is constantly evolving, and in this evolutionary process its contact with other tongues has been an important driving force for change. Throughout its remarkable history, the English language has always borrowed freely: firstly, from Celtic and Latin, later from Scandinavian and Norman French, and subsequently from the various languages spoken in the many British colonies. This extraordinary ability to absorb and incorporate different linguistic influences undoubtedly contributed to the rapid spread of English during Britain's colonisation period. As Graddol has indicated, 'when a language is imposed on a community as part of a colonial process, speakers tend to incorporate many linguistic features from their first language when speaking the new, imposed one' (Graddol et al. 1996, 185). Certainly, one of the most striking linguistic consequences of colonisation has been the creation of new, sometimes radically divergent forms of English. Most of these English language hybrids have remained local languages of relative low social status, such as English Creole – an amalgamation of English, Portuguese and Spanish developed during the slave trade between Africa and the Caribbean – which has survived with very limited use. In West Africa, for instance, such commercial activities led to the formation of English Pidgin, a simplified makeshift language mostly used in Sierra Leone (Le Page and Tabouret-Keller 1985; Todd 1984).[6]

The colonial process brought English in contact with a variety of different indigenous tongues, but it significantly did so within particular relations of power. Any account of the linguistic consequences of colonialism must also relate to the pattern of social, economic and political inequalities, which privileged the English language and those who spoke it. While the colonial conditions of language contact played an important role in shaping the new varieties of English that emerged, the influence of indigenous local languages on English was, for the most part, negligible. Territorial expansion largely saw European settlers displacing pre-colonial populations from their conquered territories. In North America, for example, colonisation witnessed the linguistic and cultural heritage of the various existing Native American peoples being virtually wiped out. As a result, these indigenous tongues had a minimum impact on the English language. In the same way as there is a lack of Celtic influence in Old English, Native Americans' languages made no significant impression on US English. Throughout the Empire, European colonists similarly limited their use of indigenous tongues to borrowing words relating to phenomena new to them

5   Graddol, D. (1997), *The Future of English?* (London: The British Council).

6   Le Page, R.G. and A. Tabouret-Keller (1985), *Acts of Identity: Creole-based Approaches to Language and Ethnicity* (Cambridge: Cambridge University Press); Todd, L. (1984), *Modern Englishes: Pidgins and Creoles* (Oxford: Blackwell).

such as local cultural practices, animal names and geographical features. It was rare for significant phonological or grammatical features of pre-colonial languages to be adopted into English. Machan and Scott explain this limited influence of pre-colonial tongues on English by pointing out that any given process of colonisation invariably results in the language of a conquered people having little effect on that of the conquerors (Machan and Scott 1992).[7]

Linguistic Consequences of De-colonisation

From the late eighteenth century onwards, the emergence of different forms of nationalistic movements within the British dominions signalled the beginning of the subsequent period of decolonisation. Ironically, the linguistic outcome of this process would see English expand further a field. For the former British Empire's model of 'inferiorisation' of indigenous languages and cultures was now to be deployed by the newly sovereign nations on their own native non-dominant linguistic groups (Le Page 1964; Smolicz and Secombe 2000).[8] As ex-colonies came to internalise hegemonic domination of their language and culture, their transition from territorially conquered to linguistically and culturally assimilated was complete.

Overseas nationalistic reactions against British domination began in North America in 1776. Other offshore colonies followed in quick succession. The British government granted a form of self-government to Canada in 1867. Dominion status was similarly conferred to Australia in 1901, to New Zealand in 1907 and to South Africa in 1910. Finally, in 1931, the totality of former British colonies became linked to Britain under its monarchy in the so-called Commonwealth of Independent States. While the nationalistic uprisings that gave birth to these countries were aimed at freeing the subordinate territories from British colonial rule, the language in which such revolutions were articulated was English. Most of the nationalistic movements in British colonies, which subsequently led to independence, were indeed instigated by English-speaking colonised peoples (Graddol et al. 1996, 182). In the United States, for instance, political independence led to the creation of a republican ideal based on the notion of 'We, the People' as an English-speaking collective. Similarly, the English language has retained some kind of official status in most of the newly created independent states, particular in post-colonial India as well as within emerging African nations. In Ghana for example, English has remained the main official language in which affairs of state, education and commerce are carried out. Use of native languages, on the other hand, is limited to regional and tribal settings. In Nigeria, English is likewise the sole official language for the many

---

7   Machan, T.W. and C.T. Scott (eds) (1992), *English in its Social Contexts: Essays in Historical Sociolinguistics* (Oxford: Oxford University Press).

8   Le Page, R.B. (1964), *The National Language Question: Linguistic Problems of Newly Independent States* (Oxford: Oxford University Press); Smolicz, J. and M.J. Secombe (2000), 'Language Resilience and Educational Empowerment: Philippines and Australia', in R. Phillipson (ed.), *Rights to Language: Equity, Power and Education: Celebrating the 60th Birthday of Tove Skutnabb-Kangas* (London: Lawrence Erlbaum Associates, Publishers), 164–69.

linguistic communities making up the nation. English is also the official language of Gambia, Sierra Leone, Uganda, Zambia and Zimbabwe. In other post-colonial countries, English has become a co-official language together with one or more additional native tongues. English is, for instance, a co-official language with French in Canada and Cameroon; with Spanish in Puerto Rico; with Swahili in Tanzania; with Cantonese in Hong Kong; and with Malay, Mandarin Chinese and Tamil in Singapore. The most complex linguistic situation regarding English is to be found in India, where this tongue performs several overlapping roles. Firstly, English is an associate official language with Hindi. In addition, it is regarded as a national language like Bengali, Hindi and Gujerati. English is furthermore an official language of eight Union Territories including the Andaman and Nicora Islands, Arunachal Pradesh, Chandigarh, Dadra and Nagar Haveli, Delhi, Lakshwadip, Mizoram and Pondicherry (Hartman 1996, 15).[9]

US-led English Language Globalisation

The end of the Cold War and the subsequent collapse of Communism saw the consolidation of the United States as the undisputed international leading nation. At the dawn of the new millennium, a combination of US political and economic might together with a worldwide technological revolution has transformed English into a global medium of mass communication (Arthur 1996, 3–15).[10] Not only world diplomacy and politics are now conducted in English, but also business, media, advertising, sports and entertainment broadcasting, and even popular music are dominated by the English language. In 1996, for instance, the *Union of International Associations' Yearbook* listed 12,500 international organisations worldwide. A random sample of 500 of these showed that 85 per cent (424) made official use of English – far more than any other language. French was the only other language to show up strongly, with 49 per cent (245) of such agencies using it officially. Thirty other languages also attracted occasional official status, but only Arabic, Spanish and German achieved over 10 per cent recognition (Crystal 1997, 79–80). English is now the language most widely taught as a foreign language – in over 100 countries, such as China, Russia, Germany, Spain, Egypt and Brazil – and in most cases it is emerging as the main language to be taught in schools, often displacing other tongues in the process (Crystal 2003, 5).[11]

Data compiled in the *Encyclopaedia Britannica* suggests that about a third of the world's newspapers are being published in those countries where the English language has an official status, and it is reasonable to assume that the majority of these would have been written in English. Similarly, the *Book of Lists* reported that the top five selling papers in the world are printed in English, these include *The*

---

9   Hartmann, R. (1996), *The English Language in Europe,* European Studies Series (Oxford: Intellect).

10   Arthur, T. (1996), 'English in the World and in Europe', in R. Hartmann (ed.), *The English Language in Europe* (Oxford: Intellect).

11   Crystal, D. (2003), *English as a Global Language,* second edition (Cambridge: Cambridge University Press).

New York Times, The Washington Post, The Wall Street Journal and two British papers, namely: *The Times* and *The Sunday Times*. Of particular importance are those English-written newspapers and magazines intended for a global readership such as the *International Herald Tribune, US Weekly, International Guardian, Time, Newsweek* and *The Economist*. It would also seem that about a quarter of the world's periodicals, literary and technical reviews, scholarly journals, comics and pornographic material are published in English-dominant countries (Crystal 1997, 85).[12]

With an average of two-thirds of a modern newspaper, especially in the United States, being devoted to advertising, the dominance of English language in this area has an enormous global impact. By 1972, for example, only three of the world's top ten publicity agencies were not US-owned (two were in Japan and one in Britain). Not surprisingly, English features as the official language of international advertising bodies such as the European Association of Advertising Agencies. English has also become the language of the film industry. It is estimated that 85 per cent of the world's entertainment market is controlled by the United States, with Hollywood films dominating box offices in most countries (Crystal 1997, 91). Despite the growth of motion pictures worldwide, English-speaking movies still largely dominate the medium, with Hollywood increasingly coming to rely on a small number of annual productions aimed at huge audiences such as the *Lord of the Rings* trilogy and the *Harry Potter* and *Pirates of the Caribbean* series. It is unusual to find a blockbuster movie produced in a language other than English, with about 80 per cent of all feature films given a theatrical release being performed in English. The Oscar system itself has always been English language oriented, featuring only one category for 'Best Foreign Film'. There is a strong English-language presence in most other film festivals too. One half of all the 'Best Film' awards ever given at the Cannes Film Festival, for example, have been granted to English-speaking productions (Crystal 1997, 91). The pop music world has also felt the international power of the English language. The 1990 edition of *The Penguin Encyclopaedia of Popular Music*, which includes 557 pop groups, already indicated that 549 (99 per cent) of them worked entirely or predominantly in English; and of the 1,219 solo vocalists featured, 1,156 (95 per cent) of them performed in English. The mother tongue of the artists appears to be altogether irrelevant. Consider for instance, the Swedish group ABBA, whose entire international career, with over twenty hit records in the 1970s and 1980s was conducted in English (Julios 2002, 185).

Perhaps the most direct evidence of globalisation of the English language has been its almost automatic transformation into the Internet's *lingua franca*. From the outset an English-speaking US-led creation, the World Wide Web has become a universal tool for accessing knowledge and exchanging information. A truly multilingual Internet remains impracticable, for servers and clients must be able to intelligently communicate with each other, whatever the data source. Most browsers are still unable to handle multilingual data presentation including writing systems

---

12 Quoted in C. Julios (2002) 'Towards a European Language Policy', in M. Farrell, S. Fella and M. Newman, *European Integration in the 21st Century – Unity in Diversity?* (London: Sage Publications), 184–85.

such as Arabic and Chinese. If the pitfalls of a technological Babel are to be avoided, the English language remains the only viable alternative (Julios 2002, 185). Here, the unparalleled domination of the international software market by US giant Microsoft seems to suggest the establishment of a growing trend, namely indiscriminate use of the English language. Significantly, Microsoft refused to translate its *Windows 95* software package into Icelandic, alleging a 'limited market' for such service (Walsh 1998).[13] While the director of the Icelandic Language Institute, Eric Kristinsson, protested that Microsoft 'are doing nothing less than destroying what has been built up here for ages', the fact remains that every school child in Iceland is taught the English language. Microsoft consequently saw no point in translating *Windows 95* into Icelandic when the Standard English version could be sold instead (Walsh 1998). Specter, in a *New York Times* article entitled: 'World, Wide, Web: Three English Words', has encapsulated the seemingly unchallenged domination of the so-called information superhighway by the English language. He suggests that 'if you want to take full advantage of the Internet, there is only one way to do it: learn English, which has more than ever become America's greatest and most efficient export' (Specter 1996).[14]

While the powerful influence of the USA and the US-led Internet has contributed to the transformation of English into a global linguistic phenomenon, there is a further factor that will ensure the continuation of this trend in the foreseeable future: world migration. A recent report by the United Nations Development Programme (UNDP) reminds us of a persistent gulf in wealth and human development between the world's richest and most developed nations and their poorer, developing counterparts. The UNDP's *Human Development Report 2000* ranks the countries of the world according to a Human Development Index (HDI) featuring a composite of measures that reflect differentials in life expectancy, adult literacy, school enrolment rates, gender equality and Gross Domestic Product (GDP) between the world's nations. Of the 174 countries rated, the top ten ranking entries include some of the world's leading industrialised states such as Canada (ranked first), Norway (ranked second), the United States (ranked third), Australia (ranked fourth), Japan (ranked ninth) and the United Kingdom (ranked tenth). In contrast, so-called 'Third World' countries in Africa, South East Asia, Central and South America and the Middle East regions dominate the lower end of the spectrum, with Mozambique (ranked 168), Ethiopia (ranked 171), Niger (ranked 173) and Sierra Leone (ranked 174) being among the least developed countries on Earth (UNDP 2000, 148–49).[15] Over ten years ago, under the headlines 'Close the Gap between Rich and Poor', *The Guardian* warned of growing socio-economic disparities between the world's richest and poorest nations (*The Guardian* 1996).[16] At the time, it was estimated that the wealth of the world's

---

13 Walsh, M. 'Microsoft set to wreck Language of Vikings', *The Guardian,* 1 July 1998, 15, quoted in C. Julios (2002) 'Towards a European Language Policy', 185.

14 Specter, M. 'World, Wide, Web: Three English Words', *The New York Times,* April 1996, quoted in C. Julios (2002) 'Towards a European Language Policy', 185.

15 United Nations Development Programme (UNDP) (2000), *Human Development Report 2000*, (Oxford University Press).

16 'Close the Gap Between Rich and Poor', *The Guardian,* 16 July 1996.

358 billionaires exceeded the combined annual incomes of countries that were home to nearly half of the Earth's population (UNDP 1996).[17] Today, the UNDP report clearly shows that such disparities in global human development and wealth still persist, with only 46 countries – out of the 174 total – ranked in the high human development category (HDI value equal to or more than 0.800), and with Canada's HDI value of 0.935 being nearly four times that of Sierra Leone (0.252). Moreover, since 1990, twenty countries have experienced reversals of human development as a result of HIV/AIDS, economic stagnation and/or conflict, particularly within Sub-Sahara Africa, Eastern Europe and the new Commonwealth of Independent States (CIS) (UNDP 2000, 148).

The linguistic consequences of these growing inequalities in wealth and human development between prosperous Western societies and Third World countries are two-fold. On the one hand, progressively larger numbers of people from developing countries are being drawn to affluent English-speaking nations in search of better living standards. On the other hand, the growing imbalance between rich and poor nations continues to increase the power of the former to culturally and linguistically influence the latter. The combination of these factors will ultimately contribute to further the process of English language globalisation. Katzner has argued that a 'snowball effect' is already taking place, for 'the more people there are in the rest of the world who already speak English, the more the rest of the world will want to, and is striving to, learn it and join the club' (Katzner 2002, 39). By the late 1990s, Hartman had already mapped out the extent of this language's universal reach by dividing the Globe into three categories: English Native Language Territories (totalling 36 nations), English as a Second Language Territories (51 nations) and English as a Foreign Language Territories (121 nations) (Hartman 1996, 15). At 208, the number of world territories using English approximates the totality of countries on Earth.

European Babel in an English-speaking World

The European Union (EU) provides a telling example of the global dominance of the English language in the face of increasing diversity. An ever expanding family of democratic countries committed to working together for peace and prosperity, the EU has grown from an original membership of six founding nations to a staggering 27 member states comprising 23 official languages and a total of 490 million people. As EUROPA, the EU's official internet portal, indicates:

> Europe is a continent with many different traditions and languages, but also with shared values such as democracy, freedom and social justice. The EU defends these values. If fosters cooperation among the peoples of Europe, promoting unity while preserving

17 United Nations Development Programme (UNDP) (1996), *The Human Report 1996* (New York: United Nations).

diversity and ensuring that decisions are taken as close as possible to the citizens (EUROPA 2007).[18]

Preservation and promotion of its members' cultural and linguistic diversity is certainly crucial to the European project. A shared belief on the principle of a citizenship of the Union and the pursuit of knowledge through lifelong learning transpires across the European institutions and policies, including both the original Maastricht Treaty and the most recent EU Agenda 2000 strategy. Linguistic diversity, in particular, is seen here as much a source of strength and mutual enrichment as a valuable economic tool, indispensable in a competitive international labour market. As Hattos has put it, 'the policy discourse in the European Union is focused on promoting diversity and developing intercultural skills for mobility' (Hattos, 2004, 446).[19] A glance at Europe's education programme, SOCRATES, with its many sub-schemes, illustrates the Union's commitment and ability to produce veritable multicultural and multilingual European citizens. As the EU's educational flagship programme, SOCRATES aims to achieve the following objectives:

To strengthen the European dimension of education at all levels
To improve the knowledge of European languages
To promote cooperation and mobility through education
To encourage innovation in education
To promote equal opportunities in all sectors of education (European Commission 2006, 4).[20]

Recent figures assessing the first five years of the programme show that almost 500,000 students undertook a period of study in another European university, 10,000 schools took part in European partnerships and thousands of projects were developed to promote European languages (European Commission 2006, 2).

Despite the undeniable success of European social and educational policies in achieving the Unions' collective pluralistic ideal, the reality of enlargement has drawn attention to the challenges faced by an ever increasing multilingual European machinery. From the outset, the institutions of the European Union have been sustained by a formidable information and communications infrastructure, responsible for translating and interpreting a wealth of daily official proceedings, policy documents and information, among others. Given that the official languages of all Member States are meant to be equally represented in the EU's output, the implementation of a European pluralistic ideal is progressively becoming costly, resource intensive, time-consuming and logistically nightmarish. In 1992, a policy

---

18 EUROPA (2007), 'Panorama of the European Union – United in Diversity' <http://europa.eu/abc/panorama/index_en.htm> (accessed 12 June 2007).

19 Hattos, A. (2004), 'Promoting Diversity through Language-in-Education Policies: Focus on Australia and the European Union, *Current Issues in Language Planning*, 5:4, 438–54.

20 European Commission (2006), *Gateway to Education*, Socrates – European Community Action Programme in the Field of Education (2000–2006) (Brussels: European Commission).

statement regarding language services already expressed concerns about the implications of further enlargement:

> Enlargement will bring additional languages to the European Union, thus enriching its cultural diversity. But more languages will also complicate its work. In the Union of 12 members there are 9 official languages in normal use; in a Union of 20 members there could be as many as 15 languages; with 30 members there could be as many as 25 languages. For reasons of principle, legal acts and important documents should continue to be translated into the official languages of all member states. To ensure effective communication in meetings, pragmatic solutions will have to be found by each of the institutions (European Commission, 1992).[21]

In 2000, a walkout by interpreters over an unrelated EU tax rate entitlement dispute highlighted the inadequacies of an over-saturated European communications system. On this occasion, the fifteen ambassadors affected by the temporary lack of interpreters avoided disaster by communicating among themselves in English and French. Similar practical shortcuts using the English language as an 'inter-lingua' are regularly used by EU interpreters performing simultaneous translations, particularly during complex meetings when the totality of Member States are present, and where over a hundred pairs of languages may require translation services (Julios 2002, 196).

Language, Berdichevsky reminds us, is both 'a medium of discourse and communication' as well as 'an ideological tool' (Berdichevsky 2004, 1).[22] Within the context of the European Union, the widespread use of English over its fellow European tongues can be said to reflect a growing gap between an aspirational pluralistic ideal and the reality of multilingualism in an English-dominated Europe; a Europe where every school child already speaks English as a second language.

During the nineteenth century, Britain's colonial rule saw English become the *lingua franca* of an international territorial empire. Throughout the twentieth century, de-colonisation together with the emergence of the United States as a political and technological super-power has seen the English language elevated to a global stage. At the same time, the United Kingdom has experienced an unprecedented growth of non-English-speaking settlements within its territory, through a combination of established communities, recent arrivals, refugee and asylum seeking intake as well as illegal migration. As the twentieth first century dawns, British society finds itself facing a major social, educational and political challenge, namely: catering for the language education needs of the country's non-English-speaking population. Common to English-speaking nations everywhere, the solution to this problem has come in the shape of so-called English as a Second Language (ESL) education policies.

---

21 European Commission (1992), *Europe and the Challenge of Enlargement* (Brussels: European Commission), quoted in C. Julios (2002) 'Towards a European Language Policy', in M. Farrell, S. Fella and M. Newman, *European Integration in the 21st Century – Unity in Diversity?* (London: Sage Publications), 195.

22 Berdichevsky, N. (2004), *Nations, Language and Citizenship* (London: McFarland and Company, Inc., Publishers).

Language Dimensions and Linguistic Hierarchies

Before exploring the nature of Britain's ESL education programmes as well as the immigration and nationality strategies specifically aimed at the non-English-speaking target group, attention must be paid to the context in which such interventions take place. In particular, consideration must be given to the power relationships that invariably develop between the dominant English language and ethnic minority tongues.

Social constructs, Hajer argues, 'do not float in the world'; they can be tied to specific institutions and actors (Hajer 1993, 46).[23] Second language education must accordingly be understood as a context-specific policy, where a multiplicity of factors and stakeholders will have an impact on ESL policy outcomes. The many external circumstances that may influence the shape of ESL education programmes include school population's socio-economic, ethnic and linguistic background, available resources, preferred pedagogical strategies, prevailing political climate and nature of the policy decision-making process. These determining factors can be broadly amalgamated into five main contextual categories or 'language dimensions' comprising demographic, socio-economic, organisational, cultural and political indicators impacting on the development of ELS education initiatives. Such language dimensions provide the backdrop against which the dominant English language and minority ethnic tongues come into contact and interact with each other.

Demographic Dimension

Migration is an inherent part of any given ESL policy, for it is population movements that create the need for English language provision in the first place. Second language-based initiatives are entirely aimed at linguistic ethnic groups, whether the Bangladeshi community in London, the Hispanic collective in New York City or the Jewish cohort in Montreal. Britain's school system, in particular, comprises an amalgamation of children from a wide range of ethnic backgrounds, income levels as well as cultural and linguistic origins. With about a third of its population (29 per cent) belonging to an ethnic minority other than white, London alone is home to over 300 community languages, including tongues as dissimilar as Spanish, Urdu, Chinese and Russian (National Statistics 2006a).[24]

In accessing ESL tuition, each of these ethnic linguistic groups brings with them a specific set of needs, mostly determined by their members' socio-economic status as well as educational and literacy levels. Factors such as family structure and parents' academic standing have long been shown to influence pupils' educational prospects as well as their school performance. The US Department of

---

23 Hajer, M.A. (1993), 'Discourse Coalitions and the Institutionalisation of Practice: the Case of Acid Rain in Britain' in F. Fisher and J. Forrester (eds), *The Argumentative Turn in Policy Analysis and Planning* (London: UCL Press), 46.

24 National Statistics (2006a), *Census 2001: Focus on London – Overview* (London: TSO) <http://www.statistics.gov.uk/CCI/nugget.asp?ID=393&Pos=2&ColRank=2&Rank=1 92> (accessed 14 April 2006).

Education, for example, has identified five such indicators, including difficulty in speaking English, poverty, single parent families, parents' educational attainment and differentials in family income (US National Centre for Educational Statistics 1997, 2–11).[25] In Britain, the link between socio-economic background, English language proficiency and academic performance is similarly well-documented.[26] The continuous arrival of new cohorts of non-English-speaking pupils entering the British education system finds educationalists and policy-makers having to perform the difficult balancing act of responding to the multiple scholastic needs of an ever increasing diverse student intake, while simultaneously raising the academic standards of all pupils, native English speakers and their non-English-speaking peers.

Organisational Dimension

The provision of ESL programmes invariably takes place within a multifaceted setting in which a multiplicity of agencies and players are involved. Numerous public, private, voluntary and community organisations as well as individuals contribute daily to the development of ESL and bilingual education programmes across the country. They specifically include government departments, Local Education Authorities, businesses, not-for-profit agencies, schools, public/private partnerships and community groups. These institutions and those who run them play different roles and exert various degrees of influence upon the second language education process. Their interests, motivations and understanding of ESL programmes often come into conflict. Any given ESL programme, for instance, may feature monolingual government officials drawing up English language proficiency targets for non-English-speaking pupils; ethnic minority leaders advocating the maintenance of their linguistic and religious heritage in the classroom; and schools striving to increase their ethnic minority intake in order to secure financial backing for their ESL programmes. Typically, a combination of competition, bargaining and compromise will characterise the relationships that develop between them.

Socio-economic Dimension

Languages, Graddol points out, 'are not equal in political or social status, particularly in multilingual contexts' (Graddol, 1997, 5). When in contact, languages inevitably enter into hierarchical relationships whereby some enjoy a dominant position, while others become relegated to a secondary or complementary level. In English-speaking

---

25 US National Centre for Education Statistics (1997), *The Conditions of Education 1997* (Washington, D.C.: US Department for Education), 2–11.

26 National Statistics (2006b), *Census 2001: Focus on Ethnicity and Identity* (London, TSO) <http://www.statistics.gov.uk/focuson/ethnicity> (accessed 14 April 2006); National Statistics (2006), *Social Trends No. 36* (London: TSO); Office of the Deputy Prime Minister (ODPM), Social Exclusion Unit (2004), *Breaking the Cycle: Taking Stock of Progress and Priorities for the Future* (London: ODPM); Cabinet Office, Strategy Unit (2003), *Ethnic Minorities and the Labour Market: Final Report* (London: SU); White, A. (ed.) (2002), National Statistics *Social Focus in Brief – Ethnicity 2002* (London, HMSO).

countries such as Britain, the United States, Canada and Australia, the English language predictably comes second to none. Linguistic hierarchies, however, seem to be present whenever languages interact with each other. Even in multilingual countries where several supposedly equal tongues are meant to coexist within a level playing field, a linguistic ranking order invariably emerges. Luxembourg's multilingual system provides a case in point. Here, Beardsmore explains, oral interaction is mainly carried out in Luxembourger, with the German language dominating written communication; while French, entering children's education at a late stage, enjoys the lowest status of them all (Beardsmore 1995, 5).[27]

Whether in English-dominant or non-English-dominant territories, languages appear hierarchically classified according to the socio-economic position they occupy in society at large. Knowledge of the officially sanctioned tongue has traditionally provided immigrants with the key to accessing the host country's services, whether they may be education, health, housing or the labour market. Proficiency in the language of the state also affords newcomers the possibility of acquiring social mobility. In Britain, the ubiquitous English language plays such an enabling role. Ignorance of the latter thus becomes detrimental to those unable or unwilling to master it; for it prevents them from fully participating in the country's everyday life, while leaving them vulnerable to exploitation and abuse. Not surprisingly, some of the most marginalised ethnic communities in Britain, such as the Pakistanis and Bangladeshis, are among the least English language proficient and academically accomplished population groups in the country. Over time, their failure to communicate with the dominant English population has seen them consigned to geographically constrained ethnic linguistic enclaves, such the London borough of Tower Hamlets' 'Banglatown' where their mother tongue and cultural heritage has come to enjoy an overwhelming presence.

As by-products of English-dominant societies, ESL education policies are mostly geared towards students' mastery of the English language, with use of community tongues being merely conceived as an aid to achieving this objective. To the extent that such linguistic divisions are institutionalised, the relative status of a language reflects that of its speakers. The British school curriculum has being designed to meet the academic needs of its dominant English-speaking population. In Wales, however, where the Welsh language dominates, the school curriculum caters for its predominantly Welsh-speaking native students.

Maintenance and development of a given tongue can ultimately be said to directly relate to the economics of a given dominant culture. While socio-economic dominant groups will be able to guarantee the preservation of their particular languages, this will not necessarily be the case for ethnic linguistic minorities. Conversely, among minority ethnic communities, those commanding the largest numbers and power-base will be better placed to exert political influence aimed at preserving their linguistic heritage than their less numerous and established peers. Both the Bangladeshi residents in Tower Hamlets and the Hispanic inhabitants of Manhattan's *los barrios*

---

27 Beardsmore, H.B. (1995), 'An Overview of European Models of Bilingual Education', in R. Khoo, U. Kreher and R. Wong (eds), *Towards Global Multilingualism: European Models and Asian Realities*, (Clevendon: Multilingual Matters Ltd.), 5.

Latinos (Latino neighbourhoods) illustrate this point. In turn, the case of Wales with its officially sanctioned regional language confirms that minority linguistic groups in a position of numerical and political superiority will mirror the behaviour of their nationally dominant indigenous counterparts.

Cultural Dimension

Every tongue belongs to a given cultural heritage and as such it expresses a unique identity. In theory, all of the world's languages can be said to have an equal share in humanity's linguistic legacy. As already indicated though, in practice, the relative worth of a tongue is determined by the socio-economic and cultural status of its speakers. The intellectual value of the English and Sylheti languages is undeniable; however, when spoken in Britain, the former becomes a priceless asset, while the latter is lowered to a secondary plane.

By their own remedial nature ESL programmes reinforce these distinctions; with the English language positioned at the top of the educational hierarchy, consistently rated as having the highest socio-economic and cultural value. Behind these language policy strategies lie peoples' motivation for learning a given tongue. The bilingual model of Wales, for instance, can be construed as a survival strategy of the Welsh against encroachments from the leading English cultural tradition. The Welsh language would appear to have been deployed to preserve the intellectual and linguistic heritage of this region. Similarly, the desire common to most first-generation immigrants for their offspring to maintain their native mother tongues can be understood as an attempt by community elders to hold back the unrelenting assimilation of the younger generation into the dominant British culture. The deployment of languages to assert both majority and minority cultural heritage highlights the significant role played by language in shaping both individual and collective identities.

Political Dimension

All language, Yanow notes, is 'symbolic', in so far as it embodies values, beliefs and ideologies (Yanow 1996, 153).[28] Within the context of ESL education policy, those involved in it will invariably use language to articulate their individual understandings of this particular intervention. Whether central or local government bureaux, private or not-for-profit agencies, community-based groups, school teachers, parents or pupils, they all espouse different perspectives regarding ESL education programmes. The rhetoric used by central government to promote the learning of English in schools, for instance, will vary from that deployed by schoolteachers advocating multilingual pedagogical approaches, or that spoken by community leaders endorsing mother tongue tuition in the classroom. Each is coloured by the particular interests and beliefs of those who articulate them. Just as language can be utilised as a cultural strategy, it can also be deployed as an ideological and political

---

28 Yanow, D. (1996), *How Does a Policy Mean? Interpreting Policy and Organisational Actions* (Washington, D.C.: Georgetown University Press), 153.

tool. The contrasting approaches to second language tuition by successive British governments in the past forty years reflect this reality.

The five language dimensions here described largely encapsulate the complexity of the environment in which second language education occurs. Demographic, socio-economic, organisational, cultural and political factors have to be considered when analysing this policy as well as those related to it, for they determine to a large extent the shape it will take. Just as important, though, are the meanings that those involved in ESL education attribute to this policy. Different approaches to the second language education question will ultimately result from values and beliefs specific to a particular group of actors, in a particular society at a particular point in time.

Conclusion

In considering the unprecedented transformation of English into a global linguistic phenomenon in modern times, two factors have been identified: firstly, the expansionism of the British Empire during the colonial period; and secondly, the elevation of the United States to the status of world's leading political and technological superpower in the twentieth century.

Having become the official language of the United Kingdom since the British state's early inception, Britain's colonial experience saw English spread further a field, well beyond the country's borders. As the *lingua franca* of a vast international Empire, English not only came to be spoken by millions of different people across several continents; but it entered into contact with 'lesser' local tongues, resulting – particularly during the slave trade – in the creation of an array of hybrid varieties of English. Dissemination of the English language continued to gain pace with the establishment of offshore colonies in the United States during the seventeenth century. Here, indigenous populations were swiftly replaced by the more powerful English-speaking newcomers. The ideal of 'We, The People' as an English-speaking entity was therefore created. As the colonial period came to an end, de-colonisation gave way to the emergence of nationalistic movements across the previous dominions. English language was to play an essential role in these uprisings. Although the campaigns for independence were aimed at freeing the territories from their colonial masters, English became the language in which such revolutions were fought. In the aftermath of the Empire, English had acquired official status in most of the newly created states. The second phase of English language expansion took placed during the twentieth century, with the raise of the United States to the position of world's leading superpower. The undisputed influence of this English-speaking nation in socio-economic, cultural and technological terms has not only extended the use of English further a field, it has catapulted this language onto a global dimension. In particular, the universal appeal of the US-led Internet has greatly accelerated this seemingly unstoppable process.

At the dawn of the twentieth-first century, persistent wealth and human development inequalities among the world's richest and poorest states will ensure that English language expansion gathers pace. For those in the developing world will continue to join the ranks of millions of 'economic' migrants who, every year, move to industrialised English-speaking western nations in search of a better life. Such population movements have, in turn, seen the creation of non-English-speaking settlements in English-speaking nations. As a result, the latter have found themselves faced with the challenge of catering for the educational and linguistic needs of the former. So-called English as a Second Language (ESL) education programmes have been adopted everywhere to address this problem.

As social constructs, ESL schemes are context-specific policy initiatives shaped by a variety of demographic, socio-economic, organisational, cultural and political factors. The combination of these circumstances provides the framework in which Britain's English-speaking Anglo-Saxon society interacts with a multiplicity of non English-speaking minority ethnic traditions. Such interactions are invariably characterised by the development of power relationships between majority and minority cultures as well as linguistic hierarchies between majority and minority languages.

Chapter 3

Ethnic Linguistic Minorities

Minorities v. Majorities

According to the *Oxford English Dictionary*, a 'minority' is a 'small group of people separated from the rest of the community by a difference in race, religion, language, etc' (Simpson and Weiner 1989, 825).[1] The *Collins Concise English Dictionary*, similarly explains the notion of 'minority' as a 'group that is different racially, politically, etc., from a larger group of which it is a part' (*Collins Concise English Dictionary* 1995, 848).[2] Ethnic linguistic minorities can thus be described as sections of a given population, which share a distinctive phenotypic, cultural and linguistic heritage. Here, a distinction must be made between a native minority and an immigrant community. Unlike the latter, the former group inhabits a national territory that has been associated with its members for a long time, often many centuries. That territory has now been placed under the jurisdiction of a nation-state whose hegemonic indigenous majority determines its socio-cultural outlook. Such is the situation of the Basques in Spain, the Bretons and Corsicans in France, the Native Americans in the USA and the Aborigines in Australia, among others.[3] Although the existence of these groups raises many important socio-economic and political challenges, it is not within the scope of this book to explore them. Instead, our attention will turn to those ethnic immigrant communities formed as a result of recent migratory population movements, in particular, non-English speaking settlements in Britain.

The *Census 2001* reveals the UK to be a multiethnic and multicultural nation, where an amalgamation of diverse individuals and communities coexist. Out of a population of 58.7 million people, 7.9 per cent (4.6 million) are identified as being members of an ethnic group other than white. About half of the UK's minority ethnic population (2.3 million) is of Asian descent – including Indians (1.0 million), Pakistanis (747,285), Bangladeshis (283,063) and Other Asians (247,664), a quarter (1.1million) is of Black parentage, fifteen per cent (677,117) is of Mixed background, over five per cent (247,403) is of Chinese origin and a further five per cent (230,615) is classified as belonging to Other Ethnic groups (National Statistics 2006a).[4] A

---

1   Simpson, J.A. and E.S.C. Weiner (1989), *The Oxford English Dictionary*, 2nd edn (Oxford: Clarendon Press), vol. IX, 825.

2   *Collins Concise English Dictionary* (1995), 3rd edn, (Glasgow: Harper Collins Publishers), 848.

3   Note: the broad distinction between native and immigrant minority seems somewhat arbitrary, with instances such as the Gypsy community being difficult to classify.

4   National Statistics (2006a), *Census 2001: Focus on Ethnicity and Identity*, National Statistics <http://www.statistics.gov.uk/focuson/ethnicity> (accessed 14 April 2006).

striking aspect of Britain's multiculturalism is the existence of an array of different religions, faiths and belief systems among its populace. While a predominantly Christian nation (40 million people), Britain is home to 1.6 million Muslims, over half a million Hindus, 336,179 Sikhs, 267,373 Jews and 149,157 Buddhists, as well as over 8 million 'people with no religion' or who ascribe themselves to no spiritual ideology at all (National Statistics 2006b).[5] Once a nation of mostly white citizens of European stock, mass migration during the second half of the twentieth century has seen Britain transformed into a veritable melting pot of peoples from different ethnic, cultural and linguistic backgrounds. Between 1991 and 2001, the number of people entering Britain from an ethnic group other than white grew by an unprecedented 53 per cent, from 3.0 million in 1991 to 4.6 million in 2001. Demographic projections point towards the continuation of this trend (UNDP 2000).[6]

In contrast to the dominant English speaking white Anglo-Saxon indigenous population, new minority ethnic arrivals in Britain bring with them a host of different cultural, religious and linguistic traditions. Their entry into Britain is also accompanied by a set of socio-economic and educational circumstances imported from their countries of origin. The relative social standing of a given population group in its native state can be said to shape its members' experience of life in their newly adopted nation. As the largest ethnic linguistic group in the UK, the case of the Bangladeshi community illustrates this point. The majority of the 300,000 Bangladeshis living in Britain have migrated from the Great Sylhet Region of Bangladesh, with up to 95 per cent of them having originated there (Husain 1996, 67).[7] Located in the north east of Bangladesh, the Greater Sylhet Region features an extremely deprived rural area, where Sylheti – a surviving oral dialect of Bengali – is the main spoken tongue. While Bengali speakers worldwide account for the sixth largest linguistic group on Earth (with some 220 million speakers), the bulk of Sylheti speakers is largely confined to the Great Sylhet Region (Husain 1996, 67). The Bangladeshi community in Britain is not only the largest ethnic linguistic group in the country; it is also the largest collective of Sylheti speakers anywhere outside Bangladesh. Given the particular socio-economic, educational and linguist circumstances Sylheti-speaking migrants experience in their country of origin, Bangladeshi newcomers often arrive in Britain with low levels of educational attainment and professional skills, high levels of illiteracy and poverty as well as lack of English language proficiency.

Common to many immigrant communities in the UK, such traits find members of these population groups geographically clustered, typically concentrated in urban conurbation settlements across the country, mostly in England (Cohen 1995; Castles

---

5   National Statistics (2006b), *Census 2001: Focus on Ethnicity and Identity – Religious Populations*, National Statistics <http://www.statistics.gov.uk/cci/nugget.asp?id=954> (accessed 14 April 2006).

6   United Nations Development Programme (UNDP) (2000), *Human Development Report 2000*, (Oxford: Oxford University Press).

7   Husain, H.M. (1996), 'Raising Our Educational Standards and Performance Levels', paper presented at the Greater Sylhet Development and Welfare Council (GSDWC) Conference 1996, London, 67.

and Miller 1993).[8] Nearly half (45 per cent) of the UK's non-white population lives in the London region, where they comprise 29 per cent of all residents; the second largest proportion of non white groups is found in the West Midlands (13 per cent); followed by the South East (eight per cent) and Yorkshire and the Humber (7 per cent). In contrast, less than 4 per cent of non-White groups live in the North East and South East regions (2 per cent of each region's population). Minority ethnic presence both in Scotland and Wales amounts to only 2 per cent of their respective populations and less than 1 per cent in Northern Ireland (National Statistics 2006c).[9] Sprawling ethnic communities of South East Asian immigrants can consequently be found in large industrial cities such as Birmingham, Leeds and Bradford. In the London Borough of Tower Hamlets alone, three in five residents are either Asian of Black – compared with only one in twenty of the population nationally; and 62 per cent of the school population has a home language other than English, with 86 per cent of all mother tongue users being Sylheti speakers (Husain 1996, 66; 42 *Census* 1991).[10] Responding to the multiple needs of such a culturally and linguistically diverse population is undoubtedly one of the major challenges facing British society today.

Notwithstanding the economic benefits derived from cheap imported labour, large population movements frequently place a burden upon the host society's available resources; they invariably test statutory social, education and immigration policies, and often provoke expressions of xenophobia among native inhabitants. The unparalleled growth of sizeable non-English-speaking settlements in Britain has been underlined by deep-seated fears in the nation's psyche of an imminent threat to the prevailing *status quo*. As minority enclaves continue to grow, the increasing presence of different ethnicities, tongues and traditions in mainstream society has raised the spectrum of cultural and linguistic fragmentation. Widespread bilingual (i.e. English and Bengali) street signs in the London Borough of Tower Hamlets, for instance, reflect this reality as does the plethora of ever expanding community language-based radio and media programmes as well as written and electronic press entirely aimed at individual immigrant communities in Britain.

A comparable and uniquely acute situation is that of the United States, where the Latino community is posed to become the largest ethnic minority group in US mainland. Over a decade ago, the US Bureau of Census already predicted that by the year 2010, Central and South Americans would eclipse African-Americans as the nation's largest minority group; and by 2050, they would account for 23 per cent of the US population, followed by African-Americans at 16 per cent (US Bureau

8   Cohen, R. (ed.) (1995), *The Cambridge Survey of World Migration* (Cambridge: Cambridge University Press); Castles, S. and M.J. Miller (1993), *The Age of Migration: International Population Movements in the Modern World* (Basingstoke: Macmillan Press).

9   National Statistics (2006c), *Census 2001: Focus on Ethnicity and Identity – Geographic Distribution*, National Statistics <http://www.statistics.gov.uk/cci/nugget.asp?id=457> (accessed 14 April 2006).

10   Husain, 'Raising Our Educational Standards', 66; *Census 1991* (1991), 'Report for Great Britain', (London: HMSO).

of Census 1995).[11] This projected demographic shift has already occurred in some urban areas, notably Los Angeles and Miami. In other metropolitan areas such as New York, Chicago, Houston and San Diego, the transformation is well underway (Farnen 1994).[12] In addition to this overwhelming Latino presence, nearly 40 per cent of all immigrants to the United States speak the same language: Spanish. The official tongue of Spain, Mexico and most countries in Central and South America – with the notable exception of Portuguese-speaking Brazil, Spanish is spoken by individuals form a dozen different Latino nations. The seemingly unstoppable growth of Spanish-speaking communities across the United States is lowering the socio-economic costs of not speaking English, while raising the benefits of communicating in Spanish. While the original European immigrants at the turn of the twentieth century were more numerous than the non-European counterparts, they were scattered across a wide range of linguistic and national groups such as Polish, German, Italian and Greek. For these European newcomers the only viable *lingual franca* was English. Today, that is no longer the case; for Latino immigrants are now less likely to learn English than their European counterparts were at the turn of the century. The continuing development of Spanish-speaking enclaves not only reduces the incentives and opportunities to learn English, but also other North American cultural and behavioural traits. Contingency theorists have already predicted what it looks like an inevitable outcome in the shape of 'a two-way assimilation' with Euro-Americans learning Spanish and consuming Latin cultural products as well as Hispanics learning English and consuming Anglo-American products (Massey 1995, 631–52; Cohen 1994).[13] In such scenario, the economic benefits and prospects for social mobility would accrue to those able to speak both languages and operate within both traditions.

There is no evidence to suggest that the presence of sizeable ethnic linguistic communities in Britain may result in the country's eventual linguistic and cultural fragmentation. But, while this may well be the case, the continuous growth of non-English-speaking communities in UK' soil is undoubtedly having a profound impact on the country's public discourse. Mass influxes of non-English-speaking students into mainstream education have not only transformed the composition of the school population, they have given rise to alternative teaching practices, shaped social and education policies, challenged traditional perceptions of British citizenship and ultimately raised questions about the future of our country as one British nation.

---

11 US Bureau of Census (1995), *Statistical Abstract of the United States 1995: The National Database Book, and Country and City Data Book 1994, A Statistical Abstract Supplement* (Washington DC: US Bureau of Census).

12 Farnen, F.R. (ed.) (1994), *Nationalism, Ethnicity and Identity: Cross National and Comparative Perspectives* (New Brunswick, USA: Transaction Publishers).

13 Massey, D.S. (1995), 'The New Immigration and Ethnicity in the United States', *Population and Development Review*, 21:3, 631–52; Cohen, R. (1994), *Frontiers of Identity: the British and Others*, (London: Longman).

English as a Second Language (ESL) Education

Understanding how British society responds to the linguistic needs of the country's non-English speaking population will shed some light on these issues. It will also afford us an insight into the values inherently attached both to the dominant English-speaking Anglo-Saxon tradition and its non-English-speaking minority counterparts.

From the outset the task of defining what second language education amounts to appears problematic, with various existing pedagogical approaches including denominations such as ESL tuition, English for Speakers of Other Languages (ESOL), bilingual education and language immersion programmes, among others.[14] Beardsmore, for instance, has broadly defined a bilingual education programme as 'one where two (or more) languages serve as the medium of education' (Beardsmore 1994, 1–12).[15] In contrast, Pakir, specifically referring to the Singaporean language experience, understands bilingualism 'not as proficiency in any two languages, but as proficiency in English and in one other official language' (Pakir 1994, 13–27).[16] Second Language tuition in the United States, on the other hand, is understood as the medium through which non-English speaking children are fast-tracked into English in the shortest space of time possible. Perceptions of second language education therefore vary greatly between different societies, according to their demographic composition, historic and socio-political circumstances as well as sanctioned educational practices.

While the particulars of ESL education in Britain will be explored as part of the wider national identity question; the following sections provide a contextual backdrop to the British case. A variety of second language education settings relevant to the British experience is therefore here considered including, firstly, the unique bilingual

---

14 Note: for a review of the literature on multicultural education practices see Baker, C. and N. Hornberger (eds) (2001), *An Introductory Reader to the Writings of Jim Cummins,* (Clevendon, PA: Multilingual Matters); Phillipson, R. (ed.) (2000), *Rights to Language: Equity, Power and Education: Celebrating the 60ᵗʰ Birthday of Tove Skutnabb-Kangas,* (London: Lawrence Erlbaum Associates, Publishers); Cummins, J. (1986), *Bilingualism in Education: Aspects of Theory, Research and Practice,* (London: Longman); Leung, C. (2001), 'English as an Additional Language: Distinctive Language Focus or Diffused Curriculum Concerns?' *Language and Education,* vol. 15, no. 1, 33–55; Mohan, B.C. Leung and C. Davison (eds) (2001), *English as a Second Language in the Mainstream: Teaching, Learning and Identity,* (London: Longman); Skutnabb-Kangas, T. (1984), *Bilingualism or not: the Education of Minorities,* (Clevendon, PA: Multilingual Matters); August, D., K. Hakuta and Board on Children, Youth and Families (U.S.) (1998), Committee on Developing a Research Agenda on the Education of Limited-English-Proficient and Bilingual Students, *Educating Language-minority Children: A Research Agenda,* (Washington, DC: National Academy Press); Bourne, J.(1989), *Moving into the Mainstream: LEA Provision for Bilingual Pupils,* (Windsor: NFER-Nelson).

15 Beardsmore, H.B. (1994), 'An Overview of European Models of Bilingual Education', in R. Khoo, U. Kreher and R. Wong (eds), *Towards Global Multilingualism: European Models and Asian Realities* (Clevendon, PA: Multilingual Matters Ltd.), 1–12.

16 Pakir, A. (1994), 'Making Bilingualism Work: Developments in Bilingual Education', in Khoo, et al. (eds), *Towards Global Multilingualism,* 13–27.

situation of Wales within the UK; secondly, the contrasting educational experiences of the English speaking Canadian and Australian states; and thirdly, the exceptional case of United States as the world's foremost English-speaking superpower. The unparalleled socio-economic and linguistic position of the North American nation merits in itself a detailed analysis of this country's response to diversity; in particular the unprecedented growth of Spanish-speaking communities within its territory, now seemingly threatening social cohesion and national unity. Examining the development of second language education in the US over time will moreover reveal the various public narratives through which the North American national identity has been constructed, de-constructed and re-constructed. Significantly, despite the existence of considerable historical, geopolitical and cultural differences between the United States and Britain, the public discourse of the former appears to have followed a remarkably similar trajectory to that of the latter.

Bilingualism in Wales

The existence of bilingual education programmes in Wales represents an exception within an otherwise UK English-monolingual education system (Stubbs 1995, 25–39).[17] In the Catalonian tradition, Wales is a country's region where the dominant/minority linguist *status quo* has been reversed.[18] In Wales, Welsh – as opposed to English – has become the dominant language. As in the case of Spain's Catalonian region, language policy in Wales has been shaped by a strong cultural and nationalistic ethos. The Welsh tongue has come to be identified with the long historical struggle that eventually saw it reclaim its place next to the English language. This 'gentle revolution' which has witnessed the steady growth of bilingual schools in Wales has slowly unfolded during the past four decades (Baker 1995, 152–64).[19]

Although Celtic tongues are still spoken both in Ireland and Scotland, their overall social impact – unlike that of Welsh in Wales – has been negligible. According to Edwards, the attitude of speakers of Celtic languages towards their native tongues varies according to the tongue in question (Edwards 1994, 61–77).[20] Most speakers of Welsh, for instance, regard their linguistic heritage as an important issue, which deeply affects their sense of identity as well as their everyday lives. Personal feelings concerning the Welsh language certainly appear to be more powerful than any

---

17 Stubbs, M. (1995), 'Educational Language Planning in England and Wales: Multicultural Rhetoric an Assimilationist Assumptions', in O. Garcia and C. Baker (eds), *Policy and Practice in Bilingual Education: Extending the Foundations* (Clevendon, PA: Multilingual Matters), 25–39.

18 Note: for an insight into Catalonia's language experience see Artigal, J.M. (1995), 'Multiways towards Multilingualism: the Catalan Immersion Programme Experience', in T. Skutnabb-Kangas (ed.), *Multilingualism for All*, European Studies on Multilingualism, vol. 4, (Denmark: Swets and Zeitlinger), 169–81.

19 Baker, C. (1995), 'Bilingual Education in Wales' in C. Baker and O. Garcia (eds), *Policy and Practice in Bilingual Education: Extending the Foundations* (Clevendon, PA: Multilingual Matters), 152–64.

20 Edwards, C.G. (1994), 'Education and Welsh Language Planning' in Khoo, et al. (eds), *Towards Global Multilingualism,* 61–77.

political sentiment regarding nationalism. In contrast, the Gaelic language of Ireland can be said to have become more of a symbol of its political independence than a core element within the nation's broader socio-cultural context. Likewise in Scotland, despite a surge of interest in Scottish nationalism as a political force, the ancient tongue has arguably never been a significant factor in the Scottish psyche (Edwards 1994, 61–77). It remains to be seen whether the recent formation of a devolved Scottish Assembly will inject a new life into the region's indigenous language. While there are over 500,000 Welsh-speakers in Wales, fewer than 100,000 people are speakers of Scottish Gaelic in Scotland (OPCS 1991; Welsh Office 1992, 1).[21] Similarly, the use and maintenance of Irish Gaelic continues to be limited to a small number of schools in Northern Ireland. In addition, the long-term political instability of this region until recent times has made predictions about the future status of Irish Gaelic particularly difficult.

The origins of bilingual provision in Wales can be traced back to the beginning of the twentieth century when Welsh had no official status. In common with the Catalan example, schools began responding more or less informally to the linguistic and political demands of local communities by setting up classes to teach Welsh and sometimes to teach through the medium of Welsh (Bourne 1997, 49–65).[22] This unofficial method of teaching continued unabated in Wales amid progressive availability of educational funds from the Welsh Office. In 1965, a committee of inquiry under the chairmanship of Sir David Hughes Parry produced a report on the *Legal Status of the Welsh Language* which recommended the introduction of the principle of 'Equal Validity' (Welsh Office 1965, para. 172, 39).[23] Equal Validity broadly meant raising the legal status of Welsh to the same level enjoyed by the English language. The report therefore recommended that:

> The Principle of Equal Validity should be adopted as the basic principle governing the future use of Welsh in the administration of justice and the conduct of public administration (Welsh Office 1965, para. 3, 58).

By the mid-1980s, a large number of officially designated Welsh-medium primary and secondary schools were already operating throughout Wales. When the *Education Reform Act, 1988* (ERA) was finally passed, it provided for the Welsh language to become compulsory in Wales for pupils aged 5–16. The National Curriculum consequently included the following subjects for Wales: Key Stages 1 and 2: English (except at Key Stage 1 in Welsh-speaking classes), Welsh, Mathematics, Science, Technology (Design and Technology, and Information Technology), History,

---

21 Office of Population, Censuses and Surveys (OPCS) (1991), *Census 1991* (London: HMSO); Welsh Office (1992), *Welsh Social Survey 1992: Preliminary Results* (London: Government Statistical Service), 1.

22 Bourne, J. (1997), 'The Grown-ups know Best: Language Policy-Making in Britain in the 1990s', in W. Eggington and H. Wren (1997), *Language Policy: Dominant English, Pluralist Challenges* (Philadelphia: John Benjamin's Publishing Company), 49–65.

23 Welsh Office (1965), *Legal Status of the Welsh Language: Report of the Committee under the Chairmanship of Sir David Hughes Parry, 1963–1965* (London: HMSO), para. 172, 39.

Geography, Art, Music and Physical Education. Key Stage 3: as at Key Stages 1 and 2 plus a Modern Foreign Language. Finally, Key Stage 4: English, Welsh (except in non-Welsh-speaking schools), Mathematics, Sciences and Physical Education (DfEE Welsh Office 1995).[24]

In addition to the Welsh language requirement, the National Curriculum for Wales emphasised the need for pupils to be given opportunities to develop and apply their knowledge and understanding of the cultural, economic, environmental, historical and linguistic characteristics of Wales (DfEE Welsh Office 1995). Before the enactment of the ERA, county and local authorities in Wales had been wholly responsible for their individual language policies. This led to variations in the quality and scope of education programmes, and consequently raised doubts about the provision of language programmes in Wales.

Baker has long voiced concerns about whether Welsh language policy had become 'long-term, systematic, planned and co-ordinated enough to ensure that language education in Wales can play its part in the survival of the language' (Baker 1985, 64).[25] Edwards has similarly argued for a stronger emphasis on Welsh learning in the classroom. As he explains, pupils are readily exposed to a vast range of experiences in the English language outside school, especially through mass media and daily contact with their English-speaking peers. Welsh students' competence in English is thus 'expected to develop naturally' (Edwards 1994, 61–77).[26] Rawkins has gone as far as to say that when dealing with language learning in Wales, often 'piecemeal measures in response to short-term political pressures are preferred to a long range co-ordination of policy' (Rawkins 1979, 101).[27]

Since the introduction of the ERA, however, the National Curriculum has provided a centralised language policy strategy, considerably strengthening the position of Welsh in schools. Subsequent education practices have seen designated bilingual schools delivering lessons in Welsh, while English has come to be taught as a content subject. The process of linguistic redemption in Wales culminated with the promulgation of the *Welsh Language Act, 1993*. This important piece of legislation established the *Bwrdd yr Iaith Cymraeg* or Welsh Language Board, which would seek to protect and nurture the use of Welsh. In its opening statement the Act clearly declared its purpose:

> An Act to establish a Board having the function of promoting and facilitating the use of the Welsh language, to provide for the preparation by public bodies of schemes giving effect to the principle that in the conduct of public business and the administration of justice in Wales the English and Welsh languages should be treated on a basis of equality,

---

24   Department for Education and Employment (DfEE) Welsh Office (1995), *The National Curriculum* (London: HMSO).

25   Baker, C. (1985), *Aspects of Bilingualism in Wales* (Clevendon, PA: Multilingual Matters), 64.

26   *Welsh Language Act, 1993*, quoted in Edwards (1994), 'Education and Welsh Language Planning', 61–77.

27   Rawkins, P.M. (1979), *The Implementation of Language Policy in the Schools of Wales* (Strathclyde: University of Strathclyde Centre for the Study of Public Policy), 101.

to make further provision relating to the Welsh language, to repeal certain spent enactment relating to Wales, and for connected purposes (*Welsh Language Act* 1993, chp. 38, 1).[28]

Not only did the Act decree the official use of Welsh for matters of government and the administration of justice, it placed a duty on all public bodies to design Welsh language strategies accordingly. By giving effect to the original principle of 'Equal Validity', the *Welsh Language Act, 1993* ultimately provided for the establishment of a *de facto* bilingual Wales.

Since 1981, a question on speaking Welsh has been included on every *Census*, when more than half (54 per cent) the population said they did. Since then, the proportion of people speaking Welsh had fallen appreciably until reaching an all time low (19 per cent) in 1991. The *Census 2001* asked respondents, for the first time, about their 'understanding' of Welsh; nearly a quarter (24 per cent) of them said they could indeed understand the language. Over a fifth (21 per cent) of the population said they could speak Welsh, with a similar proportion (20 per cent) able to read and write (18 per cent) Welsh. Sixteen per cent reported that they had all these skills (National Statistics 2006d).[29]

Canada's Language Immersion Programmes

Canada has developed a so-called language immersion model that allows English-speaking Canadians to achieve some proficiency in French (Beardsmore and Kohls 1985, 6:1, 1–15).[30] By producing bilingual speakers, Canadian immersion programmes ultimately aim to integrate both majority and minority languages (Stephen and Caron-Caldas 1999, 12:1, 42–58).[31] Immersion schooling consists of a home-school language switch, whereby English-speaking students are engaged with the French language early on. French is not only taught as a subject matter, it is also used as a medium for learning core subjects such as History, Maths or Sciences (Johnson and Swain 1997).[32] Native English-speaking Canadian children thus learn how to speak, read and write in French while attending mainstream school. As pupils progress through the Canadian school system, French eventually becomes the classroom language. There are three main variants of immersion programmes (i.e. early, middle and late), which can be distinguished by the starting age. Early immersion takes place during the earliest years of schooling in kindergarten or

---

28 *Welsh Language Act, 1993* (1993) (London: HMSO), chp. 38, 1.

29 National Statistics (2006d), *Census 2001: Wales: Its People – Welsh Language* (London: TSO) <http://www.statistics.gov.uk/CCI/nugget.asp?ID=447&Pos=&ColRank=1& Rank=374> (accessed 14 April 2006).

30 Beardsmore, H.B. and J. Kohls (1985), 'Designing Bilingual Education: Aspects of Immersion and European School Models', *Journal of Multilingual and Multicultural Development*, 6:1, 1–15.

31 Stephen J. and S. Caron-Caldas (1999), 'Language Immersion and Cultural Identity: Conflicting Influences and Values', *Language, Culture and Curriculum*, 12:1, 42–58.

32 Johnson, R.K. and M. Swain (eds) (1997), *Immersion Education: International Perspectives* (Cambridge: Cambridge University Press).

Grades 1 or 2 (Lapkin 1998).[33] Middle immersion instruction starts around Grades 4 or 5, with students being taught through the French language between 50 to 100 per cent of the time. Late immersion teaching generally starts around Grades 6 or 7, with students receiving intense tuition in French (usually a minimum of 80 per cent of the time) for about one or two years. Once the pupils reach High School, the exposure to French is progressively reduced (Cummins 1995, 159–168).[34]

While Canadian students may become reasonably proficient in French, their linguistic prowess in this language is second to their English language skills. Skutnabb-Kangas has pointed out that the linguistic expectations of immersion programmes for eventual fluency in French 'in no way match up to native speakers' norms'(Skutnabb-Kangas 1995, 24). Cummins suggests that the reason behind this lays in the superior status enjoyed by English in relation to the French language (Cummins 1995, 159–168). Throughout Elementary School, English certainly remains the major language of instruction, whereas French is frequently not introduced until Grade 4. The absence of native French-speaking peers constitutes a further limiting factor on the level of expressive French attained by Canadian students in immersion programmes.

There is a further element challenging the efficiency of immersion schooling in Canada, namely: immigration. Canadian immersion programmes have traditionally catered for a relatively homogenous school population mainly consisting of English-speaking white indigenous students. As changes in Canada's demographic composition gather pace, language education practices will have to adapt to respond to the country's increasing cultural and linguistic diversity. It is estimated that ESL students already account for about 70 per cent of Toronto's school population alone (Genesee 1995, 118–138).[35] Within this context, the applicability of immersion programmes for non-English-speaking children has been called into question. For the latter neither enjoys a similar socio-linguistic status nor have the same educational needs than the majority of the English-speaking Canadian school population (Cummins and Danesi 1990).[36] Notwithstanding, Canadian immersion programmes are widely regarded as successful strategies of multilingual education through which students acquire functional competence in French, while being able to become academically accomplished in their native English language (Genesee 1995, 118–138).

---

33   Lapkin, S. (ed.) (1998), *French Second Language Education in Canada: Empirical Studies* (Toronto: University of Toronto Press).

34   Cummins, J. (1995), 'The European Schools Model in Relation to French Immersion Programmes, in Canada', in T. Skutnabb-Kangas (ed.), *Multilingualism for All*, 159–168.

35   Genesee, F. (1995), 'The Canadian Second Language Immersion Programme', in O. Garcia and C. Baker (eds), *Policy and Practice in Bilingual Education: Extending the Foundations* (Clevendon, PA: Multilingual Matters), 118–138.

36   Cummins, J., and M. Danesi (1990), *Heritage Languages: The Development and Denial of Canada's Linguistic Resources* (Toronto: Garamond).

Multicultural Education in Australia

Australia is probably unique in the degree to which, in principle, the country's language policy has officially embraced the minority languages of its many ethnic communities (Clyne 1988, 3:3, 237–280; Herriman 1996, 35–61).[37] The *National Policy on Language 1987*, also known as the *Lo Bianco Report* after its main architect, constitutes the inaugural cornerstone of language education provision in Australia. This early piece of legislation was driven by a pluralist ideology concerned as much with ethnic identity and language rights as with ESL teaching and access to education. Overall, the *Lo Bianco Report* comprised four basic educational goals: firstly, availability of English and English literacy for all; secondly, support for Aboriginal languages; thirdly, adequate provision of modern foreign languages tuition; and fourthly, equality of access to language education services (Lo Bianco 1987; Lo Bianco 1998, 6:2, 1–7).[38] The *Lo Bianco Report*, Gibbons suggests, put 'multilingualism alongside multiculturalism as a national ethos' (Gibbons 1995, 103–12).[39]

In contrast, the subsequent *National Language and Literacy Policy 1991* envisaged a somewhat narrower approach to language education, which focused on the learning and teaching of English. Rather than the broad social goals which had concerned its predecessor, the *National Language and Literacy Policy* emphasised the need to provide English language education and training. While allowing for the learning of tongues other than English, Australian language policy clearly conferred a prominent status to English. The 1990 White Paper *Australian Language and Literacy Policy* stated that:

> All Australian residents should develop and maintain a level of spoken and written English which is appropriate for a range of contexts, with the support of education and training programmes addressing their diverse learning needs. The learning of languages other than English must be substantially expanded and improved to enhance educational outcomes and communication both within the Australian and international community. Aboriginal and Torres Strait Islander languages should be maintained and developed where they are still transmitted. Other languages should be assisted in an appropriate way, for example, through recording. These activities should only occur where the speakers so desire and in consultation with their community, for the benefit of the descendants of their speakers and for the nation's heritage. Language services provided through interpreting and translating,

---

37 Clyne, M. (1988) 'Australia's National Policy on Language and its Implications', *Journal of Educational Policy*, 3:3, 237–280; Herriman, M (1996), 'Language Policy in Australia', in M. Herriman and B. Brunaby (eds), *Language Policy in English-Dominant Countries: Six Case Studies* (Clevendon, PA: Multilingual Matters), 35–61.

38 Lo Bianco, J. (1987), *National Policy on Languages,* Commonwealth Department for Education (Canberra: Australian Government Publishing Service); Lo Bianco, J. (1998), 'ESL: is it Migrant Literacy? Is it History? *Australian Language Matters*, 6:2, 1–7.

39 Gibbons, J. (1995), 'Multilingualism for Australians', in T. Skutnabb-Kangas (ed.), *Multilingualism for All*, 103–12.

print and electronic media and libraries should be expanded and improved (DEET 1991, xiii).[40]

In spite of the seemingly pluralistic ethos of this document, evidence suggests that the reality of multiculturalism in Australia has overwhelmingly favoured English language programmes (Astill and Keeves 1999, 2:1, 1–12; McKay 1998).[41] A look at language education funding practices in any given year illustrates this point. In 1994, for example, the average Australian government's funding for language programmes comprised the following: Adult ESL (AU$120.35 million), Children's ESL (AU$117.76 million), Adult English Literacy (AU$52.63 million), Aboriginal Literacy and Language (AU$8.25 million), Advisory Councils and Research (AU$6.44 million), Adult LOTE (Languages Other Than English – i.e. Modern Foreign Languages) (AU$5.35 million) and Children's English Literacy (AU$5.1 million) (Herriman 1996, 59). The overwhelming financial support afforded to ESL tuition and English literacy programmes at the expense of community and Modern Foreign Languages initiatives provides an insight into the Australian government's educational priorities. As Gibbons has indicated, in Australia, 'the funding for maintenance of minority languages in mainstream education continues to be negligible, and for second language education in minority languages almost non-existent' (Gibbons 1995, 103–112). Herriman has gone as far as to say that Australian language policy amounts to a 'short-term rationale for the funding of particular programmes, a situation that seems to leave policy to the whim of political parties, ephemeral issues and sudden changes. It also creates a precedent for future political overriding of an area that ideally should be part of a national consensus' (Herriman 1996, 55; Ozolins 1993).[42]

As in the British and North American cases, there are practical considerations impinging on the development of a consistent and long-term language strategy in Australia. The most significant factor is the existence of an English-based school curriculum, which allows for national standardised examinations to be conducted in English. As a result, Australia's ESL education has long been conceived as a necessary transitional stage towards achieving fluency in English. In 1980, for instance, the Australian Institute of Multicultural Affairs produced a *Review of Multicultural and Migrant Education in Australia* in which lack of English proficiency was seen as 'the major barrier to effective participation in Australian society' (AIMA 1980, 13).[43] As Gibbons has indicated, it is perhaps the overwhelming socio-economic, political

---

40 Australian Department for Employment, Education and Training (DEET) (1991), *The Australian Language: Australia's Language and Literacy Policy Companion* (Canberra: AGPS), xiii.

41 Astill, B.R. and J.P. Keeves (1999), 'Assimilation, Absorption or Separatism in a Culturally and Linguistically Diverse Population', *International Journal of Bilingual Education and Bilingualism*, 2:1, 1–12; McKay, P. (1998), *The Literacy Benchmarks and ESL* (Canberra: Australian Council of TESOL Associations).

42 Ozolins, U. (1993), *The Politics of Language in Australia* (New York: Cambridge University Press).

43 Australian Institute of Multicultural Affairs (AIMA) (1980), *Review of Multicultural and Migrant Education* (Melbourne: AIMA), 13.

and cultural strength of the English language that ultimately hinders the realisation of a *de facto* pluralistic language policy in Australia (Gibbons 1995, 103–12).

Bilingual Education in the United States – A Case-study

A Discourse of Laissez-faire: We, the English-speaking People

Bilingual education in the United States is by no means a recent invention (Crawford, 1992a).[44] The origins of US second language education can be traced back to the colonial era, when German-English schooling was authorised by law in several states and flourished unofficially elsewhere. In response to pressure from immigrant communities, Kloss explains, other European tongues were also taught on their own or in conjunction with English (Kloss 1977; Cavanaugh 1996, 85:8, 40–44).[45] In spite of the fact that the peoples inhabiting this vast country had never been monolingual, the United States did not develop a federal bilingual education policy until the second half of the twentieth century. This lack of an officially sanctioned language strategy or any public institution specifically devoted to language issues is rather remarkable for a nation of its size and linguistic heritage. Ricento reminds us that 'the United States has never had an official language or a language academy' (Ricento 1996, 122–158).[46] To this day, English remains the *de facto*, as opposed to the *de jure*, national language (Piatt 1990, 3).[47] The reason behind such lack of a 'comprehensive language policy' for over a hundred years can be found in a prevailing *laissez-faire* public discourse (Ricento 1996, 128). This approach is mainly characterised by a taken-for-granted attitude towards the dominance of the Anglo-Saxon culture and its English language and a disregard of minority ethnic cultures and languages.

In the aftermath of the colonial period, Independence gave way to an enduring single hegemonic American ideal: the notion of 'We, The People'. Integral to the foundations of the federal state, it came to epitomise the core of the American nation. Cohen has long argued that such an ideal, in reality, only represented the powerful select few who had formulated it (Cohen 1994). The original British colonists in the United States had produced a social order moulded in their own national, political, cultural, religious and linguistic experience. As a result, the ideology of Americanisation that later emerged encapsulated the values cherished by the dominant English-speaking white Anglo-Saxon protestant elite. Their *laissez-faire* discourse thus pervaded all the institutions and symbols upon which the American

---

44 Crawford, J. (ed.) (1992a), *Language Loyalties: A Source Book on the Official English Controversy* (Chicago: The University of Chicago Press).

45 Kloss, H. (1977), *The American Bilingual Tradition* (Rowley, Mass.: Newbury House); Cavanaugh, M.P. (1996), 'History of Teaching English as a Second Language', *English Journal*, 85:8, 40–44.

46 Ricento, T. (1996), 'Language Policy in the United States', in M. Herriman and B. Burnaby (eds), *Language Policies in English-Dominant Countries: Six Case Studies* (Clevendon, PA: Multilingual Matters), 122–158.

47 Piatt, B. (1990), *English Only? Law and Language Policy in the United States* (Albuquerque: University of New Mexico Press), 3.

nation had been built. It was strong enough for the many immigrant communities, subsequently entering the country, to assert a collective American citizenship. In spite of the multicultural and multilingual nature of the US population, successive generations of immigrants invariably became transformed into English-speaking American citizens. The English language has played a prominent nationalistic role in this process of acculturation. Would-be US citizens have been largely expected to learn the English language and become integrated into the American way of life. While their many ethnic tongues survived at home, in community and church settings, they never posed a serious challenge to the supremacy of the English language. As Zentella has pointed out, by the time third generation US-born immigrants are old enough to communicate orally, a language shift into English has invariably occurred (Zentella 1997).[48] By devising a school curriculum that promotes the English language as well as US Anglo-Saxon values, the United States' education system has further perpetuated newcomers' cultural and linguistic integration. As a result, the problem of bilingual education largely avoided the public political agenda until the second half of the twentieth century, when the country's demographic landscape began to change in fundamental ways. Without previous significant demands for bilingual services, Crawford explains, 'the language of government' was certainly not at issue (Crawford 1992a, 9).

The period between the colonial days and the 1960s can therefore be described as a *laissez-faire* phase, mostly featuring the preservation of the *status quo*. Prior to that, Americans have had relatively limited experience with conflicts over language. For most of the country's history, the hegemony of the English language had seemed self-evident; seldom did anyone perceived a threat from other languages (Crawford 2000, 1).[49] The US government consequently did not see the need to either enact legislation protecting language rights or to make English the official language of the country. The federal government adopted a 'no policy' on language, explicitly defined and national in scope (Crawford 2000, 1; Kirp 1979).[50] During this time, ethnic linguistic minorities entering the United States were largely expected to abide by this 'un-official' view on bilingual education policy. Not surprisingly the impact of bilingual education in the political agenda was negligible. The fact that bilingual education was broadly believed to be a non-issue, Yanow would argue, conveys a message about the prevailing *laissez-faire* ideology behind such perception (Yanow 1996, 9).[51]

---

48 Zentella (1997), *Growing Up Bilingual: Puerto Rican Children in New York City* (New York: Blackwell).

49 Crawford, J. (2000), *At War with Diversity: US Language Policy in an Age of Anxiety* (Clevendon, PA: Multilingual Matters Ltd.), 1.

50 Kirp, D.L. (1979), *Doing Good by Doing Little: Race and Schooling in Britain* (Berkeley, CA: University of California Press).

51 Yanow, D. (1996), *How Does a Policy Mean? Interpreting Policy and Organisational Actions*, (Washington, DC: Georgetown University Press), 9.

A Discourse of Multiculturalism: Ethnic Minorities' Language Rights

The 'by default' endorsed *laissez-faire* discourse was based on the so-called doctrine of 'separate but equal', whereby racial segregation was believed to be compatible with American democracy (Bailey 1979).[52] Laws, official customs and practices had long segregated American citizens in public places, schools, restaurants, residencies, recreational facilities and the likes. By the mid-1950s, nearly half of the states in the nation had laws that assigned children to public schools solely on the basis of their race (Bailey 1979, 6). This publicly sanctioned ghettoisation translated into the non-white community experiencing widespread educational disadvantage. Towards the end of the decade, though, a shift in public attitudes began to take place, with the publication of the *Ashmore Report,* in 1954, inaugurating this process (Ashmore 1954).[53] The *Ashmore Report* brought into the open the plight of America's coloured citizens, by laying bare the acutely adverse conditions reining in all-black schools across the country, compared with the vastly more favourable ones existing in all-white establishments. Crucially, this document identified 'racial segregation' as the root of unequal educational opportunities (Ashmore 1954).

Brown v. Board of Education of Topeka, 1954 Two days after the Ashmore Report was published, the US Supreme Court adopted a landmark anti-discrimination decision in the *Brown v. Board of Education of Topeka* (US Supreme Court 1954, 347 US 483, 74 s. ct. 686).[54] In Kansas, where the Brown case originated, state law permitted Topeka's Board of Education to segregate elementary school children by race. This lawsuit was initiated by African-American parents, suing for the right to an integrated education for their children. Their legal action dealt with racial discrimination as a basis for educational inequality. Brown – the leading plaintiff – complained, among other things, about the lack of safety, which resulted from bussing his daughter Linda to a 'coloured school' some 21 blocks away, as opposed to sending her to the neighbourhood school, only seven blocks away from his home (Bailey 1979, 7). The *Brown v. Board of Education* case was ultimately an attack on racial separateness. When the lawsuit reached the Supreme Court, appended to it was a document called 'The Effects of Segregation and the Consequences of Desegregation: A Social Science Statement' that had been signed by thirty-two prominent social scientists. It summarised what was then known about the adverse effects of statutory racial segregation on minority children. Segregation was explicitly defined as, 'that restriction of opportunities for different types of associations between the members of one racial, religious, national or geographical origin, or linguistic group and those of other groups, which results from or is supported by the action of any official body

52 Bailey, S.K. (1979), *Prejudice and Pride: the Brown Decision after Twenty-Five Years, May 17th 1954 – May 17th 1979, Report from the US National Academy of Education* (Washington, DC: US Department of Health, Education and Welfare).

53 Ashmore, H. (1954), *The Negro and The Schools* (Chapel Hill: University of North Carolina Press).

54 US Supreme Court (1954), *Brown v. Board of Education of Topeka* (Washington, DC: US Supreme Court), 347 US 483, 74 s. ct. 686.

or agency representing some branch of government' (Bailey 1979, 7). In explaining the Court's ruling, Chief Justice Warren wrote:

> Does segregation of children in public schools solely on the basis of race, even though the physical facilities and other tangible factors may be equal, deprive children of the minority group of equal educational opportunities? We believe it does. We conclude that in the field of public education, the doctrine of 'separate but equal' has no place. Separate educational facilities are inherently unequal (US Supreme Court 1954, 347 US 483, 74 s. ct. 686).

This Supreme Court decision was based on the belief that separate and segregated facilities provided for non-white US citizens were not, in fact, equal. On the contrary, existing patterns of segregation were no more than a manifestation of prejudice pervading North American society. By setting coloured students apart from the white majority, the latter were both discriminated against as well as rendered academically disadvantaged. Regardless of the existence of equality of facilities, racial segregation was inherently discriminatory. The Supreme Court recognised that intentional segregation amounted to an official caste system that ghettoised coloured citizens (Bailey 1979, 6). While the removal of school segregation would not necessarily abate racial prejudice, ethnic minority pupils would at least not be deprived of the opportunity to access society's services on their own merits. As Bailey has put it, 'what the lawyers and justices associated with the *Brown* decision actually demanded was that race should be an irrelevant issue in all public policy – including educational policy' (Bailey 1979, 6).

Following the *Brown* ruling, states courts throughout the country began to recognise that racial segregation did inherently promote inequality (Bailey 1979, 7). Faced with evidence that school authorities consistently made decisions regarding, among others, attendance areas, faculty assignment and grade structure in ways that would racially separate children, these courts eventually decided that 'desegregation' was required (Bailey 1979, 8). Congress, in turn, came to view the *Brown* decision in the same light; with the *Civil Rights Act of 1964* clearly spelling out 'desegregation' as 'the assignment of students to public schools, and within such schools without regard to their race, colour, religion, or national origin'(Bailey 1979, 7). Every American citizen was therefore now guaranteed equal treatment before the law, regardless of race or ancestry. Within the context of bilingual education, the *Brown v. Board of Education* ruling signalled the beginning of a process of policy reframing, which would culminate with the replacement of the prevailing *laissez-faire* discourse with a multiculturalist narrative. The first step in this transformation had seen the government's long-held views on schooling practices being challenged. Both the African-American community as well as the country's judiciary had understood the ideology of 'separate but equal' to be discriminatory. Moreover, as integrated education became a reality across the country, the educational needs of non-English-speaking children would soon cease to be considered a non-issue. By the late 1960s, Crawford notes, bilingual education had already become a civil rights concern (Crawford 2000, 91). When the *Bilingual Education Act of 1968* was eventually passed, the academic underachievement of Limited English Proficient

(LEP) students was a matter of public debate throughout the United States (Crawford 2000, 84).

Bilingual Education Act (BEA), 1968   The federal government's first attempt to deal comprehensively with the educational needs of non-English-speaking students was arguably the *Bilingual Education Act of 1968*.[55] The original purpose of this piece of legislation was to address the learning needs of Mexican-American children in the Southwest who had either been segregated in 'inferior' schools or placed in English-only classes (Lyons 1992, 363–66).[56] Senator Yargorough, a Texan populist, introduced the legislation in an attempt to break what he saw as a cycle of injustice. War and annexation, Crawford explains, had reduced Spanish speakers to 'a powerless minority' which, in turn, 'encouraged their economic exploitation, perpetuated by the educational neglect of their children in English-only classrooms' (Crawford 1992b, 75).[57] Senator Yargorough had conceived bilingual education as a special entitlement for Spanish-speaking Mexican-Americans, rather than a programme to cater generally for ethnic linguistic minorities. In the event, the legislation went on to acknowledge the country's rich cultural diversity, and consequently it addressed the scholastic needs of all its ethnic communities:

> In recognition of the special educational needs of the large numbers of children of limited English-speaking ability in the Untied States, Congress hereby declares it to be the policy of the United States to provide financial assistance to local educational agencies to develop and carry out new and imaginative elementary and secondary school programmes designed to meet these special needs (U.S.C., quoted in Anderson and Boyer 1970, vol. 2, appxs., 1).[58]

Title VII of the Act introduced a standard 'Bilingual Education Programme' as one designed to cater for the educational requirements of 3 to 18 year olds whose first language is not English (U.S.C., quoted in Anderson and Boyer 1970, 8). The main aim of this second language programme was to allow non-English-speaking children to 'develop greater competence in English, to become more proficient in the use of two languages and to profit from increased educational opportunity' (U.S.C., quoted in Anderson and Boyer 1970, 8). Although Title VII clearly affirmed the importance of English, it also recognised the relevance of mother tongue teaching:

---

55 Note: the *Bilingual Education Act* of 1968 derived from an earlier *Elementary and Secondary Education Act of 1965*, which it amended and extended. See U.S.C. (United States Congress), *Bilingual Education Act, Title VII, Elementary and Secondary Education Act of 1965*, as amended in 1967, Public Law 90–247, appx. A, sect. 702, stat. 816, 2 January 1968.

56 Lyons, J.J. (1992), 'Secretary Bennett versus Equal Opportunity', in Crawford (ed.), *Language Loyalties*, 363–66.

57 Crawford, J. (1992b), *Hold Your Tongue: Bilingualism and the Politics of 'English Only'* (Teading, MA: Adison-Wesley), 75.

58 U.S.C. (1970), *Bilingual Education Act*, quoted in T. Anderson and M. Boyer, *Bilingual Education Learning in the United States* (Austin, Texas: Southwest Educational Development Laboratory), vol. 2, appxs., 1.

A child's mother tongue which is other than English can have a beneficial effect upon his education. The mother tongue, used as the medium of instruction before the child's command of English is sufficient to carry the whole load of his education, can help to prevent retardation in school performance. The literacy thus achieved in the non-English tongue, if further developed, should result in a more liberally educated adult (U.S.C., quoted in Anderson and Boyer 1970, 8).

The Act went as far as to define bilingual education as instruction in two languages and the use of those two languages as mediums of instruction for any part or the entire school curriculum. Study of the history and culture associated with a student's mother tongue was ultimately considered an integral part of bilingual programmes. The government's endorsement of the Act can be said to signify an ideological shift, away from the prevailing *laissez-faire* ideology and towards a more equitable multiculturalist perspective. It could be argued that the values embedded in the *Bilingual Education Act* of 1968 ultimately reflect the way in which federal policy-makers made sense of bilingual education policy at the time (Yanow 1996, ix). Throughout the 1960s and 1970s, the debate over bilingual education continued to move further in the direction of language rights and equal opportunities. It became, in the words of Crawford, a clash of attitudes, 'nativist bias versus tolerance toward newcomers, Anglo-conformity versus an appreciation of diversity' (Crawford 1992a, 87).

Lau v. Nichols, 1974 Twenty years after the *Brown v. Board of Education* case, another community-based lawsuit was to strengthen the government's re-interpretation of bilingual education as an equal opportunities issue. The so-called *Lau v. Nichols* of 1974 was a class-action suit initiated by the parents of nearly 2,000 Chinese students within the 16,500 strong San Francisco public school system. Here, approximately one-third of all the Chinese students received supplemental instruction in the English language; the remainder received no special tuition (Lyons 1995, 4).[59] The legal challenge was initiated by Lau – a Chinese student – and his guardians on behalf of 1,800 children of non-English-speaking ability. They litigated against Nichols, Chancellor of the San Francisco Public Schools, for the purpose of 'seeking relief against alleged unequal education opportunities resulting from the officials' failure to establish a programme to rectify the students' language problem' (*Lau v. Nichols*, quoted in Santiago 1978, 55).[60] The plaintiffs argued that the inability of the San Francisco Unified School District officials to remedy existing inequality of opportunity violated the Fourteenth Amendment to the *US Constitution* as well as Title VI of the *Civil Rights Act of 1964* (*US Constitution* and *Civil Rights Act*, quoted in Maidment and McGrew 1986, 201; Crawford 1992a, 253).[61] The petitioners asked

59 Lyons, J.J. (1995), 'The Past and Future Directions of Federal Bilingual-Education Policy', in O. Garcia and C. Baker (eds), *Policy and Practice in Bilingual Education: Extending the Foundations* (Clevendon, PA: Multilingual Matters), 4.

60 *Lau v. Nichols*, 414 US 563, 1974, quoted in I. Santiago (1978), *A Community's Struggle for Equal Educational Opportunity: ASPIRA v. Board of Education* (Princeton, NJ: Office for Minority Education Testing Service), 55.

61 Note: the Fourteenth Amendment to the *US Constitution* states that 'no state shall … deny to any person within its jurisdiction the equal protection of the laws', while Title VI

that the Board of Education be directed to apply its expertise to the problem and rectify the situation (Crawford 1992a, 252). The case was first argued before the District Court of California. The lower court in San Francisco was very sympathetic but unresponsive. *Lau v. Nichols* was then appealed to the United States Court of Appeals for the Ninth Circuit, which affirmed the decision of the lower court. Finding 'no violation' cither of the *US Constitution* or Title VI of the *Civil Rights Act of 1964*, the Court stated:

> Every student brings to the starting line of his educational career different advantages and disadvantages caused in part by social, economic and cultural background, created and continued completely apart from any contribution by the school system (*Lau v. Nichols,* 414 US 563, 797 quoted in Santiago 1978, 55).

The lower federal court went on to absolve the San Francisco School District of any responsibility for ethnic minority children's 'language deficiency' (Crawford 1992a, 252). The case was then appealed to the US Supreme Court. Astonishingly, the highest court in the land unanimously disagreed with the federal court's decision. In reversing the judgement of the Ninth Circuit Court, the US Supreme Court found that English-only instruction to non-English-speaking public school students in San Francisco was a violation of Title VI of the *Civil Rights Act of 1964.* The basis of the Court's ruling rested on the understanding that these children's deficiency in English had prevented them from meaningful participation in the education programmes offered by their School District. It was consequently deemed that, by merely treating all students the same, school administrators had not met their obligations to provide equal educational opportunities. On the contrary, they had neglected their responsibility to offer special help to those pupils unable to understand English. In delivering the decision, on 21 January 1974, Justice Douglas stated:

> It seems obvious that the Chinese-speaking minority receives fewer benefits than the English-speaking majority from the respondents' school system, which denies them a meaningful opportunity to participate in the educational program (*Lau v. Nichols,* 414 US 563, 568 quoted in Santiago 1978, 55).

In short, it was recognised that when children arrived at school with little or no English-speaking ability, 'sink or swim' instruction was a violation of their civil rights. There was no such a thing as equality of treatment simply by providing students with the same facilities, textbooks, teachers and curriculum. For pupils who did not understand English were effectively precluded from attaining any meaningful education (Crawford 1992a, 253). As the US Supreme Court Justice indicated, 'basic English skills are at the very core of what these public schools teach. Imposition of a requirement that, before a child can effectively participate in the educational programme he must already have acquired those basic skills is to make a mockery

---

of the *Civil Rights Act of 1964* bans discrimination based 'on the grounds of race, colour, or national origin' in 'any programme or activity receiving federal financial assistance', quoted in R. Maidment and A. McGrew (1986), *The American Political Process* (London: Sage), 201; Crawford (ed.) (1992a), *Language Loyalties*, 253.

of public education' (*Lau v. Nichols,* 414 US 563, 568 quoted in Santiago 1978, 56). The US Supreme Court however, stopped short of decreeing the official provision of bilingual programmes, thus leaving the door open to other pedagogical treatments for LEP students. As Justice Douglas indicated:

> No specific remedy is urged upon us. Teaching English to the students of Chinese ancestry who do not speak the language is one choice. Giving instructions to this group in Chinese is another. There may be others. Petitioner asks only that the Board of Education be directed to apply its expertise to the problem and rectify the situation (*Lau v. Nichols,* 414 US 563, 563, quoted in Crawford 2000, 93).

The US Office of Education interpreted this decision as the remedy of choice whenever a school district was found to be violating the civil rights of LEP students (Crawford 2000, 93). As a result, *Lau v. Nichols* soon became a mandate for bilingual education in the country. In the aftermath of the ruling, the Office of Civil Rights convened a group of experts to recommend approaches for implementing the Supreme Court's decision. The ensuing *Lau Remedies* outlined the necessary procedures districts should follow to be in compliance with the Court's decision including programme selection, identification of students' primary language, personnel requirements, parental notification and evaluation (Fernandez 1987, 90–123).[62] Enforcement of these measures from 1975 to 1981 saw bilingual education imposed in nearly 500 school districts nationwide through consent agreements known as *Lau Plans* (Crawford 2000, 93). For the first time, large numbers of school districts were compelled to pay attention to their LEP students and to effectively address these children's educational needs Before the mid-1970s, few had done either of these things (Crawford 2000, 93).

The *Lau v. Nichols* ruling set a major legal precedent on language rights in the USA, whereby the federal government was obliged to provide adequate language programmes to safeguard fundamental civil rights (Crawford 2000, 92). By successfully defending the language rights of non-English-speaking minorities, the *Lau v. Nichols* decision consolidated the government's re-framing of bilingual education policy as an equal opportunities matter. The main architects of such an ideological transformation had been none other than the linguistic ethnic minorities themselves. Together with the judiciary, they have managed to find common ground in a shared understanding of bilingual policy. In a nation noted for its respect for law and order, Castellanos suggests, 'American minorities were turning to the courts in their attempt to leave a more hopeful legacy for their children than they themselves had inherited from their forebears' (Castellanos and Leggio 1983; 117).[63]

Bilingual Education Act, 1974   The fact that Congress re-authorised and substantially revised the *Bilingual Education Act of 1968* illustrates the prominence that bilingual

---

62 Fernandez, R.R. (1987), 'Legislation, Regulation, and Litigation: the Origins and Evolution of Public Policy on Bilingual Education in the United States', in W.A. Van Horne (ed.), *Ethnicity and Language* (Milwaukee: the University of Wisconsin), 90–123.

63 Castellanos, D. and P. Leggio (1983), *The Best of Two Worlds: Bilingual-Bicultural Education in the US* (Trenton, NJ: New Jersey State Department for Education), 117.

education policy had acquired by the mid-1970s. The new amended *Bilingual Education Act of 1974* expanded the previous programme by approving, among others, new grants for training and technical assistance for state educational agencies. It also established a National Clearinghouse for Bilingual Education (NCBE) for the collection, analysis and dissemination of information on bilingual programmes. In accordance with the now prevailing multiculturalist discourse, the Act recognised three basic educational facts previously overlooked: firstly, the existence of 'large numbers of children of limited English-speaking ability' nationwide; secondly, that such children 'have educational needs which can be met by the use of bilingual educational methods and techniques'; and thirdly, that 'a primary means by which a child learns is through the use of such child's language and cultural heritage' (U.S.C. 1976, vol. 88, part 1, Title VII: *'Bilingual Education Act'*, stat. 88, sec. 702 (a) (1) (2) (3) (4) (5), 503–04).[64] The *Bilingual Education Act of 1974* was therefore instituted to provide equality of opportunities for all:

> Congress declares it to be the policy of the United States, in order to establish equal educational opportunity for all children, to encourage the establishment of an operation, where appropriate, of educational programmes using bilingual educational practices, techniques and methods; and for that purpose, to provide financial assistance to local educational agencies and to State educational agencies for certain purposes, in order to enable such local educational agencies to develop and carry out such programmes in elementary and secondary schools, including activities at the pre-school level, which are designed to meet the educational needs of such children; and to demonstrate effective ways of providing, for children of limited English-speaking ability, instruction designed to enable them, while using their native language, to achieve competence in the English language (U.S.C. 1976, Title VII: *'Bilingual Education Act'*, stat. 88, sec. 702 (a), 503–04).

The term 'programme of bilingual education' hence referred to language tuition designed to cater for 'children of limited English-speaking ability in Elementary or Secondary schools' (U.S.C. 1976, Title VII: *'Bilingual Education Act'*, stat. 88, sec. 703 (a) (4), 504). The use of these students' native languages was only to be allowed in so far as it contributed to pupils' progress in English. Although upholding LEP students' language rights, the *Bilingual Education Act of 1974* clearly reinforced the compensatory nature of bilingual education policy. The *Lau* decision had not given LEP students the right to learn their own language, but only the right to learn English. Empowered with such a newly acquired entitlement, ethnic linguistic communities across the country made their voices heard. During the 1970s several school districts became the target of lawsuits by parents, who argued that failure to address their LEP students' language needs meant failure to provide them with equal opportunities to learn (Crawford 2000, 91). One of such

---

64 U.S.C. (1976), *United States Statues at Large 1974,* containing the laws and concurrent resolutions enacted during the second session of the 93rd Congress of the United States of America 1974 and proclamations, vol. 88, part 1, Public Laws 93–246 through 93–446 (Washington, DC: US Government Printing Office), Title VII: *'Bilingual Education Act'*, stat. 88, sec. 702 (a) (1) (2) (3) (4) (5), 503–04.

legal actions, the so-called *ASPIRA v. Board of Education*, involved the Hispanic community in New York City.

ASPIRA v. Board of Education of New York City, 1974 Following the *Lau v. Nichols* decision, the *ASPIRA v. Board of Education* lawsuit grappled with similar issues relating to the education of children of limited English-speaking ability. On the 20 September 1972, ASPIRA, a Puerto Rican community organisation, filed a suit against the Board of Education of New York City. ASPIRA claimed that the 182,000 Puerto Rican children of limited or non-English-speaking ability enrolled in New York City schools had been denied the right to equal educational opportunities (Santiago 1978, 6). The discrimination experienced by these children was alleged to have been a function of both their ethnic origin as well as their lack of English-language skills. The complaint filed with the court by ASPIRA maintained that:

> Plaintiffs and the members of the class they represent are Puerto Rican and other Spanish-speaking persons who speak English poorly or not at all. They are linguistically, culturally and historically different from the dominant culture in New York City. Yet the defendants have failed to recognise these differences in designing and implementing educational services and courses of study for plaintiffs. Specifically, they have failed to take into account the plaintiffs' inability to speak and understand English, and learn in classes conducted in the English language. Moreover, the defendants have not effectively taught the plaintiffs and their classes the English language. The failures of the defendants' public officials have been catastrophic. The rates of illiteracy, dropout and truancy in public schools for plaintiffs and their classes are shocking (US District Court, Southern District of New York (SDNY), quoted in Santiago 1978, 50).[65]

The Puerto Rican Legal Defence and Education Fund (PRLDEF) – attorneys for the plaintiffs – contended that children of limited or no English-speaking ability were precluded from fully participating in the learning process, because they were not able to understand either their teachers or the classroom texts. In accordance with the *Lau* case, the *ASPIRA* suit claimed that non-English-speaking children had been both denied equal educational opportunities as well as having their civil rights violated. It was argued that the Board of Education of New York City and its administrators had infringed Title VI of the *Civil Rights Act of 1964* together with the equal protection clause of the Fourteenth Amendment of the *US Constitution* (Santiago 1978, 50). The PRLDEF claimed that the Board of Education had failed to provide any adequate pedagogical programmes and services to meet these children's special linguistic needs. Consequently, ASPIRA petitioned the United States District Court to order the New York City Board of Education to provide bilingual programmes for all children in need of them (Santiago 1978, 6).

The *ASPIRA v. Board of Education* case turned out to be a lengthy and hard fought lawsuit. One in which the New York City Board of Education attempted to have the claim dismissed, while ASPIRA spent a considerable amount of time

---

65   US District Court, Southern District of New York (SDNY) (1974), *ASPIRA of New York Inc. v. Board of Education of the City of New York,* 72 civ. 4002 SDNY (New York: SDNY), quoted in Santiago (1978), *A Community's Struggle*, 50.

and resources gathering evidence to the contrary. On January 1973, US District Judge Frankel denied the Board's motion to dismiss the case on the grounds that the questions presented to the court were of 'evident gravity and complexity' (US District Court, SDNY, 58 FRD 62 SDNY, quoted in Santiago 1978, 53). During the time the *ASPIRA v. Board of Education* trial was in progress, the *Lau v. Nichols* case in California had reached the US Supreme Court. Recognising the similarity of the questions and issues raised both by *Lau* and *ASPIRA*, the judge delayed litigation until a decision had been reached in the *Lau v. Nichols* lawsuit. In the event, the unanimous ruling of the US Supreme Court in favour of *Lau* had a direct impact on the *ASPIRA v. Board of Education* case.

Although the eventual ruling provided legal protection for the language rights of non-English-speaking minorities, the Supreme Court's decision left many questions relating to the actual delivery of bilingual programmes unanswered. Among others, matters such as classification and assessment of LEP students, qualification and training of bilingual teachers, as well as evaluation and funding of bilingual programmes remained unsolved. Months of negotiations between ASPIRA and the Board of Education followed, in which both parties tried to agree on the best way to deliver bilingual education services. In April 1974, Judge Frankel ordered them to develop separate plans for the provision of bilingual education to LEP students. Upon receipt of the latter and after reviewing the legal issues involved, he concluded that there was sufficient ground for mutual agreement, and asked both parties to produce jointly a consent agreement (Santiago 1978, 65). On the 2 August 1974, they finally signed the so-called *APIRA v. Board of Education Consent Decree*. This document established a responsibility on the part of the Board of Education to: firstly, design and implement 'an improved method for accurately and systematically identifying and classifying children who are Spanish speaking or Spanish surnamed'; secondly, 'to provide all children attending public schools, both English-speaking and non-English-speaking pupils, with programmes in which they can effectively participate and learn'; thirdly, to promulgate a policy of 'minimum educational standards' to all districts and high schools in the New York City school system; and fourthly, to apply 'maximum feasible efforts to obtain and spend the funds required to implement' bilingual education (US District Court, SDNY 1974, 2–10).[66] The basic bilingual programme proposed by the *Consent Decree* comprised tuition in English as well as support for LEP children's Spanish language skills. This dual objective was to be achieved through an educational strategy involving: firstly, the development of 'the child's ability to speak, understand, read and write the English language'; secondly, 'instruction in substantive courses in Spanish (e.g. courses in mathematics, science and social studies); and finally, reinforcement of 'the child's use of Spanish' (US District Court, SDNY 1974, 4). The *Consent Decree*'s overriding concern was to ultimately provide equal educational opportunity as well as the highest quality of instructional programmes. In a memorandum accompanying the court order, Judge Frankel indicated:

---

66   US District Court, SDNY (1974), *ASPIRA of New York Inc. v. Board of Education of the City of New York*, 72 civ. 4002 (MEF) (New York: SDNY), 2–10.

The result appears to be a meaningful and hope-inspiring decree. There are problems still to be solved. There remain subjects of potential disputes in the future. But the main lines seem clear enough. And, most importantly, the court ventures to predict that the spirit of collaborative building that helped to bring us here should prove a vital force later on in meeting the further challenges we may face (US District Court, SDNY 1974, 7–8).

He considered the *Consent Decree* to be the result of 'a painstaking course of skilled, imaginative and high-minded endeavours' and explained how in the last critical months of negotiations, there had been 'an impressive display of constructive and creating lawyering' (US District Court, SDNY 1974, 6–7). In line with the Judge's positive remarks, Chancellor Anker, of the New York Central Board of Education, stressed that in entering into a consent agreement with ASPIRA, they were 'launching a major effort to implement further fundamental Board policy that every opportunity should be offered for all children in the city's public schools to be successful in learning' (New York City Board of Education (NCBOE) News Bureau 1974, 1–2).[67] He went on to say that 'we have an agreement we are happy with and we look forward to continue harmonious relationships with ASPIRA on behalf of our young people' (NCBOE News Bureau 1974, 2). While the two main players in the *ASPIRA v. Board of Education of New York City* case had found common ideological ground, their position was not universally endorsed. An array of different and often conflicting reactions to the newly established bilingual education programmes were reflected in the national press. The Spanish-speaking newspaper *El Diario ('The Daily')*, for instance, hailed the court's decision as 'a victory for bilingual education' (*El Diario* 1974).[68] The *New York Daily News*, on the other hand, viewed the *Consent Decree* as a 'bilingual headache', which the Board of Education had brought upon itself for failing to make a strong enough case for the provision of English-only instructional programmes (*The New York Daily News* 1975).[69] In contrast, the *New York Times* saw bilingual education as a matter of being 'dragged into progress' (*The New York Times* 1974).[70] In spite of such diverse responses to this educational phenomenon, bilingual programmes became institutionalised. Crawford has explained how in the process of doing so, bilingual education followed the course of many social reforms of the 1960s. Bilingual education, he argues, was 'conceived as an innovative approach to a social problem, it was taken up as a demand by ethnic militants and parents' organisations, supported by federal funds, and accepted by corps of experts, lawyers and bureaucrats' (Crawford 2000, 96). Just as the *Lau v. Nichols* ruling had done earlier, the *ASPIRA v. Board of Education Consent Decree* came to inform the officially sanctioned bilingual policy. In accordance with federal guidelines, hundreds of school districts nationwide now adopted bilingual education programmes. Against this background, it can be argued that having successfully reframed bilingual education in terms of equal opportunities and language rights, the current multiculturalist discourse had finally come to dominate the realm of

---

67   New York City Board of Education (NCBOE) News Bureau (1974), *Press Release no. N–13–1974/75* (New York: Office of Public Affairs), 1–2.

68   *El Diario,* 4 September 1974.

69   *The New York Daily News,* 6 January 1975.

70   *The New York Times,* 2 September 1974.

public policy. As Hajer would put it, both 'discourse structuration' and 'discourse institutionalisation' had now taken place (Hajer 1993, 46).[71]

A Discourse of Integration: English Only or English Plus?

At a press conference called by New York City's Board of Education in 1974 to announce the signing of the *ASPIRA v. Board of Education Consent Decree*, Chancellor Anker expressed concerns about the dangers inherent in bilingual education policy. He conceded that bilingual education was a necessity for Spanish-speaking students with 'discomfort' in English, but warned that 'many people ... believe that bilingualism could become a source of divisiveness' (Chancellor Irving Anker, quoted in Santiago 1978, 67).[72] From the moment bilingual education became a policy mandate, opposition to the very same policy had also been born. Crawford reminds us that 'prescriptiveness breeds resistance' (Crawford 2000, 93–94). Bilingual education policy might well have remained a marginal experiment had it not been imposed on school districts nationwide via the *Lau Remedies*, court orders and federal guidelines. Instead, as Chancellor Anker had warned, it ultimately became a point of conflict between federal authorities and local school boards.

Bilingual education policy was left open to criticism on two fronts. On the one hand, the legitimacy of second language education as a civil rights issue was questioned. In so far as bilingual education had become the domain of teachers, educationalists and professionals, its significance as a community concern and a social movement diminished. As a result, attention turned to the actual effectiveness of bilingual programmes, which were increasingly viewed with scepticism. Government agencies, educational bodies and school districts have certainly done little to explain the pedagogical basis of bilingual education to outsiders, particularly parents, many of whom were new to the United States and had no memory of earlier struggles for bilingual education. The broader public, which had never been clear about the rationale of native language instruction, grew increasingly wary of its results (Crawford 2000, 96). On the other hand, as bilingual education became standardised and the numbers of linguistic ethnic minority students kept on rising, nationwide deep-seated fears regarding the prospect of cultural and linguistic fragmentation surfaced. From the 1980s onwards, the multiculturalist public discourse – which had dominated the previous decade – started to give way to an emerging integrationist public narrative advocating English language nationalism. The closing years of the twentieth century would see this integrationist discourse successfully transform the issue of bilingual education policy – as an entitlement of linguistic ethnic minorities – into a legal struggle for the sanctioning of English as the country's official language.

---

71   Hajer, M.A. (1993), 'Discourse Coalitions and the Institutionalisation of Practice: the Case of Acid Rain in Britain', in F. Fisher and J. Forrester (eds), *The Argumentative Turn in Policy Analysis and Planning* (London: UCL Press), 46.

72   Chancellor Irving Anker speaking at the NYCBOE on 29 August 1974, quoted in Santiago (1978), *A Community's Struggle*, 67.

The Official English Movement   During the 1960s unprecedented mass migration from Asia and Latin America into the United States had already raised fears of cultural and linguistic fragmentation. These ethnic groups' continuous maintenance of their customs and heritage, in particular, had been widely perceived as either inability or unwillingness to assimilate into mainstream US society.[73] Throughout the 1970s, the development of bilingual education policy was therefore accompanied by a growing anti-immigration sentiment. In the aftermath of the *Lau* and *ASPIRA* decisions, such xenophobic feelings were compounded by concerns regarding both English language use as well as access to government and public services in tongues other than English. Within this context, a nationwide political movement aimed at protecting the English language by conferring it official status gradually emerged. It included an amalgamation of government agencies and political lobbying bureaux, public and private sector organisations as well as educational institutions and community groups.

From its inception in the early 1980s, the so-called 'Official English Campaign' sought an amendment to *The United States Constitution* that would make English the official language of the country. In 1981, Republican Californian Senator Hayakawa, a critic of linguistic minorities' voting rights, introduced for the first time ever such an amendment. The proposed amendment not only acknowledged English as the national language, it emphasised the transitional nature of bilingual education programs:

> The English language shall be the official language of the United States. Neither the United States nor any State shall make or enforce any law which requires the use of any language other than English. This article shall apply to laws, ordinances, regulations, order, programs and policies. No order or decree shall be issued by any court of the United States or of any State requiring that any proceedings, or matter to which this article applies, be in any language other than English. This article shall not prohibit educational instruction in a language other than English as required as a transitional method of making students who use a language other than English proficient in English. The Congress and the States shall have power to enforce that article by appropriate legislation (*S.J. Res. 72, 1981*, sects. 1–6, quoted in Crawford 1992a, 112).[74]

This early English Language Amendment went largely ignored, and it died without a hearing in the 97th US Congress. Prior to the English Language Amendment, Americans have seldom fought over their language. It seemed inconceivable that English may need legal protection in a country where, according to the *US Census, 1980,* it was spoken by all but two per cent of residents above the age of four, and where only 11 per cent of the population were regular speakers of another tongue (Crawford 1992a, 1). A new Babel appeared hardly imminent. Senator Hayakawa's

---

73 Note: for a historical view of the development of nativist groups in the United States see Piatt (1990), B., *English Only? Law and Language Policy in the United States* (Albuquerque: University of New Mexico Press).

74 *S.J. Res. 72, 1981*, sects. 1–6, proposed English Language Amendment to the *US Constitution* sponsored by Senator S.I. Hayakawa, quoted in Crawford (ed.) (1992a), *Language Loyalties*, 112.

action however, inaugurated what has become one of the most divisive debates in US politics to this day. Within the context of bilingual education policy, the English Language Amendment signalled a change in public perceptions regarding the issue of second language education. The entitlement of non-English-speaking immigrants to equal opportunities was now being challenged by the linguistic rights of the English-speaking population, who perceived their own language to have come under threat.

Hajer has argued that in the process of framing policy problems 'actors try to impose their views of reality on others, sometimes through debate and persuasion, but also manipulation and the exercise of power' (Hajer 1993, 45). The many flagship organisations belonging to the Official English Movement can be said to have deployed their growing budgets, nationwide membership and political influence to promote their specific views on bilingual education policy. Pressure groups such as US English and English First have certainly transformed the Official English campaign into a major force in US politics. The US English Agency alone has raised and spent millions of US dollars promoting their particular understanding of the English language question. Between 1983 and 1990, for example, it commanded a $28 million budget (Crawford 1992b, 4). While lobbying to legalise the official status of English, these groups have also sponsored the abolition of bilingual education programmes. Organisations such as the Centre for Equal Opportunity (CEO) and One Nation/One California, for instance, have consistently advocated the notion of 'one nation, one common language', while at the same time exposing 'the failure of bilingual education' (Chavez 1995, 1–4).[75] This ideological approach and the methods used to propagate it are ultimately symptomatic of the values underlying the Official English Movement.

Two concerns, in particular, have become central to the Official English campaign. On the one hand, there is the issue of national unity. As Linda Chavez, President of the Centre for Equal Opportunity has indicated, 'with 20 million immigrants now living in our country, it's more important than ever to teach newcomers to think of themselves as Americans, if we hope to remain one people, not simply a conglomeration of different groups. And one of the most effective ways of forging that sense of unity is through a common language' (Chavez 1995, 1–4). Hence, the need to ensure legal protection of English as the United States' official language. On the other hand, there is the perceived failure of bilingual education programmes to deliver their intended results (Unger 1995, 9).[76] The escalating costs of bilingual education over time make a compelling case. In the 1960s, federal allocation for second language education programmes comprised only a relatively small grant of $7.5 million. By the 1980s, in contrast, with some 2.4 million pupils already eligible to receive bilingual tuition, well over $5.5 billion were spent on their educational needs nationwide. It is estimated that New York City alone spent $400 million annually on its 147,500 bilingual students, which amounts to $2,712 per pupil (Chavez 1995, 1–4). Ron Unz, Chairman of One Nation/One California, has pointed out that there

---

75 Chavez, L. (1995), 'One Nation, One Common Language', Centre for Equal Opportunity (CEO), 1–4 <http://www.ceousa.org/html/chavez.html> (accessed 12 June 2002).

76 Unger, H. 'Babel Babble', *Education*, 18 August 1995, 9.

is no conclusive evidence of the effectiveness of bilingual programmes, but instead mounting data to the contrary. Writing in the *Los Angeles Times*, he refers to the results of ELS education programmes as 'utterly dismal'. As he explains, 'of the 1.3 million Californian schoolchildren – a quarter of our state's total public school enrolment – who begin each year classified as not knowing English, only about 5 per cent learn English by the year's end, implying an annual failure rate of 95 per cent for existing programmes' (Unz 1997, M6).[77]

The Official English Movement has not only mobilised a white middle-class conservative base, but it has managed to attract the support of members of linguistic ethnic communities across the country. Linda Chavez, a prominent Hispanic public figure, for instance, has strongly advocated English-Only educational policies (Chavez 1995, 1–4). Former House Speaker, Newt Gingrich, has also repeatedly called for a 'partial end of bilingual education'. He argues, that 'English is the common, commercial language in America … when we allow children to stay trapped in a bilingual programme, where you do not learn English, we are destroying their economic future' (Roman 1998, A–1).[78] The late President Reagan similarly stated his opposition to bilingual education programmes:

> Where there are predominantly students speaking a foreign language at home, coming to school and being taught English, and they fall behind or are unable to keep up in some subjects because of lack of knowledge of the language, I think it is proper that we have teachers equipped who can get at them in their own language and understand why it is they don't get the answer to the problem and help them in the way. But it is absolutely wrong and against American concepts to have a bilingual education program that is openly, admittedly dedicated to preserving their native language and never getting them adequate in English so they can go out in the job market and participate (Reagan, quoted in Lyons 1995, 1–4).[79]

Reagan, who had made attacks on federal red tape during his early election campaign, withdrew the *Lau* Regulations as one of his first official acts as President (Crawford 2000, 94). Against a backdrop of 3.6 million LEP students nationwide, his administration presided over progressive cuts on bilingual education funding (Bell 1982, 3).[80] During the fiscal years of 1980 and 1988, real spending under the *Bilingual Education Act of 1974* was reduced by 47 per cent. In contrast, total support for all education programmes declined by only eight per cent (Lyons 1995, 6). Lack of support for bilingual programmes continued to gain pace during the 1990s, in spite of the Clinton administrations' favourable view of bilingual education (Hakuta,

---

77 Unz, R.K. 'Bilingualism v. Bilingual Education', *Los Angeles Times,* 19 October 1997, M6.

78 Roman, N.E. 'Gingrich lays out Goals to reform Government', *The Washington Times*, 6 January 1998, A–1.

79 Public address by former President Ronald Reagan, quoted in Lyons (1995), 'The Past and Future Directions', 1–14.

80 Bell, T.H. (1982), *The Condition of Bilingual Education in the Nation* (Washington, DC: Department for Education), 3.

1993).[81] Since the early 1980s, this trend has been compounded by the refusal of the Office of Civil Rights to articulate a preference for any pedagogical approach to bilingual education (Crawford 2000, 94).

Critics of the Official English Movement's integrationist ideology have rallied behind the so-called 'English Plus Campaign'. This pro-bilingual education initiative is supported by an amalgamation of educationalists and political lobby groups as well as members of the research and academic communities across the country. Organisations such as the National Association for Bilingual Education (NABE), the Puerto Rican Defence and Educational Fund (PRDEF) and the National Council of *La Raza* (National Council of Race) have long advocated the provision of bilingual education programmes, while denouncing what they perceive to be a hidden US Anglo-Saxon nationalistic agenda. Supporters of the English Plus Campaign have come to voice a wide range of concerns regarding the direction US bilingual education policy is heading towards. Under the headline 'English-Only Laws will foster Divisiveness, not Unity: they are Anti-Hispanic, Anti-Elderly and Anti-Female', Zentella, for instance, has warned against the Official English Movement's views as being discriminatory and damaging to the American nation (Zentella 1998, B1–B3).[82] Mulero has further criticised English-only programmes for 'valuing English above community languages' (Mulero 1995, 7).[83] Woodward has furthermore highlighted the 'anti-immigrant' character of English-only legislation, which is based on misguided fears of that which is neither English nor Anglo-Saxon and is perceived to threaten the *status quo* (Woodward 1995, 76).[84] The essence of the current debate on second language education has been encapsulated by Crawford, who argues that bilingual education policy has become 'a discussion about national identity: what it means to be an American in the late twentieth century, and what will hold Americans together during a time of bewildering change. It [bilingual education] is about how much diversity a nation can tolerate, even a nation of immigrants' (Crawford 1992a, 87).

Despite the efforts of English Plus supporters during the past twenty years, the integrationist discourse embodied in the Official English Movement has ultimately come to dominate the US public narrative on second language education. Two main reasons that can be said to account for the success of this policy discourse. On the one hand, there is a significant ideological shift taking place among members of ethnic communities towards integration into US society. Second generation US-born English-speaking immigrants, in particular, seem to be moving away from bilingual programmes and towards the provision of English-only education. A *Los Angeles Times* poll carried out in 1997, showed that 84 per cent of Hispanic Californians favoured English-only public school instruction over bilingual tuition;

---

81   Hakuta, K. (1993), (ed.), *Federal Education Programmes for Limited-English-Proficient Students: A Blueprint for the Second Generation* (Stanford, CA: Stanford Working Group).

82   Zentella, A.C. 'English-Only Laws will foster Divisiveness, not Unity; They are Anti-Hispanic, Anti-Elderly, and Anti-Female', *The Chronicle of Higher Education,* 23 November 1998, B1–B3.

83   Mulero, L. 'Dole pone por Encima el Ingles' ('Dole puts English First'), *El Nuevo Dia ('The New Day'),* 13 October 1995, 7.

84   Woodward, C. 'Push for English-Only is on', *The San Juan Star,* 19 October 1995, 76.

while another *Los Angeles Times*-CNN poll a year later indicated that almost 40 per cent of Latinos already supported the abolition of bilingual education programmes (*Los Angeles Times*, quoted in Crawford 2000, 96–103).[85] On the other hand, the economic argument against bilingual programmes seems to be taking root. As the cost of bilingual tuition continues to rise, so do doubts about the long-term viability of such educational strategy.

With the activities of the Official English Movement having progressively intensified over time, the drive to legitimise English as the United States' official language has also accelerated. Between 1981 and 1990, sixteen English Language Amendments were introduced in Congress, in addition to various statues and resolutions. There have been two basic versions of the proposed amendments: on the one hand, there is the one-liner, which simply establishes English as the nation's official language. This leaves Congress and the federal courts to decide in which circumstances use of other languages may be allowed. On the other hand, there is the English-only mandate, which outlaws uses of other languages by federal, state and local governments. A few exceptions are specified here, such as emergency situations and foreign language classrooms (Crawford 1992a, 112). Although the Senate convened hearings on Official English in 1984, as did the House in 1988, the English Language Amendment has never come to a congressional vote. Ratification of an Official English Constitutional Amendment at the federal level would require the approval of three-fourths of the state legislatures, after passage by a two-third majority in both Houses of Congress. It therefore appears to be the strategy of proponents of these measures to obtain English statutes in most states first, and then argue that ratification of the federal provision would be no major departure from existing laws. Such tactics have been extremely successful. Since Senator Hayakawa first proposed an English Language Amendment to *the United States Constitution* in Congress in 1981, Official English legislation has been considered in forty-eight states, with a total of twenty-one states having now some form of Official English laws including: Arizona, Arkansas, California, Colorado, Florida, Georgia, Hawaii, Illinois, Indiana, Kentucky, Mississippi, Nebraska, North Carolina, North Dakota, South Carolina, Tennessee and Virginia (Piatt 1990, 21–22).

California: from Bilingualism to Monolingualism   Among the fifty states comprising the United States, few have so distinctively shaped the debate on bilingual education policy as California has. The so-called 'Golden State' is often thought to be a national 'trend setter' at the forefront of social developments; as Shiffman has put it 'things happen in California' (Shiffman 1996, 248).[86] The early free-speech entitlement, the hippie movement of the 1960s, the election of a former US movie actor as Governor in 1966 – re-elected in 1970 and later 40th US President, the anti-war movement of the 1970s, the race-related riots of the 1990s and the election of a second film start – this time, an Austrian immigrant – as Governor in 2003, all happened first in California. With regard to bilingual education policy, California has also been the

---

85 *Los Angeles Times,* 1997 and 1998, quoted in Crawford 2000, 96–103.

86 Shiffman, H.F. (1996), *Linguistic Culture and Language Policy* (London: Routledge), 248.

state where some of the most groundbreaking language legislation has originated, not least the *Lau v. Nichols* of 1974. During the 1970s, for instance, California was instrumental in placing bilingual education in the public political agenda, ultimately helping to frame the language question as an 'equal opportunities' issue. In contrast, throughout the 1980s and 1990s, California has been at the forefront of Official English legislation. Ironically, it has been this cutting-edge and influential state, the one which has helped facilitate the re-formulation of bilingual education within an integrationist public narrative. From the late 1980s onwards, the state legislature has passed a string of measures specifically aimed at legally protecting the English language as well as abolishing bilingual education. In 1986, for example, Proposition 63 was passed in California with 73 per cent of the vote (Ricento 1996, 151). This legislative landmark amended the State Constitution, making English the official language of California. Although Colorado and Florida have preceded California in similar rulings, the significance of the later addition cannot be underestimated, with fourteen more states following down the Californian route in quick succession.

In 1994, further Official English legislation followed. *Proposition 187*, the so-called SOS (Save Our State) by its US English sponsors, was approved by Californian voters by a three to two margin (Ricento 1996, 150). In a state affected by large-scale migration, this proposition sought to discourage illegal immigration by denying publicly funded benefits to undocumented aliens. Its most controversial provision barred illegal immigrants from public Elementary and Secondary Schools. As *The New York Times* indicated at the time, the proposal also stipulated that children, who were US citizens – although born to undocumented parents – would be expelled from schools (*The New York Times* 1994, A17).[87] This measure was to be enforced even though these children may have grown up in the United States, be fluent in English and know little about their parents' native country (*The New York Times* 1994, A17). A particularly contentious aspect of *Proposition 187* was the requirement that public schools and agencies providing health and welfare services would have to verify the status of 'suspected' undocumented persons. Ricento has indicated that this would in effect mean that 'teachers and public officials will become agents for the immigration services, an Orwellian concept even for those who are sympathetic to the stated goals of the proposition' (Ricento 1996, 150). *The New York Times* pointed out that the implications would be far-reaching, with non-English-speaking people with 'foreign accents' becoming prime suspects, and undocumented persons refusing to seek emergency medical attention to avoid detection (*The New York Times* 1994, A17).

In spite of such concerns, four years later another monolingual initiative was passed in California. On 2 June 1998, the so-called 'English for the Children' initiative was approved, by a landslide of 61 to 39 per cent of the vote. The initiative specified that:

> All children in California's public schools shall be taught in English by being taught in English. In particular, this shall require that all children be placed in English language schools. Children who are English learners shall be educated through sheltered English

---

87 *The New York Times,* 11 November 1994, A17.

immersion during a temporary transition period normally intended not to exceed one year (Unz and Tuchman 1997, sec. 1, chp. 3, art. 2, 305).[88]

California's *Proposition 227* constituted a turning point in the development of bilingual education policy, for it effectively reversed the principles behind the *Lau v. Nichols* ruling. Whereas the latter understood bilingual education as the key to equality of opportunities, the former now established that English-only tuition played that role instead. To all intents and purposes, *Proposition 227* had reverted to the traditional 'sink or swim' educational system prevailing in the period prior to the *Lau v. Nichols* ruling. In the run-up to *Proposition 227*, Ron Unz, Chairman of the 'English for the Children' initiative campaign, had already described bilingual education as being 'completely unworkable as well as unsuccessful' (Unz 1997, M6). As he explained:

> Even after 20 or 30 years of effort, California has had absolutely no luck in finding the enormous supply of properly certified bilingual teachers to match the 140 languages spoken by California's school children. All sides of the debate agree that the old-fashioned sink or swim method of learning English is the worst alternative; yet more of California's school children today are submerged into this approach than are in properly structured bilingual programmes, although courts have ruled the former unconstitutional and the latter legally mandatory. Bilingual or nothing, in practice, often means nothing (Unz 1997, M6; Unz 2002).[89]

Accordingly, *Proposition 227* not only openly criticised bilingual education programmes, it made a case for English-only tuition:

> The public schools of California currently do a poor job of educating immigrant children, wasting financial resources on costly experimental language programmes whose failure over the past two decades is demonstrated by the current high drop-out rates and low English literacy levels of many immigrant children. Young immigrant children can easily acquire full fluency in a new language, such as English, if they are heavily exposed to that language in the classroom at an early age (Unz and Tuchman 1997, 305).

From this perspective, *Proposition 227* was understood to have granted Californian children the right to be taught in English. For it ultimately afforded them the opportunity to fully engage with US society's services.

Arizona's Proposition 203, 2000 and Beyond   By an electoral landslide of 63 per cent of the 1.5 million votes cast on 7 November 2000, Arizona became the second state to adopt an English-only schools initiative (Crawford 2001, 15:2).[90] Sponsored

---

88 Unz, R.K. and G.M. Tuchman (1997), *English Language Education for Children in Public Schools (Proposition 227),* sec. 1, chp. 3, art. 2, 305 <http://www.onenation.org/fulltext/html> (accessed 9 September 1999).

89 R. Unz 'Not Unfair', *National Review (letters),* 28 January 2002 <http://www.onenation.org/0201/012802.htm> (accessed 3 June 2006).

90 Crawford, J. (2001), 'Bilingual Education: Strike Two', *Rethinking Schools Online,* 15:2 <http://ourworld.compuserve.com/homepages/JWCRAWFORD/RS–az.htm> (accessed 3 June 2006).

by the English for the Children of Arizona organisation, Proposition 203 – largely modelled on California's Proposition 227 – advocates the provision of English-only classes throughout the State of Arizona. In line with the now dominant integrationist ideology, Proposition 203 establishes that 'all Arizona's school children have the right to be provided by their local schools with English language education' (Mendoza and Ayala 1999, 15–754).[91] Arizona's government and school system are understood to have 'a moral obligation and a constitutional duty to provide all Arizona's children, regardless of their ethnicity or national origins, with the skills necessary to become productive members of our society' (Mendoza and Ayala 1999, 15–754). Of those basic skills, English language proficiency is considered to be paramount. In practice, Crawford explains, this effectively means 'banning bilingual education for virtually all children learning English as a second language' in the state (Crawford 2001, 15:2). The years following the California and Arizona's electoral victories have witnessed a growing number of states, including Colorado and Massachusetts, launching similar ballot campaigns aimed at replacing bilingual education with English-only instruction for immigrant children (Hubler 2001; Stuner 2001).[92] Despite the varying degrees of success they have enjoyed, there is little doubt that a shift has taken place in the national psyche away from bilingualism and towards English language monolingualism.

The trend towards ever-increasing enactment of English-only legislation across the country can be said to reflect the current predominance of an integrationist public narrative. The linguistic rights of ethnic minorities have now been superseded by the entitlement of English speakers to protect their own language. The case of California, in particular, illustrates how the meanings attributed to bilingual education have changed over time. During the 1970s, when bilingual education was perceived as an equal opportunity issue, Californians provided the country with its most progressive bilingual education programmes. Two decades later however, as the protection of English language becomes a key national priority, Californians have endorsed the country's most far-reaching English-only legislation. As the Official English Movement continues to broaden its nationwide appeal and successive generations of English-speaking US-born immigrants embrace the American way of life, the future predominance of this integrationist discourse seems guaranteed.

Conclusion

The accelerated transformation of Britain into a diverse, multicultural and multifaith nation during the second half of the twentieth century has been accompanied by the creation of increasingly large settlements of non-English speaking communities

91   Mendoza, M. and H. Ayala (1999), *English Language Education for Children in Public Schools (Proposition 203)*, sec. 3, chp. 7, art. 3.1, 15–754 <http://www.onenation. org/fulltext/html> (accessed 20 February 1999).

92   Hubler, E. 'Bilingual Fray may go to Ballot', *Denver Post*, 20 June 2001, front page <http://www.onenation.org/0106/062001a.htm> (accessed 3 June 2006); Stuner, S., 'Bilingual Reform facing Battle', *Worcester Telegram & Gazette*, 1 August 2001, front page <http:// www.onenation.org/0108/080101c.htm> (accessed 3 June 2006).

within its territory. Often originating in developing countries, these newcomers' social standing has arguably been shaped by their high levels of poverty, academic underachievement and lack of English language proficiency. Over the past fifty years, successive waves of immigrants have not only altered Britain's demographic landscape; they have challenged existing social and educational provision, ultimately raising the spectrum of cultural and linguistic fragmentation.

The universal response to increased diversity by English-speaking nations has come in the shape of second language education programmes; each tailored to the individual needs of their particular constituent groups. Within the UK, the unique case of bilingual provision in Wales has seen a minority ethnic tongue elevated to the same status of the dominant English language. The Canadian immersion model, on the other hand, has sought to enable English-speaking Canadians to acquire some fluency in French. While Australia's pluralistic approach to second language education has only revealed a gap between the ideal of 'multilingualism' and the reality of language use in a diverse, yet English-dominated, nation.

As the world's foremost English-speaking superpower – and a nation experiencing an unprecedented ethnic linguistic minority presence inland, the United States' response to the diversity challenge has been examined in detailed here. In tracing the development of US bilingual education policy over time, a succession of different public narratives espousing contrasting approaches to English language learning has been unveiled. From early colonial times until the first half of the twentieth century, the prevalence of a *laissez-faire* ideology, which took for granted the preservation of the dominant English-speaking Anglo-Saxon tradition, resulted in the educational needs of linguistic ethnic minorities going largely unnoticed. With a school population of mostly white European stock, English was the only viable *lingua franca* for those settling in the United States. Throughout the 1970s, as large numbers of non-English-speaking pupils of non-European descent flooded the country's school system, the way in which bilingual education had been perceived hitherto began to change. A number of community-instigated court rulings, which translated into bilingual legislation, eventually brought about the re-formulation of bilingual education policy. In the event, a multiculturalist narrative, championing equality of access to education for non-English-speaking pupils – as part of their civil rights, became to dominate the realm of public discourse. From the 1980s onwards, as bilingual education became institutionalised, bilingual student numbers grew and the cost of financing the programmes soared, public perceptions about bilingual education began to shift. The Official English Movement, with its two-pronged approach aimed at ending the provision of bilingual programmes while legitimising English as the USA's official language, has come to epitomise the new set of integrationist values now prevailing in the public psyche. The success of the Official English campaign, which has resulted in the enactment of a string of English-only legislative measures across the country, clearly illustrates that the re-framing of bilingual education policy by an Anglocentric, English-biased discourse has ultimately taken place.

The different responses of English-speaking countries to a growing ethnic linguistic minority presence here described highlight the scale of the challenge facing these nations. Their contrasting second language education policy strategies have moreover provided an insight into the hierarchical relationships that invariably develop when majority and minority languages enter into contact. In line with the US experience, an in-depth analysis of the evolution of Britain's public narratives over time will similarly reveal the value systems ruling such interactions.

PART 2
Migrants and the Public Discourse

Chapter 4

1900s–1950s: A Discourse of *Laissez-faire* – Preserving the *Status Quo*

British citizens and 'the Others'

Colley has traced the origins of 'Britishness' as far back as the eighteenth century, when following the *Act of Union of 1707*, a sense of British nationalism was created to bind English and Scots together (Colley 1994).[1] Travelling further back in time to the Middle Ages, Crick has pointed to the dominance of 'Englishness' as the prime influence shaping the character of Britishness. He explains how despite the British nation having emerged as a 'melting pot' of different cultures and influences; historically 'it was the feudal kingdom of England that became militarily and politically dominant. So Englishness predominates in Britishness, but that Englishness, the national spirit and culture of the growing state, was influenced by, as well as influencing, the other nations' (Crick 2001, 11).[2]

An enduring legacy of Britain's colonial past, our national identity has been forged over time through a combination of imperial expansion, trade, religion and war. In this process, the notion of Britishness has been shaped as much by the institutions and symbols of the earlier Union as by those of the subsequent Empire. Since the late nineteenth century, the monarchy, the Union, the Church of England and Parliament – the very foundations of our modern nation-state – have indeed come to embody the essence of Britishness. Underlying them all is the ubiquitous English language; perhaps Britain's greatest export and the Empire's ultimate tool of cultural domination. The past hundred years have thus witnessed the emergence of a distinctive British identity modelled on an English-speaking white Anglo-Saxon Protestant ideal (Cohen 1994).[3] In his exposition of the ideological origins of the British Empire, Armitage has encapsulated the essence of such an ideal:

> the British Empire had certain characteristics which distinguished it both from past empires and from contemporary imperial polities such as the Spanish Monarchy. Its inhabitants believed it to be primarily Protestant despite the variety even of Protestant denominations that could be found within the Three Kingdoms [of Britain and Ireland] and among the islands and colonies ... The British Empire was an arena of hemispheric and international trade. Its character was therefore commercial. The attachment to commerce – and the means by which commerce connected the various parts of the Empire to one another

---

1   Colley, L. (1994), *Britons: Forging the Nation, 1707–1837* (London: Pimlico).

2   Crick, B. (2001), 'The Sense of Identity of the Indigenous British', in B. Crick, *Crossing Borders – Political Essays* (London: Continuum).

3   Cohen, R. (1994), *Frontiers of Identity: the British and Others* (London: Longman).

– made the British Empire different from its predecessors or its rivals, most of which (it was believed) had been integrated by force or had been operated more for reasons of power (often over subject people) than plenty. For the far-flung British Empire to be successful in its commerce, it had also to be maritime ... The waters around Britain itself had always been defended by the Royal Navy, and a series of naval myths provided the legendary foundations for such maritime supremacy. Protestantism, oceanic commerce and mastery of the seas provided bastion to protect the freedom of inhabitants of the British Empire. That freedom found its institutional expression in Parliament, the law, property and rights, all of which were exported throughout the British Atlantic world. Such freedom also allowed the British, uniquely, to combine the classically incompatible ideals of liberty and empire. In sum, the British Empire was, above all and beyond all such polities, Protestant, commercial, maritime and free (Armitage 2000, 8).[4]

A by-product of the colonial era, the British national ideal of the turn of the twentieth century was to largely prevail during the post-Second World War years, when Britain's population was predominantly of white British stock, the legacy of Empire very much alive, and the country's reconstruction effort well underway (General Register Office, 114–15).[5] As part of the overall imperial contribution to the development of British identity, Ward has singled out the key role played by one significant pillar of our civic society, namely: the monarchy:

Between 1876, when Disraeli gave Queen Victoria the title of Empress of India, and 1953, the monarchy was fundamentally entwined with the idea and reality of the British Empire. They were seen together as forming two basic foundations upon which Britishness could be built ... The coronation of Elizabeth II in 1953, after the loss of India from Empire (though not from the Commonwealth), continued to link monarch to Empire ... The monarchy was seen as a device to maintain the loyalty of the dominions and colonies (Ward 2004, 14).[6]

The Crown is also seen by Crick as an important symbol of British identity and national unity, if only because in Britain 'unlike say in the United States, there is no constitution to respect or worship and Parliament by itself is too partisan and too prone to the kind of disrespect that even a royal family can accidentally earn' (Crick 2001, 9). To this day, the relationship between the monarch and their subjects has to a large extent shaped Britain's particularly brand of citizenship. According to law, naturalised British citizens nowadays are still required to profess their allegiance to 'Her Majesty Queen Elizabeth the Second, Her Heirs and Successors' (*Nationality Act* 2002, c. 45, sch. 5).[7] A seemingly anachronistic vestige of our nation's feudal history, today's monarchy has effectively turned twenty-first century British nationals into citizen-subjects. This is perhaps not surprising given that the concept of British nationality originated from that of 'British subject', whereby an individual would

---

4   Armitage, D. (2000), *The Ideological Origins of the British Empire* (Cambridge: Cambridge University Press).

5   General Register Office, *Census 1951,* (London: HMSO), 1951, table 32, Birthplaces and Nationalities of all Population, 114–15.

6   Ward, P. (2004), *Britishness Since 1870* (London: Routledge).

7   *Nationality, Immigration and Asylum Act 2002* (2002), (London: TSO).

owe allegiance to their sovereign. In earlier times, the Home Office reminds us, 'the sovereign claimed the allegiance of all persons born within his dominions, and Parliament later extended this in various ways to persons of British descent born elsewhere' (Home Office 1977, para.1, 1).[8] While the Commonwealth developed, the new self-governing Dominions went on to enact their own nationality laws; notwithstanding increased autonomy, the common status of British nationality and the link to the British monarch remained.

As the fullest expression of the relationship between an individual and the state, citizenship not only implies membership of the nation, but the acquisition of complete political rights. The conferring of such rights, however, is a complex process beset with difficulties. In the ancient Greek city-state, Aristotle already wrestled with the arduous task of unravelling the meaning of citizenship. The state, he wrote, is 'a compound made up of citizens; and this compels us to consider who should properly be called a citizen and what a citizen really is. The nature of citizenship, like that of the state, is a question which is often disputed: there is no general agreement on a single definition: the man who is a citizen in a democracy is often not one in an oligarchy' (Brubaker 1992, preface).[9] Allowing for inevitable differences in historical and ideological circumstances, Aristotle's observation is as relevant today as it was then and indeed at the turn of the twentieth century. Given the sheer territorial and geo-political scale of the British Empire and its Commonwealth, defining what those rights might amount to and who might be entitled to them proved invariably burdensome. In time, it led to the disaggregating of British citizenship into a hierarchy of different categories, whereby some individuals enjoyed a full set of rights, while others did not. The inherent difficulties in delineating the contour of British citizenship are illustrated by Sargant's attempt at classifying this concept:

> If by British citizenship we mean this full citizenship, ignoring such compound terms as citizen-elector and citizen-subject, then not only women and minors be excluded, but also every British subject with electoral rights in the overseas Dominions, since as a colonial citizen he may not join in the making of laws inconsistent with an Act of the British Parliament. We should thus have to speak in a descending scale, first of parliamentary electors within the United Kingdom as alone possessed of British citizenship, then of those in the self-governing Dominions overseas as Canadian citizens, Australian citizens, etc. Next would follow various classes of Crown colonists, distinguished as citizens of Jamaica, etc. then a group of British Indian citizens (since the word 'citizenship' is used in the Indian proclamation of the late King-Emperor), and lastly, women electors, who would be merely citizens of London, Montreal, etc., unless they were domiciled in Australia or New Zealand, when they would rise in the foregoing scale. Finally would come the class of un-enfranchised (and disfranchised) persons and minors, who, if not aliens, would, like all the classes already mentioned, be British subjects (Sargant 1912, 4).[10]

---

8   Home Office (1977), *British Nationality and Citizenship of the United Kingdom and Colonies* booklet (London: Home Office).

9   Aristotle, quoted in Brubaker, R. (1992), *Citizenship and Nationhood in France and Germany* (Harvard: Harvard University Press).

10   Sargant, E.B. (1912), 'British Citizenship: A Discussion Initiated' Reprint of discussion on citizenship 'United Empire' by the *Journal of the Royal Colonial Institute*, November (London: Longmas, Green and Co.).

Through the years, as New Commonwealth migration continued to transform the demographic landscape of Britain, the ever wider spectrum of nationality rights spawned new varieties of British citizenship. Just a the monarchy had played a central role in determining individuals' relationship with the state, mass influxes of New Commonwealth migrants would ultimately influence their collective sense of identity and nationhood.

New Commonwealth Migrants

The history of mass immigration to Britain can be traced back as far as the early nineteenth century. From that period onwards, three major waves of immigrants entered the country, namely: the Irish migration during the years 1800–1861; the East European Jewish migration during the years 1870–1911; and the New Commonwealth migration during the years 1950–1971. Evidence relating to earlier periods of social policy development in Britain suggests that first the Irish and subsequently the East European Jews had been of comparable importance as newcomers. Their mere presence in the country contributed to highlight the shortcomings of welfare service provision as well as exposing government interventions aimed at them as a focus of host-immigrant resentment (Jones 1977, 4).[11] The significance of New Commonwealth migration in influencing the development of contemporary social and nationality policies and its impact upon race relations, however, is by far the most relevant of the three.

According to the *Registrar General* of 1966, the term 'New Commonwealth immigrants' embraced all those Commonwealth entrants that did not hail from the 'Old Commonwealth' countries of Canada, Australia and New Zealand (Census 1966, vii).[12] This was, to say the least, a definition that left much scope for variety within the ranks. Even so, New Commonwealth immigrants seemed to share certain common characteristics: they were typically poor, typically unskilled and to varying degrees non-white. On the whole, New Commonwealth immigration can be divided into two periods: before and after the implementation of the *Commonwealth Immigrants Act 1962* (*Commonwealth Immigrants Act 1962*).[13] This piece of legislation, which was mainly aimed at managing growing migration into Britain, had three core objectives: firstly, 'to make temporary provision for controlling the immigration into the United Kingdom of Commonwealth citizens'; secondly, 'to authorise the deportation from the United Kingdom of certain Commonwealth citizens convicted of offences and recommended by the court for deportation'; and thirdly, 'to amend the qualifications required of Commonwealth citizens applying for citizenship under the British Nationality Act, 1948' (*Commonwealth Immigrants Act 1962*, Chapter 21, 1). The *Commonwealth Immigrants Act 1962* constitutes a landmark in immigration policy not simply because it brought about the reduction in the total annual inflow of New Commonwealth immigrants, but it contributed to a shift in the balance of this inflow,

---

11 Catherine Jones (1977), *Immigration and Social Policy in Britain*, (Cambridge: Tavistock), 4.

12 *1966 Census* (1991), 'Commonwealth Immigrant Tables', (London: HMSO), vii.

13 *Commonwealth Immigrants Act 1962* (1962) (London: HMSO).

away from a predominantly West Indian stock and towards a markedly Asian entry. The two periods of New Commonwealth migration preceding and following the Act respectively tend to be associated with the bulk arrival years of these migrant communities whose members were generally non-English speaking individuals of non-European descent.

The period between June 1948 (when the former German pleasure cruiser, the Empire Windrush set sail from Kingston, Jamaica with some 492 intending immigrants on board) and June 1962, can be termed as the years of the colonial/ New Commonwealth entry as of right to the Mother Country. Just as in the case of Irish immigrants or Jewish immigrants prior to the *Aliens Act 1905*, there existed no government machinery either to prevent their coming in, or definitively to compute their numbers (Layton-Henry 1992, 7).[14] Following the Second World War, West Indian immigration was the first to assume noticeable proportions. By the mid-1950s it was significant enough for the Home Office to begin supplying the House of Commons with annual estimates of the net inward movement of citizens from the West Indies and from the Mediterranean (Jones 1977, 123).[15] It was only during the late 1950s and, more particularly during the pre-Act scramble of the 1960s onwards, that immigration from India and Pakistan began to attract serious preponderance right up to the implementation of the *Commonwealth Immigrants Act 1962*. Despite considerable fluctuations in overall numbers from one year to the next, at no point after July 1962 did the net annual inflow from the West Indies equal that from India; and at no point after 1966 did it equal even the net annual inflow from Pakistan. In 1971, for the first time, the balance of migration between the UK and the West Indies was to show a net loss of some 1,163 persons as against a net inflow of some 6,584 people from India and 5,643 from Pakistan (Jones 1977, 124).[16] The significance of this turnabout in entry patterns after July 1962 was two-fold: on the one hand, it meant that while the majority of West Indians residents in the UK by the latter 1960s must be immigrants of relatively long standing (having arrived before the implementation of controls), the majority of Indian and Pakistani residents had to be of post-July 1962 vintage. At the same time, so marked a shift in entry proportions exercised an inevitable cumulative effect on the relative strength of these groupings within the resident New Commonwealth population. Through the years, the government's response to Britain's growing diversity would see the country enact a succession of legislative and policy measures aimed at dealing with newcomers' demographic and socio-economic impact on the nation's civic society. At the time of the New Commonwealth migrants' early arrival though, such state mechanisms were barely in existence.

---

14 Layton-Henry, Z. (1992), *The Politics of Immigration*, (Oxford: Blackwell), 7.

15 Note: the Home Office had kept figures before 1955, but these had been estimates of total arrivals rather than of net immigration. See Jones, C. (1977), *Immigration and Social Policy in Britain* (Cambridge: Tavistock), 123.

16 *Commonwealth Immigrants Acts 1962 and 1968*; 'Control of Immigration: Statistics 1962-1971'. Figures taken from Jones, C. (1977), *Immigration and Social Policy in Britain,* 124.

The Aliens Act, 1905

Governments everywhere have long struggled with the challenge of migration and border control. Whether dealing with large influxes of new arrivals, economic migrants, illegal entries or refugee and asylum seekers; managing population movements remains a colossal task at the best of times. As Pellew has put it, 'there is a certain timelessness about the administrative problems that have arisen in governments' attempts to control immigration. Politically, it has nearly always been an emotive issue, where liberal ideals of welcoming strangers have conflicted with a variety of fears about letting them in unrestricted' (Pellew 1989, 369).[17] In order to regulate the numbers and types of newcomers allowed admission into the UK, the British government has come to develop four main areas of legislation over time: firstly, Acts of Parliament to control aliens; secondly, Acts to control Commonwealth immigrants; thirdly, Acts to regulate British nationality; and finally, Acts to harmonise race relations in Britain (Peach et al. 1988, 567).[18] Since the beginning of the 1990s, legislation to control aliens seemed largely concentrated before and after the First World War; with the blurred distinction between 'desirable' and 'undesirable' migrants invariably depending on the government of the day and their particular circumstances. Peach explains how earlier legislative measures were mostly aimed at controlling the Jewish refugee movements from Eastern Europe, while the later legislation reflected a deteriorating relations with Germany instead (Peach et al. 1988, 568). The *Aliens Act 1905* falls within the former category.

As the first modern piece of legislation to regulate immigration into Britain, the *Aliens Act 1905* was passed to prevent mainly Jewish and gypsy refugees from seeking asylum in Britain. The arrival of thousands of Eastern European Russian and Polish Jews fleeing persecution in London's East End, in particular, had been accompanied by a dramatic deterioration of already overcrowding living conditions; ultimately resulting in a heightened sense of crisis. The Conservative MP for Stepney, Major William Evans Gordon, called for legislation amid cries that native English families were being 'ruthlessly turned out to make room for foreign invaders' who were bringing disease and crime with them (Pannick 2005).[19]

The Act represented a first attempt by the British state to manage alien intake by labelling different groups of immigrants according to their perceived desirability; a trend that has lasted to this day. Striving to keep out of Britain not-sought-after migrants, the Act gave the Home Secretary powers to refuse entry to those who could not support themselves and their dependants, those whose infirmities were likely to see them becoming a burden and certain criminals (Layton-Henry 1992, 7).[20] On

---

17 Pellew, J. (1989), 'The Home Office and the Aliens Act, 1905', *The Historical Journal*, 32:2, 369–65.

18 Peach, C., V. Robinson, J. Maxted and J. Chance (1988), 'Immigration and Ethnicity', in A.H. Halsey (ed.) *British Social Trends since 1990 – A Guide to the Changing Social Structure of Britain* (London: Macmillan Press), 561–615.

19 Pannick, D., QC 'A century ago immigration control was an alien concept - how it has changed', *The Times*, 28 June 2005 <http://www.timesonline.co.uk/tol/life_and_style/career_ and_jobs/legal/article537244.ece> (accessed 29 June 2007).

20 Layton-Henry, Z. (1992), *The Politics of Immigration*, 7.

the other hand, in reaffirming the principle of political asylum, the Act effectively conferred protection to prospective migrants. An immigrant would therefore be allowed entry if they could show to have been the subject of political or religious prosecution.

On the whole, the *Aliens Act 1905* must be seen as an early government response to prevailing deep-seated fears of white European migration to Britain. Pannick has referred to the Act as 'an illuminating episode' in British legal history, because of the ease with which bigotry resulted in legislation being enacted; legislation which nevertheless provided for the protection of immigrants' (Pannick 2005). As he expounds:

> By comparison with what followed, the 1905 Act was a surprisingly moderate measure, for all the anti-Semitic prejudice that provoked parliamentary action. The day after war was declared on Germany in August 1914, Parliament considered and approved in less than 24 hours the Aliens Restriction Act, which conferred broad powers on the Home Secretary to prohibit or restrict aliens from landing in this country. The 1914 Act was introduced as a temporary, wartime measure. But it was extended in 1919 for one year, and then for many years afterwards. If the 1905 Act had remained in force, a large proportion of the European Jews murdered by the Nazis would have been entitled to find refuge in this country (Pannick 2005).

In 1948, the arrival of the first cohorts of non-white New Commonwealth immigrants to British shores would inaugurate an unprecedented era of immigration, nationality and race relations legislation aimed at their successors and lasting to the present day.

The Empire Windrush

The outbreak of the First World War enabled the government to introduce an elaborate system of strict border controls restricting foreign entry into Britain. As Pannick indicated, the *Aliens Restriction Act 914* was passed in just one day as part of the impending national emergency, with its draconian powers meant only to last as long as the national emergency required them to remain in place. Nevertheless, the legislation went on to be extended both by the *Aliens Restriction (Amendment) Act 1919* and the subsequent *Aliens Order, 1920*. The end of the Second World War, in contrast, removed the threat of overseas armed invasion and signalled the beginning of reconstruction of the British economy. This process would require the use of immigrant labour on an unprecedented scale.

After the War, Britain's economy indeed suffered severe deficiencies in human capital, labour market resources and skills. In 1945, shortly after the end of the war, the desperate state of the economy became apparent when the Trade Union Congress (TUC) reported that 'we are meeting the problem of manpower scarcity at every turn, and the whole of the vital services of this country are very near breaking point' (Paul 1997, 4).[21] A year later, a Cabinet Working Paper estimated

---

21 TUC quoted in Paul, K. (1997), *Whitewashing Britain: Race and Citizenship in the Postwar Era* (Cornell: Cornell University Press), 4.

the extent of the shortages at between one million and a million and a half of people (Spencer 1997, 38).[22] By 1949, the Royal Commission on Population reported that immigrant workers of 'good stock' would be welcome 'without reserve'; in reality however, the appeal for new employees was primarily aimed at the white European workforce who had largely dominated immigration to Britain from the beginning of the twentieth century (National Archives 2007).[23] The recruitment of 'European volunteer workers', mostly displaced individuals from refugee camps in Germany, Poland and throughout Eastern Europe, saw the employment of thousands of migrant workers; mainly allowed in Britain to work across industry sectors where their contribution was most directly needed (McDowell, 2004, 23–56).[24] Despite the economic benefits brought about by labour migration, underlying reservations about foreign migrants, particularly coloured workers, remained. British government officials, Spencer argues, were keen to reduce rather than increase the sources of coloured Commonwealth skilled labour; as illustrated by their attempts to repatriate Caribbean technicians recruited in Jamaica and Barbados to work in factories in the north-west of England during the war (Spencer 1997, 38). It was the Colonial Office that eventually took the view that given the extensive use of white European labour in post-war reconstruction, the British government should consider offering similar employment opportunities to British subjects from Commonwealth countries. As Spencer explains:

> It [the Colonial Office] had been pressed to do so [lobby government] by the Governors of Officers Administering in Barbados, British Guiana, Trinidad and Jamaica each of whom wrote to London in 1947 advertising the needs of their surplus, skilled and often ex-service labour. The demands of the Governors of Trinidad and Jamaica were provoked by – and they referred directly to – the use of labour imported from continental Europe in reconstruction in the United Kingdom … In 1948, at the behest of the Colonial Office, an Interdepartmental Working Party on the employment in the United Kingdom of surplus colonial labour chaired by the Under-Secretary of Sate for the Colonies, was set up to inquire into the issues raised by the Caribbean authorities (Spencer 1997, 39).

The first time a memorandum was eventually circulated to Cabinet members on the subject of 'coloured immigration', it came from the Colonial Secretary, Arthur Creech Jones; this being partly the reason behind the public and parliamentary interest aroused by the arrival of the Empire Windrush (Spencer 1997, 51).

On 22 June 1948, the merchant vessel Empire Windrush sailed into Tilbury Dock in England carrying 492 passengers, most of whom were ex-servicemen from the Caribbean who have fought for Britain during the Second World War. They had come to Britain to assist with the post-war reconstruction effort. Often hailed as the

---

22 Spencer, I.R.G. (1997), *British Immigration Policy since 1939: the Making of Multi-Racial Britain* (London: Routledge).

23 National Archives (2007), 'Citizenship – Brave New World: Postwar Migration' <http://www.nationalarchives.gov.uk/pathways/citizenship/brave_new_world/immigration. htm> (accessed 29 June 2007).

24 McDowell, L. (2004), 'Narratives of Family, Community and Waged Work: Latvian European Volunteer Worker Women in Post-war Britain', *Women's History Review*, 13:1, 23–56.

beginnings of a 'postwar black history', their arrival must be understood within the wider context of a series (as opposed to one) of coloured diasporic movements to the Mother Country. On the occasion of the two hundredth anniversary of the symbolic docking of the *Windrush*, Procter reflected on the significance of such event and the somehow distorted manner in which popular narratives have come to portray it:

the ritually recorded anecdote of the *Windrush* docking at Tilbury has privileged Jamaican male settlement as a primal moment in the establishment of a Black British heritage, when, in fact, the boat was actually carrying men *and* women, black *and* white passengers from a number of different Caribbean islands (not just Jamaica, as it is frequently stated). More than this, that narrative of West Indian exodus forgets that the *Windrush*'s arrival was facilitated by the Nationality Act (1948), a piece of legislation partly motivated by Indian Independence in 1947. Here '1948' cannot be reduced to the year in which a single boat docked at Tilbury, but needs to be understood within the context of the broader political act/Act, which led directly to Britain's borders being opened to its colonies and former colonies for the first time. In this context, Caribbean, African *and* South Asian migrations to the 'motherland' demand recognition within the 'pioneer' narratives of early postwar immigration (Procter 2000, 3).[25]

Allowing for adequate contextualisation, there is no doubt that the arrival of the passengers onboard the *Windrush* represents nevertheless the beginnings of a lengthy socio-demographic shift; one that would see Britain transformed from a nation of predominantly white-European stock to a modern multiethnic and multicultural state. In 1948 though, the arrival of New Commonwealth immigrants highlighted the extent of prevailing public sentiment regarding the desirability and impact of non-white migration to Britain; such attitudes would find expression in the introduction of statutory controls targeting coloured workers from the West Indies, South Asia and other part of the Commonwealth and Dominions. It is against this backdrop that the introduction of the *British Nationality Act 1948* must be understood.

British Nationality Act 1948

The story of post-war migration to Britain, Hansen writes, is 'the story of citizenship'; and the latter was officially defined for the first time by the *British Nationality Act 1948* (Hansen 2000, 35).[26] Prior and subsequently to this legislation, a number of British Nationality Acts had been enacted, including the *British Nationality and Status of Aliens Act 1914*, the *British Nationality Act 1948* and the *British Nationality Act 1964*. The *British Nationality Act 1948* however, was arguably the most influential of them (Peach et al. 1988, 568).

The significance of this piece of legislation is two fold: on the one hand, it created a legal framework that facilitated mass entry of New Commonwealth migrants into Britain, perhaps in a manner not anticipated. Members of the British Commonwealth,

---

25 Procter, J. (2000), *Writing Black Britain, 1948–1998: An Interdisciplinary Anthology* (Manchester: Manchester University Press).

26 Hansen, R.S. (2000), *Citizenship and Immigration in Post-War Britain: the Institutional Origins of a Multicultural Nation* (Oxford: Oxford University Press).

Colonies and Protectorates were consequently conferred the status of British citizens and had their full rights of access to settlement in the UK recognised. On the other hand, the legislation provided a comprehensive classification of the notion of British citizenship, which considered every eventuality regarding the circumstances of prospective British citizens, whether it may be citizenship by birth or descent, registration, naturalisation or incorporation of territory. In doing so, the Act ultimately established the parameters for future government interventions on the nationality and citizenship question.

According to the *British Nationality Act 1948*, British nationality by virtue of citizenship was conferred as follows:

(1) Every person who under this Act is a citizen of the United Kingdom and Colonies or who under any enactment for the time being in force in any country mentioned in subsection (3) of this section is a citizen of that country shall by virtue of that citizenship have the status of a British subject.

(2) Any person having the status aforesaid may be known either as a British subject or as a Commonwealth citizen; and accordingly in this Act and in any other enactment or instrument whatever, whether passed or made before or after the commencement of this Act, the expression 'British subject' and the expression 'Commonwealth citizen' shall have the same meaning.

(3) The following are the countries hereinbefore referred to, that is to say, Canada, Australia, New Zealand, the Union of South Africa, Newfoundland, India, Pakistan, Southern Rhodesia and Ceylon (*British Nationality Act* 1948 Chapter 56, part 1, para. 1).[27]

The Act, Hansen argues, clearly defined the constitutional status of British subjects within the United Kingdom and Empire and, in turn, the institutional links between Britain and the members states of the Commonwealth. It is in this manner that it bequeathed to subsequent policy-makers a legal framework that shaped, and ultimately limited, their ability to articulate a policy response to this migration (Hansen 2000, 35).

Under the Act, British citizenship of newly-independent countries such as India and Pakistan as well as old Commonwealth states continued. This potentially meant that nearly 1,000 million people could in theory claim British citizenship. It is precisely, Peach has pointed out, when prospective claims began to translate into actual submissions that further controls were implemented (Peach et al. 1988, 569). Subsequent legislation such as the *Commonwealth Immigrants Act 1962*, would see the right of access of even those who had no citizenship other than that of the UK and colonies curtailed. The *Immigration Act 1971*, in turn, created categories of citizenship claims based on the degree of 'Britishness' of the origin of the person; in particular, the Act removed the right of those born in Britain to have an automatic claim to citizenship (Peach et al. 1988, 569). From 1971 onwards, the right of abode was therefore limited to those with a prior link to the UK, such as a parent

27   *The British Nationality Act 1948*, (1948) (London: HMSO).

or grandparent who was born in Britain. This ultimately had the effect of virtually ending primary immigration.

Migration, Paul points out, has a long history as a 'political tool' in Britain, and many groups have successively being welcomed or discouraged according to their perceived value (Paul 1997, 65). During the first half of the twentieth century, hostile public attitudes to New Commonwealth migration were not only disproportionate to the scale of their presence in Britain; but reflected the underlying prejudices of a white-dominated Anglo-European society towards a coloured minority population. From the outset, government's reaction to New Commonwealth migrants had been geared towards the preservation of the *status quo*. Despite their ties to the Mother Country, sustained contribution to the war effort and the subsequent reconstruction of the British economy, discriminatory legislative measures were consistently deployed to limit the numbers of New Commonwealth migrants, while restricting their entry into the country. Tracing the steady erosion of these migrants' rights, Peach et al. have explained how this process evolved over time:

> From a situation in which every person born in Britain or any part of its previous Empire could claim British citizenship with the right of free access to Britain, British citizenship was pruned back to a more exclusive and restrictive definition in which the aim of racial exclusion was clearly visible. Political control centred first on the exclusion of potential workers, next on the control of dependants. Political pressure was then aimed at attempts to promote repatriation, and more recently has viewed the higher birthrate of coloured minorities with foreboding. Even those born in Britain can no longer automatically claim British citizenship (Peach et al. 1988, 570).

In spite of the political backlash that followed mass arrivals of West Indians and South Asians in Britain, New Commonwealth migration had a profound effect on the demographic and social landscape of the country. Over the course of the twentieth century, their presence would furthermore affect public perceptions of national identity and citizenship.

Educating the Children of Empire

Once in Britain, New Commonwealth migrants were largely expected to settle down into British society and fit with the nation's way of life. As part of an alien's qualifying criteria for British citizenship, the *British Nationality Act 1948* already listed among others, their being 'of good character' and having 'sufficient knowledge of the English language'. In addition, they were required to swear an oath of allegiance to 'His Majesty King George the Sixth His Heirs and Successors' according to law (*British Nationality Act* 1948, first and second schedules). The intention behind such displays of acculturation, Paul argues, was 'to transform aliens into subjects by clothing them in a discourse of potential Britishness'. As she puts it:

> This discourse itself aided the reconstructive process by giving aliens a category within which to live their lives in Britain and through which they might more quickly become British. Critical to this reconstruction was the demographic acceptability of aliens. Selection of the 345,000 postwar immigrants was guided by the consciousness that

recruiting for the labour market in the short term was tantamount to recruiting for the population of Britain in the long term (Paul 1997, 65).

An important aspect of this assimilation strategy was the absorption of New Commonwealth migrants and their children into the country's education system. Given that many of these newcomers did not speak English as their mother tongue, mastery of Britain's dominant language became paramount. At the time of their arrival though, the educational and linguistic needs of non-English speaking migrants were largely overlooked; with the provision of so-called English as a Second Language (ESL) education having only come to light in recent times. Not until the second half of the twentieth century, when growing numbers of linguistically challenged school children finally attracted the government's attention, did British policy makers actually develop some kind of systematic ESL education provision. In the meantime, interest in the language needs of New Commonwealth children seemed to be in direct proportion to the relative negligible size of their school population. This is perhaps not surprising given that Britain's own education system was in its infancy, struggling itself to make available adequate and consistent scholarly instruction for the country's native population.

The Education Act 1944

The British government's first concerted attempt at raising Britain's school children's performance was the *Education Act 1944*. The Butler Act (so-called after R.A. Butler, President of the Board of Education) prescribed far-reaching changes in the organisation of the country's Primary, Secondary and Tertiary education (*Education Act 1944*).[28] The focus of the Act was the overall re-structuring of a deficient education system operating both in England and Wales (Ikin 1944).[29] In its opening section, the Act provided for the creation of a Minister of Education who was to be responsible for attaining a standardised national education service:

> It shall be lawful for His Majesty to appoint a Minister (hereinafter referred to as 'The Minister'), whose duty it shall be to promote the education of the people of England and Wales and the progressive development of institutions devoted to that purpose, and to secure the effective execution by local authorities, under his control and direction, of the national policy for providing a varied and comprehensive educational service in every area. The Minister shall for all purposes be a corporation sole under the name of the Minister of Education, and the department of which he is in charge shall be known as the Ministry of Education (*The Education Act 1944*, Chapter 31, part 1 (1), paras. 1 and 2, 224).

Not until the passage of the *Education Act 1944* did central government assume full responsibility for universal free Primary and Secondary education up to the age of 15 (16 since 1971). The Act dealt in detail with matters comprising the organisation, structuring and regulation of the entire national educational system, including local and central government provision, availability of public funds, school management

---

28　*The Education Act 1944,* (1944) (London: HMSO).

29　Ikin, A., *The Education Act 1944*, (1944) (London: Sir Isaac Pitman and Sons Ltd.).

and inspections (*The Education Act 1944*, 220–24).[30] The *Education Act 1944* introduced a tripartite system of Secondary education based on grammar, modern and technical schools with selection by the 11+ examination. Fee-paying in secondary schools was abolished and the school leaving age was raised to 15 (Coxal and Robins 1998, 23).[31] Butler pointed to the Act's overhauling of education in the area of local government, whereby 'the number of local education authorities was reduced from 315 to 146, which certainly made for more efficient administration' (Butler 1966, 6).[32] The legislation was judged by Dent to be 'a very great Act, which makes possible as important and substantial an advance in public education as this country has ever known' (Dent 1955, 3).[33] Overall, the Act can be said to have addressed the need to bring education provision and its organisation in line with the needs of a twentieth century British society (Young and Rao 1997, 51–86).[34]

In spite of its significance and scope, the *Education Act 1944* neither acknowledged nor made provision for the educational needs of non-English-speaking pupils. At the time, ESL education was simply regarded as a non-issue in the government's political agenda. Policies, Yanow argues, must always be understood with regard to 'the values, feelings and believes which they express' (Yanow 1996, 9).[35] The *Education Act 1944* can thus be said to reflect a prevailing *laissez-faire* attitude towards the New Commonwealth migrant question; one which simply catered for the academic needs of Britain's indigenous English-speaking school population. In recent times, such early *laissez-faire* attitude regarding the country's minority ethnic population has been denounced by the Commission on the Future of Multiethnic Britain (Runnymede Trust 2000).[36]

Conclusion

From the outset, a by-product of Britain's colonial past, the notion of 'Britishness' became intrinsically linked with the legacy of Empire. Forged by the forces of war, territorial and commercial expansion as well as religion, Britishness became synonymous with the Union, the monarchy, the Church of England and Parliament. Such pillars of our civic society came indeed to embody all that was considered to be British. As Britain inaugurated the twentieth century, her national identity was

---

30 *The Education Act 1944* (1944), chapter 31, 220–24.

31 Coxall, B. and L. Robins (1998), *Contemporary British Politics,* 3rd edn (London: Macmillan Press Ltd.), 23.

32 Butler, R.A. (1966), *The Education Act of 1944 and After* (London: Longman), 6.

33 Dent, H.C. (1955), *The Education Act 1944: Provisions, Regulations, Circulars and Later Acts,* 5th edn (London: University of London Press Ltd.), 3.

34 Young, K. and N. Rao (1997), *Local Government since 1945*, (London: Blackwell), 51–86.

35 Yanow, D. (1996), *How Does a Policy Mean? Interpreting Policy and Organisational Actions* (Washington, DC: Georgetown University Press), 9.

36 The Runnymede Trust (2000), *The Future of Multiethnic Britain: Report of the Commission on the Future of Multiethnic Britain: The Parekh Report* (London: Profile Books).

firmly anchored on a white Anglo-Saxon Protestant ideal. The supremacy of such an ideal however, would come under pressure with the arrival on British soil of unprecedented numbers of foreign migrants.

In the early years of the century, white European Russian and Polish Jews fleeing persecution first entered the country – although in most cases their communities had long enjoyed a presence here. After the Second World War, they were followed by further influxes of mostly displaced Eastern European refugee workers, allowed in as part of the post-war reconstruction effort. Despite the newcomers being of white European descent, their presence was invariably met by legislative measures aimed at curbing their entry. Notwithstanding the latter; white phenotypical characteristics afforded these migrants invisibility on entry, thus facilitating their incorporation into British society. Unlike their 'invisible' European counterparts, New Commonwealth migrants could only enjoy a highly visible presence on arrival.

Given the prevailing public discourse at the time, it is not surprising that the entrance of the first cohorts of coloured New Commonwealth immigrants during the late 1940s was met with disproportionate levels of hostility. Such antagonism towards them was to materialise in a series of often overtly discriminatory legislative measures that would see a progressive erosion of their rights of abode. Those who succeeded in overcoming such barriers to entry were largely expected to master the English language, embrace British customs and quickly become immersed into society's everyday life. Adequate educational and social support was, nevertheless, not forthcoming. After all, this was a predominantly English-speaking white Anglo-Saxon British society whose public discourse was ultimately geared towards the preservation of the *status quo*.

Chapter 5

1960s–1980s: A Discourse of Multiculturalism – Living with Difference

Racial Politics

In the post-war years, New Commonwealth immigration to Britain began to change the country's demographic landscape. West Indian immigration was the first to assume noticeable proportions followed by mass arrivals from India and Pakistan. On their coming into Britain, New Commonwealth immigrants found themselves disproportionately concentrated in the least skilled, least desirable and worst remunerated occupations where the demand for labour was at its highest. Immigrant settlements grew rapidly within declining, twilight inner-city areas whose native population was already on the move out. By 1961, approximately 80 per cent of all West Indians and 59 per cent of all Indians and Pakistanis in Britain were conurbation dwellers (Jones 1997, 129–30).[1] At the time, relatively little was known about the deprived socio-economic conditions experienced by these newcomers. Perhaps not surprisingly, prevailing public attitudes towards them overwhelmingly favoured migration controls. In May 1961, a Gallup poll of English attitudes towards Third World immigrants revealed this to be the case. The survey included the question, 'Do you think that coloured people from the Commonwealth should have the right to completely free entry into Britain, should there be restrictions on entry, or should they be kept out completely?'. The majority of respondents (67 per cent) advocated restrictions, whereas only 21 per cent favoured free entry; in addition, six per cent wanted 'blacks' completed excluded and a further six per cent were undecided (Institute of Race Relations 1961, 1).[2]

Over the following two decades, a startling transformation in public perceptions towards migration was to take place. Not only migrants would come to be seen as an integral part of the British nation, but their presence would also alter traditional views of national identity and nationhood. The long ideological journey on the road to multiculturalism though was neither smooth nor consistent; often provoking strong reactions and polarising public opinion. During the 1960s–1970s in particular, government and opposition espoused strikingly different standpoints on the subject.

---

1   Jones, C. (1997), *Immigration and Social Policy in Britain,* (Cambridge: Tavistock), 129–30.

2   Institute of Race Relations (1961), 'Supplement', *Institute of Race Relations Newsletter*, August, 1.

The search for a coherent 'politics of race' at the time, Katznelson has pointed out, was primarily as search for coherence 'within' each party. Not only their ideological differences, but hierarchies of interests, social priorities and membership's makeup appeared to be dissimilar (Katznelson 1973, 131).[3]

Conservative Powellism

The decision of the Conservative government to introduce controls on New Commonwealth migration in 1962, which even *The Times* (*The Times* 1962, 11)[4] considered racially discriminatory, was arguably the result of growing pressures from a public mobilised by grassroots anti-immigration campaigners. As the broadsheet indicated, 'the [Commonwealth Immigrants] Bill, dress it as the government may, is racially discriminating ... Its application is expressly ordered to be a non racial basis. But it was racial prejudices, pressures, and jealousies which constituted the support for it' (*The Times* 1962, 11).

The nationalistic rhetoric used by Enoch Powell, Conservative Shadow Defence Spokesman, not only acted as a focus for those calling for tighter controls in immigration, it helped to popularise the common racialist sentiment against New Commonwealth immigrants. In his infamous 'rivers of blood' speech in Birmingham in April 1968, Powell argued that the long-term solution to the migrant problem went beyond immigration controls; it required the repatriation of immigrants already settled in Britain. Using apocalyptic language, Powell sought to warn against what he saw as an unprecedented danger:

> As I look ahead, I am filled with foreboding. Like the Roman, I seem to see 'the River Tiber foaming with much blood'. The tragic and intractable phenomenon which we watch with horror on the other side of the Atlantic, but which there is interwoven with the history and existence of the States itself, is coming upon us here by our own volition and our own neglect (*The Occidental Quarterly* 2006, 1).[5]

He went on to conjure up images of the white British indigenous population increasingly turning into isolated strangers in their own country:

> They [white Britons] found their wives unable to obtain a hospital bed in childbirth, their children unable to obtain school places, their homes and neighbourhoods changed beyond recognition, their plans and prospects for the future defeated (*The Occidental Quarterly* 2006, 2).

---

3   Katznelson, I. (1973), *Black Men, White Cities*, (London: Oxford University Press), 131.

4   'Racial Discrimination', *The Times*, 27 February 1962, issue 55326, col. B, 11.

5   *The Occidental Quarterly* (2006) 'full text of Enoch Powell's famous speech to the Annual General Meeting of the West Midlands Area Conservative Political Centre, Birmingham, England, April 20, 1968', 1 <http://theoccidentalquarterly.com/vol1no1/ep–rivers.html> (accessed 2 July 2007); 'Immigrants Main Election Issue at Smethwick – Labour Accusation of Exploitation', *The Times*, 9 March 1964, issue 55955, col. C, 6; 'Mosley Speeches recalled – Powell figures 'fantasy'', *The Times*, 22 April 1968, issue 57232, col. A, 2.

Powell's enunciation of his overt hostility to migrants in crude populist terms brought him overwhelming public support. His cause was aided by a national media which allowed him reach to a mass audience, whilst reinforcing the image of migrants as 'a problem, a threat, a category of unprincipled scroungers and muggers' who were justifiably viewed as an object of reasonable fear, hatred and even violence (Husband 1982, 161).[6] Despite being dismissed from the Shadow Cabinet, Powell's popular appeal and continuing media profile ensured the issue of migration and nationhood was firmly kept in the political agenda, right up to the Conservative Party electoral victory in 1970. Throughout this time though, Conservative policy towards New Commonwealth immigrants was characterised by a seemingly inconsistent dual approach; one which was based on stricter controls for those intended to enter the country, while at the same time ensuring the right to equal treatment for those immigrants already in Britain. In 1965, a letter sent to *The Times* by three MPs (i.e. Donald Chapman, Eric Lubbock and Joan Vickers) regarding 'the immigrant problem' illustrates the extent to which it had become a highly politicised and divisive issue. They wrote:

> Many members of all parties have realised the danger to Britain's good name and to the future of the Commonwealth in letting coloured immigration become a regular feature of our party strife. They recoil with distaste from the prospect of this country's ending up in the long list of nations that have failed on this issue. We believe that the British Government should seize the present chance to take immigration out of party politics, and we suggest that leading representatives of the Opposition parties should be invited to join talks with the Government ... We believe that all-party talks of this kind would show a wide area of agreement and the subject could then quite quickly cease to be a brickbat in party politics (*The Times* 1965, 13).[7]

Labour's Policy of Appeasement

Although the Labour party in opposition fought against the first *Commonwealth Immigrants Bill*, once in government, its administration performed a U-turn by embracing the view that border control was essential. The capitulation of the Labour government to the Right-led anti-immigration campaign was not only a betrayal of principle; it exposed the complex and highly sensitive nature of the issue as well as the difficulties inherent in dealing with it. Ben-Tovin and Gabriel have argued that the racial justification for immigration controls had not been publicly presented by the government as an accommodation of white racism; but rather explained in terms of the adverse socio-economic impact resulting from coloured migration. The presence of growing numbers of New Commonwealth immigrants was portrayed as exacerbating the already existing social problems of housing, employment and healthcare, ultimately to the detriment of the indigenous white British working classes (Ben-Tovim 1982, 149).[8]

---

6   Husband, C. (ed.) (1982), *'Race' in Britain*, (London: Hutchinson), 161.

7   'The Immigration Problem', *The Times*, 5 March 1965, issue 56262, col. E, 13.

8   Ben-Tovim. G. and J. Gabriel (1982), 'The Politics of Race in Britain , 1962–79: A Review of the Major Trends and of Recent Debates', in Husband (ed.), *'Race' in Britain*, 149.

It is easy to anticipate here the development of a racialist culture featuring crude stereotypes, negative images and feelings of difference and superiority deeply embodied in the state's legal and institutional practices. Labour policy of appeasement saw the government placating white opinion ostensibly as a response to problems caused by coloured migrants, rather than directly tackling deep-seated racial inequalities disproportionally affecting the latter. In doing so, the government not only nourished and gave legitimacy to anti-immigrant sentiment, but ultimately deepened racialist trends in British society. The resulting racially discriminatory legislation was overtly aimed at stripping New Commonwealth immigrants off their rights to settle down in Britain and generally preventing them from entering the country. At the same time, measures would be introduced to reduce racial tensions and promote good community relations among those immigrant groups already in the country. The Labour government's seemingly ambivalent approach to the migration question as much as that of the Conservative opposition came to characterise these rather turbulent, formative years.

Dealing with Migration

During the decade of the 1960s–1970s, the prevailing approach to New Commonwealth migration materialised in a series of consecutive immigration legislative measures imposing tight controls on the numbers of immigrants entering Britain, together with a similar set of race relations legislation aimed at promoting racial harmony among settled communities.

Commonwealth Immigrants Act 1962

The *Commonwealth Immigrants Act 1962* constituted a watershed for Britain's commitment to Commonwealth migrants; as it mainly sought to prevent their entry into the 'mother country'. A distinction was introduced between citizens of the UK and colonies and citizens of independent Commonwealth countries, resulting in Commonwealth passport-holders becoming subject to new immigration controls (*Commonwealth Immigrants Act 1962*, ch. 21, ss. 1 (2) (a), (b) and (c)).[9] While admissions would be administered through a system of employment vouchers issued by the Ministry of Labour, immigration officers were empowered to refuse entry to new migrants under the previous rules (Solomos 1989, 52).[10]

The Conservative government legitimised the need to 'curb the dangers of unrestricted immigration' by reference to the limited ability of the host society to assimilate coloured immigrants (Solomos 1989, 51). In contrast, the Labour opposition and some sections of the media denounced the Act as a bigoted piece of legislation specifically aimed at coloured immigrants in response to public pressure. Hugh Gaitskell, Leader of the Labour Party, headed a particularly strong attack on

---

9   *Commonwealth Immigrants Act 1962* (1962) (London: HMSO), ch. 21, ss. 1 (2) (a), (b) and (c).

10   Solomos, J. (1989), *Race and Racism in Contemporary Britain*, (London: Macmillan), 52.

the Bill in Parliament and its crude amalgamation of immigration with race. He denounced 'this miserable, shameful, shabby bill' calling it 'an appalling confession of failure by the government ... It means in effect that Great Britain cannot absorb or integrate with our community more than 1 per cent of the population' (Hansard 1961, vol. 709, cols. 334–45).[11] Ben-Tovim and Gabriel, have similarly argued that the official equation of blackness with second-class citizenship enshrined in the Act provided a legal framework for the institutionalisation of racism (Ben-Tovim 1982, 146).

Notwithstanding the controversy, between 1962 and 1965 both parties moved towards a new ideological consensus aimed at achieving a 'balanced policy towards immigration and immigrant communities' (Hansard 1965, vol. 709, cols. 334–45).[12] Katznelson has interpreted this change of strategy as a shared desire to relegate the issue of 'race' from the centre of the political agenda (Katznelson 1973, 139–51). When Harold Wilson took office as Labour Prime Minister in 1964, he accordingly preserved the *Commonwealth Immigrants Act 1962*. The Labour opposition, he explained, had originally criticised the Act mainly because it was 'based on race and colour discrimination'; he therefore undertook to rectify the 'loopholes in the Act' and called for more effective tightening of the deportation provisions (Katznelson 1973, 145).

On its return to office, Labour was reeling from the narrowness of electoral majorities and appalled at the racist victory in Smethwick of the Conservative candidate, Peter Griffiths. He have fought the election campaign largely on the basis of defending the interests of the white majority against the 'influx of immigrants'; using slogans such as 'If you want a nigger for a neighbour, vote Labour' (*The Times* 1964, 4).[13] The defeat of Patrick Gordon Walker, Foreign Secretary – and widely regarded as a liberal on migration, at the Leyton by-election in January 1965, further stunned the government and reduced its majority to a mere hair's breadth of three seats overall (Layton-Henry 1992, 50).[14] Opinion surveys at the time clearly showed that 'race' had played a crucial role in the election results (Katznelson 1973, 147).[15] Determined to benefit from the powerful public tide in favour of immigration controls, but at the same time needed to retain something of its liberal credentials; the Labour government sought to obtain opposition support for its anti-discrimination legislation. In 1965, the government produced a White Paper on *Immigration from the Commonwealth*, which called for controls to be maintained in an even stricter form alongside measures to promote the integration of immigrants (Solomos 1989, 53).

---

11 Hansard (1961), *House of Commons, Session 1960–61*, (London: HMSO), vol. 649, cols. 792–803.

12 Hansard (1965), *House of Commons, Session 1964–65*, (London: HMSO), vol. 709, cols. 334–45.

13 'No Race Problem in Leyton', *The Times*, 19 December 1964, issue 56199, col. F, 4; 'Mr Wilson wants a Bigger Role for Navy – More Men Afloat: Helping to Keep Peace', *The Times*, 10 March 1964, issue 55956, col. A, 9.

14 Layton-Henry, Z. (1992), *The Politics of Immigration* (Oxford: Blackwell), 50.

15 Lineal, A.T., quoted in Katznelson, I. (1973), *Black Men, White Cities*, 147.

Race Relations Act 1965

The *Race Relations Act 1965* had come into existence as a result of bipartisan consensus. The main emphasis was therefore on conciliation rather than on criminal sanctions; it urged people to do what was right without penalising them for doing what was unfair or unjust (Layton-Henry 1992, 50). The Act outlawed discrimination in specific places of public resort such as hotels, restaurants, cinemas, dance halls and transport facilities, while making it a criminal offence to deliberately stir up racial hatred by publishing or distributing written matter or by speaking in public (Glazer and Young 1983, 51).[16] In addition, the Act set up the Race Relations Board (RRB) to deal with complaints of discrimination.

Commonwealth Immigrants Act 1968

The earlier *Commonwealth Immigrants Act 1962* had the effect of provoking a rush among qualifying migrants to enter Britain before the controls became effective. Migrants were mainly African Asians hailing from newly independent states of East Africa and holding UK-issued passports by their British High Commissions overseas. When in 1967, Kenya adopted legislation that effectively expelled African Asians holding these passports from the country; they travelled en masse to Britain. Falling into the UK passport-holders category, these migrants were not subject to the control regulations applying to most coloured entrants. In order to remedy this situation and strengthen border controls, the Labour government swiftly proceed to pass the *Commonwealth Immigrants Act 1968*.

A direct response to the Kenyan Asian crisis, the Act denied any African Asian the right of entry unless he, or at least one of his parents or grandparents:

(a) was born in the United Kingdom, or
(b) is or was a person naturalised in the United Kingdom, or
(c) became a citizen of the United Kingdom and Colonies by virtue of being adopted in the United Kingdom (*Commonwealth Immigrants Act 1968*, vol. 1, ch. 9, s. 1 (a), (b) and (c)).[17]

In addition, refusal of admission by immigration officers to any Commonwealth citizen falling under the above categories remained. This effectively ensured that most white UK passport-holders from East Africa retained the right of entry to Britain, while their Asian counterparts were instead brought into the same system of voucher controls as other potential coloured immigrants (Glazer and Young 1983, 49).

While the government denied that the Act was racist, it was clearly designed to restrict the entry of British citizens without close ties to the UK, the vast majority of which were not white. At the time, *The Times* compared the behaviour of the

---

16 Glazer, N. and K. Young (eds) (1983), *Ethnic Pluralism and Public Policy*, (London: Heinemman), 51.

17 *Commonwealth Immigrants Act 1968*, (1968) (London: HMSO), vol. 1, ch. 9, s. 1 (a), (b) and (c).

Labour government to its attitude while in opposition in 1962, while recognising that 'there is a serious colour problem in this country' (*The Times* 1968, 9).[18] During the Parliamentary debates the Liberals led the opposition to the Bill, which was also opposed by some Conservative and Labour members; notably, Ian Macleod who, as Colonial Secretary, had guided Kenya to independence. The legislation, *The Times* cried, was 'probably the most shameful measure that the Labour members have even been asked by their Whips to support' (*The Times* 1968, 9).

Race Relations Act 1968

After its capitulation to anti-immigration pressure over the Kenyan Asians Bill, the government pressed ahead with race relations legislation. A milestone in equality law, the *Race Relations Act 1968* was the first attempt of its kind to promote inter-racial harmony through the promotion of universal fair treatment and equal opportunities. It established the novel concept of 'discrimination' and implicitly recognised that members of ethnic minorities in Britain may be disadvantaged on racial grounds:

> a person discriminates against another if on the ground of colour, race of ethnic or national origins he treats that other, in any situation less favourable than he treats or would treat other persons (*Race Relations Act 1968*, vol. 2, ch. 71, s. 1 (1)).[19]

The Act went on to make it unlawful to discriminate in most areas of social life:

2.– (1) It shall be unlawful for any person concerned with the provision to the public (whether on payment or otherwise) of any goods, facilities or services to discriminate against any person seeking to obtain or use those goods, facilities or services (*Race Relations Act 1968*, s. 2 (1)).

3.– (1) It shall be unlawful for an employer or any person concerned with the employment of others to discriminate against any other person (*Race Relations Act 1968*, s. 3(1)).

4.– (1) It shall be unlawful for an organisation or any person concerns with the affairs of the organisation to discriminate against a person who is not a member of the organisation (*Race Relations Act 1968*, s. 4(1)).[20]

5.– It shall be unlawful for any person having power to dispose, or being otherwise concerned with the disposal of housing accommodation, business premises or other land to discriminate (*Race Relations Act* 1968, s. 5).

6.– (1) It shall be unlawful for any person to publish or display, or to cause to be published or displayed, any advertisement or notice which indicates, or which

---

18 'Panic and Prejudice', *The Times*, 27 February 1968, issue 57186, col. A, 9.

19 *Race Relations Act 1968* (1968), (London: HMSO), vol. 2, ch. 71, s. 1 (1).

20 Note: [Emphasis added]. The Act refers to trade unions and employers' organisations.

could be reasonably understood to be indicating, an act of discrimination (*Race Relations Act 1968*, s. 6 (1)).[21]

The Race Relations Board was also expanded and given powers to secure compliance with the Act's provisions by investigating complaints of racial discrimination, instituting conciliation procedures, and if these failed, by recourse to legal proceedings. The Community Relations Commission was furthermore created with the purpose of encouraging 'the establishment of harmonious community relations' and to coordinate on a national basis the measures adopted for that objective as well as advising the Secretary of State (*Race Relations Act 1968*, vol. 2, ch. 71, s. 25).

Immigration Act 1971

The *Immigration Act 1971* introduced an entirely new and very elaborate system, which based border controls on the notion of citizenship by differentiating between citizens of the United Kingdom and Colonies who were 'patrial' and thus had the right of abode in Britain, and 'non-patrials' who did not (*Immigration Act 1971*, vol. 2, ch. 7, ss. 1 (1) and (2)).[22] The rather cumbersome definition of patrial consolidated the distinction between those Commonwealth citizens who had a close connection by descent with the UK and those who did not. Under the Act, a person was considered to be a patrial if:

(a) he is a citizen of the United Kingdom and Colonies who has that citizenship by his birth, adoption, naturalisation or registration in the United Kingdom or in any of the Islands; or
(b) he is a citizen of the United Kingdom and Colonies born to or legally adopted by a parent who had that citizenship at the time of the birth or adoption (*Immigration Act 1971*, ss. 2 (1) (a) and (b)).

Outside the UK, this division was effectively between white people and their non-white counterparts; with all aliens and Commonwealth citizens who were not patrials needing permission to enter Britain (Glazer and Young 1983, 50). Before the Act came into force, Commonwealth citizens arriving under the voucher system could settle in Britain; whereas afterwards they entered on the basis of work-permits. The latter meant that immigrants would be subject to annual work-permit controls as well as facing the possibility of non-renewal of their work permits (Solomos 1989, 58).

Race Relations Act 1976

The country's slow transition towards a multicultural ideology was greatly advanced by the enactment of the *Race Relations Act 1976*. This landmark document amended its predecessor in a number of ways. Firstly, the new Act extended the definition of discrimination to include two kinds, namely: direct and indirect discrimination:

---

21 Note: the Act refers to advertisements and notices such as those specifying 'no coloureds'.

22 *Immigration Act 1971* (1971) (London: HMSO), vol. 2, ch. 7, ss. 1 (1) and (2).

A person discriminates against another if:

(1) Direct racial discrimination:

(a) on racial grounds [colour, race, nationality or national origins] he treats that other person less favourably than he treats or would treat other persons (*Race Relations Act 1976*, vol. 2, ch. 74, ss. 1 (1) (a) and 3 (1) [emphasis added]).[23]

(2) Indirect racial discrimination:

(b) he applies to that another a requirement condition which he applies or would apply equally to persons not of the same racial group as that other but–

(i) which is such that the proportion of persons of the same racial group as that other who can comply with it is considerably smaller than the proportion of persons not of that racial group who can comply with it; and

(ii) which he cannot show to be justifiable irrespective of the colour, race, nationality or ethnic or national origins to the person whom it is applied; and

(iii) which is to the detriment of that other because it cannot comply with it (*Race Relations Act 1976*, s. 1 (1) (b) (i), (ii) and (iii) [emphasis added]).

Modelled on the US experience of affirmative action, the Act's conceptualisation of indirect discrimination borne strong similarities to the anti-discrimination provisions of the American *Civil Rights Act 1964* (MacDonald 1977, 13).[24] Both were attempts, McCrudden argues, 'to circumvent the problems of proof of intentional discrimination, to go beyond its individualised nature, and to provide a basis for intervening against the present effects of past and other types of institutional discrimination' (McCrudden 1983, 56).[25]

Secondly, the Act created a new right – subject to five exceptions, to complain directly to an industrial tribunal in employment cases and to a County Court in all others. Under the previous Act, all complaints had to be processed by the Race Relations Board or in employment cases by the existing special joint industrial machinery. Given that employment was one of the main targets of the Act, the legislation was to encourage companies to adopt positive equal opportunity policies.

Thirdly, both the Race Relations Board and the Community Relations Commission effectively disappeared and were replaced by the new Commission for Racial Equality (CRE), with much stronger powers of investigation and enforcement, whose remit included:

---

23 *Race Relations Act 1976* (1976) (London: HMSO), vol. 2, ch. 74, ss. 1 (1) (a) and 3 (1).

24 MacDonald, I.A. (1977), *Race Relations, the New Law*, (London: Butterworths), 13.

25 McCrudden, C. (1983), 'Anti-discrimination Goals and the Legal Process', in Glazer, N. and K. Young (eds), *Ethnic Pluralism*, 56.

(i) to work towards the elimination of discrimination;
(ii) to promote equality of opportunity and good race relations;
(iii) to keep the working of the Race Relations Act under review and propose amendments (*Race Relations Act 1976*, s. 43 (1) (a),(b), and (c)).

Unlike the old Board, the new Commission would be able to obtain documents and subpoena witnesses. As the government's White Paper put it, the new Act envisaged a wider strategic enforcement of the legislation 'in the public interest' (MacDonald 1977, iii). Over two decades later, the Act would be enhanced by a *Race Relations (Amendment) Act 2000*, which imposed on local authorities the duty to 'eliminate unlawful racial discrimination' and to 'promote equality of opportunity and good relations between persons of different racial groups' (*Race Relations (Amendment) Act 2000*).[26]

On the whole, the decade of the 1960s–1970s can be said to have been characterised by the seemingly ambiguous approach of successive governments to the questions of New Commonwealth migration. The amalgamation of race and immigration resulted in a twin strategy featuring both strict border controls at the same time as liberal social policies aimed at promoting racial harmony. On the one hand, colour distinctions were at the root of the immigration controls, while at the same time, integration measures implied that colour was irrelevant. As the Labour Party was later to recognise:

> Our nationality and immigration laws are confused. And they have not been improved by hasty amendments in response to fears about black immigration. As a result, the United Kingdom has been found in breach of international human rights agreements it has ratified and has been unable to ratify others (Labour Party 1980, 5).[27]

Notwithstanding the government's muddled response to the New Commonwealth question, the long-term implications were clear: a fundamental shift in public perceptions and attitudes towards these newcomers and their impact on British society was taking place.

Towards Multiculturalism

A combination of socio-economic deprivation, unemployment, lack of English language skills, academic underachievement and widespread racism placed these newcomers at considerable disadvantage in comparison with their white British counterparts. As the numbers of New Commonwealth immigrant swelled, their presence continued to stretch available public resources. One area of particular concern was the enrolment of large numbers of non-English-speaking children in local schools, which required the latter to address these pupils' educational needs. By 1966, 7,700 immigrant pupils in maintained Primary and Secondary schools were

---

26 *Race Relations (Amendment Act) 2000* (2000) (London: TSO).

27 The Labour Party (1980), 'Citizenship and Immigration: A Labour Party Discussion Document', *Socialism in the 80s* (London: The Labour Party/College Hill Press), 5.

described as having no knowledge of English, and 24,000 as having some English but needing further intensive teaching (Hansard 1967, cmnd. 307).[28] A growing problem at the time, the ever increasing diversity of Britain's school population has become one of the most contentions issues at the centre of the ongoing debate on British identity and nationhood to this day. For it presents society with the profound challenge of educating a new generation of multiethnic British citizens whose first language is not English. A closer look at the way in which British society dealt with such particular situation during this time serves to illustrate further the country's continuing ideological journey in the direction of multiculturalism.

Section 11 of the Local Government Act 1966

The government's first attempt to deal with the educational needs of linguistic ethnic minorities was *Section 11 of the Local Government Act 1966*. This piece of legislation provided for additional resources to be allocated to local authorities 'with substantial numbers of immigrants' (Brown 1984; Eversley 2000, 61–66).[29] An exchange in the House of Commons, during the spring of 1966, reflects how the issue of non-English-speaking immigrants was increasingly being perceived as a rising problem. Here, Brian Redhead, Minister of State for Education and Science, is being questioned by a member of the opposition on the matter:

Sir D. Renton asked the Secretary of State for Education and Science what have so far been the effects upon the public education system of England of the need to educate large numbers of children of Commonwealth immigrants; what extra numbers of children have been involved during the past two years; and whether he will make a statement.

Mr. Redhead: The effects have been confined to the few areas much affected. Extra numbers have sometimes *increased* staffing difficulties, particularly in places short of teachers, and there have been some teaching problems particularly where the children know little or no English. The presence of classes with a large exotic element has sometimes altered the character of lessons, not always for the worse. Approximately 49,000 children of all ages under 16 were admitted from Commonwealth countries for settlement to the United Kingdom during the two years 1964 and 1965.

Sir D. Renton: Is the Hon. Gentleman aware that dependants are still coming in large numbers and going to live in places where classes are already full? What is the government to do about it?

---

28 Hansard (1967), *House of Commons, Official Report, Session 1966–67,* comprising period from 17– 28 April 1967, (London: HMSO), fifth series, vol. 745, Written Answers to Questions, Education and Science, Immigrant Pupils (English Language), cmnd. 307.

29 Brown, C. (1984), *Black and White Britain: the Third PSI Survey,* (London: Heineman Educational); Eversley, J. (2000), 'Section 11: A Brief History', in Baker, P. and J. Eversley (eds), *Multilingual Capital,* (London: Battlebridge Publications), 61–66.

Mr. Redhead: A careful watch is being kept on this. It is impossible to generalise, because, as the Right Hon. and learned gentleman will appreciate, the problem is that of only a small minority of schools in a limited number of areas (Hansard 1967, vol. 729, Oral Answers to Questions, Education and Science, Commonwealth Immigrants, cmnds. 1638–39).

Against this background, Section 11 grant understood the arrival of large numbers of New Commonwealth immigrants as placing 'a burden' on certain local authorities affected by their presence. The original intention behind the grant was therefore for the government to financially 'compensate' such Local Education Authorities (Tomlinson 1989, 803–06). Provision of Section 11 grant nevertheless signified an official recognition, albeit a reluctant one, of a growing problem which needed to be addressed, namely the educational needs of increasingly large numbers of non-English-speaking pupils in Britain's schools.

Section 11 of the *Local Government Act 1966*, operating both in England and Wales, thus provided for the payment of such grants to local authorities and subsequently, by virtue of the *Education Reform Act 1988*, also to certain educational institutions (i.e. principally grant-maintained schools and further education colleges). Section 11 funds were administered by paying local authorities a proportion (i.e. 75 per cent) of the costs incurred in employing additional staff on projects designed to enable members of non-English-speaking ethnic minorities to overcome disadvantage. Overall, the grant was seen as a compensatory measure (Home Office 1988, 2).[30]

When Section 11 was created the area of education alone accounted for over 90 per cent of the total funding. The largest single use of the grant was to support the cost of employing additional teachers and classroom assistants to teach ESL programmes in schools (OFSTED 1994).[31] Figures for 1986/87, for instance, show that out of a Section 11 grant totalling £87.5 million to local authorities, education accounted for £70 million (79.5 per cent) of the grant, while £3.0 million (3.5 per cent) was spent on social services and around £14.5 million (17 per cent) on other items (Home Office 1988, 2). Educational provision included projects to raise academic achievement among school children by strengthening home/school liaisons, as well as the delivery of English language teaching in Further and Adult Education. Social services grant-funded projects, on the other hand, comprised the provision of interpreting and translation services, advice and training for adults, libraries and information services, as well as support in overcoming homelessness and racial harassment (Home Office 1988). According to the *PEP Report 1975*, the ethnic minorities at the time accounted for only 2.5 per cent of the total population of Britain at most. The main minority groups not included in the survey were black

---

30 Home Office (1988), A *Scrutiny of Grants under Section 11 of the Local Government Act 1966: Final Report,* (London: HMSO), 2.

31 Note: the Home Office administered a wide range of grants under Section 11, but expenditure on education posts predominated from the inception of the grants. In 1993/94, for instance, from a total Section 11 expenditure of £173 million, the education allocation was in the region of £154 million (89 per cent). See Office for Standards in Education (OFSTED) (1994), *Educational Support for Minority Ethnic Communities: A Survey of Educational Provision funded under Section 11 of the Local Government Act 1966,* (London: OFSTED).

Africans and people from Asian countries other than India, Pakistan and Bangladesh. Analysis from the *1971 Census* suggested that these excluded groups accounted for between 15 and 20 per cent of the total minority population (Smith 1976, 11).[32]

The report's findings confirmed the existence of widespread racial discrimination in the country. One of the key conclusions of this report was identifying lack of English language proficiency as a major source of disadvantage. Both the black and Asian communities had been shown to experience significant difficulties due to their poor spoken English. The West Indians for instance, spoke a Creole variety of English, which differed considerably from Standard English. People in Britain would find it rather difficult to understand this tongue. The language situation of the Asians was even more serious, since most of them had either learnt English only as a second language or not at all. Moreover, their native languages (i.e. Hindi, Urdu, Bengali, Sylheti, Gujarati and Punjabi) were very different from English (Smith 1976, 44). The *PEP Report 1975* found that Asians who spoke English were much more likely to be doing non-manual jobs, and less likely to be doing semiskilled and unskilled manual jobs than those who did not. This connexion between educational underachievement and lack English proficiency was furthermore corroborated by the *Fifth Report of the House of Commons Affairs Committee*, which, in 1981, indicated that one 'important component of racial disadvantage is educational' (Hansard 1981, para. 20, p. xii).[33] Lack of English skills, in particular, was seen as detrimental to ethnic minority students' academic performance, hence:

> What evidence there is shows that Asian and West Indian children encounter some major difficulties in their progress through the British educational system, which are not shared by white children in the same schools. Most obviously, a proportion of Asian children still speaks little or no English on entering schools in Britain. West Indian children may also suffer at school because of linguistic problems, which were and are less clearly identified and dealt with (Hansard 1981, para. 21, p. xiii).

As the *PEP Report 1975* had already shown, the average educational level of the non-English-speaking population was generally lower than that existing among whites. Throughout the 1980s, concerns with the educational needs of linguistic ethnic minorities continued to intensify amid a spate of racial disturbances across the country. Between 1980 and 1985, outbreaks of civil unrest in inner-city areas of London, Liverpool and Bristol highlighted the acute socio-economic conditions experienced by linguistic ethnic minorities. The *Scarman Report* into the early disturbances ultimately suggested that they have been driven by a sense of disadvantage. The Report's conclusions indicated that residents living in 'deprived, inner-city, multiracial localities' invariably experienced 'social and economic disadvantages' (quoted in Solomos 1989, 115). The existence of such adverse circumstances created 'a predisposition towards violent protest' which could be sparked off by incidents such as confrontations between local residents and the police (quoted in Solomos

---

32 Smith, D.J. (ed.) (1976), *The Facts of Racial Disadvantage, Volume XLII*, Broadsheet No. 560, (London: PEP), 11.

33 Hansard (1981), *House of Commons, Fifth Report from the Home Affairs Committee, Session 1980–81, Racial Disadvantage*, (London: HMSO), para. 20, p. xii.

1989, 115). Against this background, the commissioning of the Rampton Enquiry into the education of ethnic minority children reflects the significance that the issue of ESL education had come to acquire, and therefore how far public perceptions about this policy had shifted.[34]

Education for All: Report of the Committee of Inquiry into the Education of Children from Ethnic Minority Groups 1985

Published in the aftermath of the 1985 riots, the *Education for All Report* (called Swann Report after its Chairman, Lord Swann) went on to addressed the educational underachievement of all non-English-speaking children living in Britain (Verma 1985, 470–75).[35] The Committee's terms of reference stated that:

> Recognising the contribution of schools in preparing all pupils for life in a society which is both multi-racial and culturally diverse, the Committee is required to review, in relation to schools, the educational needs and attainments of children from ethnic minority groups, taking account, as necessary, of factors outside the formal education system relevant to school performance, including influences in early childhood and prospects for school leavers (DES 1985, para. 2, p. vii).[36]

In order to carry out this brief, the Swann Committee consulted a wide range of relevant policy actors involved in the provision of ESL education, including officials from the Department of education and Science (DES) as well as Her Majesty's Inspectorate (HMI), academics from several universities, councillors from local government authorities, educational advisers, language specialists, think tank researchers as well as media practitioners (DES 1985, iii–v). In addition, an array of organisations submitted evidence to the Committee, including the Commission for Racial Equality, the British Refugee Council, the Afro-Caribbean Teachers Association, the National Council of Hindu Associations, the Muslim Education Trust, the Joint Council for the Welfare of Immigrants and the National Association for Multi-Racial Education (DES 1985, 788–93). The contrasting backgrounds of those partaking in the inquiry, as well as their broad-ranging expertise reflect the pluralistic nature that the debate over ESL education had attained (Parekh 1985, 22–3).[37]

---

34 Note: in line with the Swann Report, the Rampton Enquiry expressed concerns about the educational disadvantage experienced by ethic minorities, and in particular the West Indian community. However, unlike the Swann Report, which provided extensive evidence of racism in schools, the Rampton Enquiry identified perceived entrenched attitudes and low expectations of the West Indian community as the main reason behind their children's academic underachievement.

35 Verma, G. K. (1985), 'The Swann Report and Ethnic Achievement: a Comment', *New Community*, 12:3, 470–75.

36 Department for Education and Science (DES) (1985), *Education for All: Report of the Committee of Inquiry into the Education of Children from Ethnic Minority Groups,* appointed by the Secretary of State and Science under the Chairmanship of Lord Swann, (London: HMSO), para. 2, p. vii.

37 Parekh, B. (1985), 'The Gifts of Diversity', *The Times Education Supplement*, 29 March 1985, 22–23.

The Report recognised that the multiracial nature of British society had implications for the education of all children, including the English-speaking indigenous majority. It consequently explored every aspect of multicultural education in Britain. It addressed, among other issues: the diverse nature of British society, the roots of racism, educational underachievement, ESL education policy, the employment of ethnic minority teachers, multi-ethnic and religious education as well as language across the curriculum. It also dealt with the particular educational needs of different ethnic minority groups, including Asians, West Indians, Chinese, Cypriots, Italians, Ukrainians, Vietnamese and Travellers. Within this context, the Committee advocated the development of what it called 'Education for All', understood as a national education system which aimed to preserve the cultural diversity of the country's school population. There were two distinct aspects of 'Education for All': on the one hand, catering for any particular educational needs, which ethnic minority pupils may have; and on the other hand, enhancing the education offered to all pupils (DES 1985, para. 4.13, 358). Hence, the Report indicated:

> In our view, 'Education for All' should involve more than learning more about the cultures and lifestyles of various ethnic groups; it should also seek to develop in all pupils, both ethnic majority and minority, a flexibility of mind and an ability to analyse critically and rationally the nature of British society today within a global context. The reality of British society now and in the future, is that a variety of ethnic groups, with their own distinct lifestyles and value systems will be living together (DES 1985, para. 2.7, 324).

Linguistic diversity was consequently regarded as a 'positive asset', one which the schools should impart an understanding of to all pupils (DES 1985, para. 5.6, 671). With regard to the particular wants of ESL students, the Report suggested a number of measures. On the one hand, 'the needs of learners of English as a second language should be met by provision within the mainstream school, as part of a comprehensive programme of language education to all children' (DES 1985, 5.3, 771). On the other hand, the Report indicated that 'for a child from a home where English is not the first language, pre-school provision can be particularly valuable' (DES 1985, para. 5.4, 771). The Report went on to recommend changes across a whole range of curricular areas, which would offer pupils a more balanced and relevant view of the multi-ethnic society in which they lived in (DES 1985, para. 3.1, 327). It significantly called for the provision of two different sources of funding to cater for the two distinct dimensions of 'Education for All'. The Committee members regarded Section 11 as the chief source of funding for the 'ethnic minority dimension' of education (DES 1985, para. 4.13, 358). They believed, however, that the provision of a 'multicultural' component affecting the education of all pupils was not adequately catered for:

> We feel that existing legislation does not cater adequately for present-day circumstances and that any new arrangements are bound to be hampered by the terms of the 1966 Act. We believe the time has therefore come for the government to reconsider the possibility of revising the provisions of Section 11 fully, through new legislation, in order to make it more appropriate to the needs of multi-racial schools and LEAs in Britain today (DES 1985, para. 4.13, 358–59).

Above all, as Sir Keith Joseph, Secretary of State for Education, put it 'the Swann Report is asking us to deal with the most difficult of all issues: attitudes' (Hansard 1985, cmnd. 453).[38] The transformation of Britain into a multi-ethnic nation was central to the Report. The latter not only acknowledged the multicultural and multilingual nature of Britain, the Swann Report expected its peoples to embrace it. This could only be accomplished by a change in public perceptions regarding linguistic ethnic minorities:

> This report is concerned primarily to change behaviour and attitudes. They need to change throughout Britain, and while the education system must not be expected to carry the whole of the burden of that change, schools in particular are uniquely well placed to take a lead role. Britain has evolved, over many centuries, institutions and traditions which, whatever their shortcomings, have been taken as models by many nations, and were indeed an important part of the attraction of this country to the ethnic minorities who are the essential concern of our report. It is because we believe that everyone in Britain has a direct interest in ensuring that those institutions and the attitudes, which inform them, change to take full account of the pluralism, which is now, a marked feature of British life, that we make our recommendations (DES 1985, para. 1.1, 767).

Verma has indicated that the Swann Report constituted a 'landmark in pluralism' (Verma 1989, 1).[39] The language in which the Committee articulated ESL policy reflects the multicultural values advocated by its members. Their approach to ethnic diversity had not only translated into a celebration of multicultural education, but an endorsement of ESL education policy. On publishing the Report, Sir Keith Joseph indicated that 'the government accepts the Committee's finding that many ethnic minority pupils are achieving below their potential, and recognises the concern that is felt about this among their parents ... we want the schools to preserve and transmit our national values in a way which accepts Britain's ethnic diversity and promotes tolerance and racial harmony' (Hansard 1985, cmnd. 451). It is against this background, that the *Education Reform Act 1988* (ERA) was introduced.

The Education Reform Act 1988 (ERA)

Forty four years after the *Education Act 1944* had come into being, the *Education Reform Act 1988* (ERA) was enacted. Just as the original Act had structured the then incipient education system, the new ERA would proceed to overhaul it. The *Education Reform Act 1988* was concerned with 'the school curriculum, assessment and examinations, and related arrangements', which 'will affect the education provided for all pupils of compulsory school age' (DES 1989a, 3).[40] One of the most significant innovations of the ERA was the introduction of the National Curriculum,

---

38 *Hansard* (1985), *House of Commons Official Report, Session 1984–85,* comprising period 11 March – 22 March 1985, sixth series, vol. 75, (London: HMSO), Ethnic Minority Children (Education), cmnd. 453.

39 Verma, G.K. (ed.) (1989), *Education for All: A Landmark in Pluralism,* (London: The Falmer Press), 1.

40 DES (1989a), *The Education Reform Act 1988: the School Curriculum and Assessment, Circular no. 5/89,* (London: HMSO), 3.

which provided a blueprint for the subject matter to be taught in British schools. In its opening section, the ERA stated the purpose of the National Curriculum as one which:

> Promotes the spiritual, moral, cultural, mental and physical development of pupils at the school and of society; and prepares such pupils for the opportunities, responsibilities and experiences of adult life (DES 1989b, part 1, chp. 1, sec. 1, paras. 2 (a) (b), c. 40).[41]

Organised on the basis of four Key Stages for 11–14 year olds, the ERA accordingly established two categories of subjects to be taught in schools across the country:

> The core subjects are: Mathematics, English and Science; and in relation to schools in Wales which are Welsh-speaking schools, Welsh.

> The other foundation subjects are: History, Geography, Technology, Music, Art and Physical Education; in relation to the third and fourth Key Stages, a Modern Foreign Language specified in an order of the Secretary of State; and in relation to schools in Wales which are not Welsh-speaking schools, Welsh (DES 1989b, part 1, chp. 1, sec. 3, paras. 1 (a) (b), and 2 (a) (b) (c), c. 40).

While significantly making provision for the teaching of Modern Foreign Languages as a foundation subject, prominence was given to the learning and teaching of English. This preference reflects the Act's concern with raising students' academic standards across the board. The latter had been the main thrust of the Kingman Committee, basis to the working party which established the National Curriculum (Nash 1988, 11–14).[42] The Committee had dealt at length with a wide range of issues relating to teaching and learning of the English language, such as grammatical and pedagogical matters, language acquisition and development, teacher training techniques and qualifications, as well as evaluation and assessment (DES 1988).[43] Although focusing to a large extent on English language tuition, the Kingman Committee acknowledged the problems faced by non-English-speaking students. In its final Report the Committee's members stated:

> Our report is primarily concerned with children who speak English as a mother-tongue. Children in our schools who are speakers of languages other than English, including Afro-Caribbean Creole languages, share the entitlement which we have defined, and should be given every possible opportunity to function effectively in an English-speaking society. It is not within our terms of reference to consider English as a Second Language (ESL) provision in detail, but we urge close co-operation between ESL specialists and teachers

---

41 DES (1989b), *The Education Reform Act 1988*, part 1, chp. 1, sec. 1, paras. 2 (a) (b), c. 40 <http://www.hmso.gov.uk/acts/acts1988/Ukpga_19880040_en_2.htm#mdiv2> (accessed 9 June 2002).

42 Nash, I. 'The Kingman Report: Laying the Foundation for a New Consensus', *The Times Education Supplement,* 6 May 1988, 11–14.

43 DES (1988), *Report of the Committee of Inquiry into the Teaching of English Language*, appointed by the Secretary of State for Education and Science under the Chairmanship of Sir John Kingman, (London: HMSO).

who are implementing our recommendations in primary and secondary schools (DES 1988, chp. 5, para. 17, 58).

In the same way as the Kingman Committee recognized the problem of ESL education, the contents of the National Curriculum ultimately endeavoured to reflect Britain's 'cultural diverse society' (DES 1989a, para. 17, 7). Against this background, ESL education can be said to have become increasingly regarded as part of a wider multicultural discourse; one based on the notion of equality of access to education. By the late 1990s, the educational needs of non-English-speaking pupils were certainly considered as a legitimate policy problem (Bourne 1989).[44] This process of policy reframing finally materialised in 1999, with the replacement of Section 11 grant by the so-called Ethnic Minority Achievement Grant (EMAG).

The Ethnic Minority Achievement Grant (EMAG)

In 1998, shortly after coming into office, Prime Minister Tony Blair speaking on education policy stated:

> I said in opposition that education would be our number one priority, the passion of my government. Words that are easy enough in opposition. But I believe we are turning those words into action that will revolutionise standards at every level ... I believe passionately in education as the key to the success of an individual and of a nation (No. 10 Downing Street 2002).[45]

In the first education White Paper of the new administration, *Excellence in Schools*, David Blunkett, Secretary of State for Education, spelt out the government's vision for Britain's education policy accordingly, thus:

> Education matters. It matters to you and to the children you care about. It matters to the country. Tony Blair and I have made clear that education is our top priority ... Excellence can be achieved only on the basis of partnership. We all need to be involved: schools, teachers and parents are at the heart of it. We also need the help of all of you: families and the wider community. We need your commitment if we are to get our children off to a good start. Everyone has a part to play (DfEE 1997, Foreword, i). [46]

The concept of education in a multicultural and multilingual British society had ultimately become central to the government's political agenda. During the previous three decades, the educational needs of non-English-speaking children had been mainly addressed through the provision of Section 11 grants. However, despite a promising start in the late 1960s, by the late 1990s this pioneering funding scheme

---

44 Bourne, J. (1989), *Moving into the Mainstream: LEA Provision for Bilingual Pupils*, (Windsor: NFER-Nelson).

45 No. 10 Downing Street (2002), 'Speech by Prime Minister Tony Blair on education policy', 14 April 1998 <http://www.number–10.gov.uk/output/page1589.asp> (accessed 9 June 2002).

46 DfEE (1997), *Excellence in Schools White Paper*, (London: HMSO), Foreword by the Secretary of State for Education, i.

had been widely criticised (Meakin 1996, vol. 766, 12; Gillborn 1998, 26).[47] In 1981, the *Fifth Report from the Home Office Affairs Committee on Racial Disadvantage* admitted that 'there is no single aspect of Section 11 payments which has escaped criticism', hence:

> It should be emphasised that the [Section 11] money is intended to repay local authorities for something extra which they have to do. The statute does not define what that extra is, which is left to local authorities to decide. Home Office guidance apparently goes no further than suggesting that as a general rule staff in posts claimed for should spent at least half of their time in dealing with 'Commonwealth immigrants'. Nobody from central government attempts to persuade local authorities to undertake new programmes and to reclaim the money spent. (Hansard 1981, vol. 1, sec. (i), para. 50, xxiii–xxiv).

It went on to list a number of specific concerns about Section 11 including: 'the absurd formula of payments … under which payment is made when certain expenditure attributable to the presence of Commonwealth immigrants exceeds a norm', 'the exclusion of non-Commonwealth ethnic minorities with similar needs', 'the Home Office interpretation of Commonwealth immigrants being limited to those who had been in this country for less than ten years', 'lack of supervision by the Home Office of the expenditure and its effectiveness' and 'lack of any strategic approach by authorities'(Hansard 1981, vol. 1, sec. (1), paras. 53, 54 and 55, xxv–xxvi; Tomlinson 1989, 803–6).

The Report suggested that if Section 11 was to be maintained, it had to be radically reformed; although 'the little evidence available suggests however that there is no general understanding of the purpose of Section 11, and little by the way of accepted good practice' (Hansard 1981, vol. 1, sec. (1), para. 59, xxvii). By 1988, the situation developed further as a Home Office report entitled *A Scrutiny of Grants Under Section 11 of the Local Government Act 1966* reflects:

> £100 million of taxpayers' money is spent under Section 11 with the intention of benefiting the ethnic minorities. The money is spent on additional teachers for ethnic minority children, together with social workers, housing officers, business advisers and other local authority staff. Yet there is no clear objective for the grant and no effective system for assessing results. The Home Office team is cracking under the strain of examining in great detail the 1,200 existing applications for new posts received each year, while 12,000 existing posts continue with little or no scrutiny. The application process is bureaucratic and wasteful. Local authorities and communities believe the Home Office has lost all commitment to the grant, and that its days are numbered. Authorities vary considerably in their use and management of Section 11 resources. We saw evidence of the grant acting as a valuable catalyst for change in mainstream programmes. But we also saw it funding token ethnic minority posts and subsiding programme expenditure. The ethnic minorities, who are ultimately the customers for Section 11 grant, argue that there is no effective consultation, and feel little benefit for the expenditure of much of the £100 million. The

---

47 Meakin, J. (1996), 'What Future for Section 11 Funding?' *Municipal Review and AMA News*, vol. 766, 12; Gillborn, D. 'Naïve Multiculturalism: Social Justice, "Race" and Education Policy under New Labour', *Times Education Supplement*, 4 September 1998, 26.

legislation now 20 years old is out of date in important respects (Home Office 1988, para. 1, iii).

While the findings of the report identified serious flaws with the provision of Section 11 grants, it was felt that dismantling the programme would be perceived by ethnic communities as a 'downgrading of the government's commitment to tackling racial disadvantage' (Home Office 1988, iv). Instead, the Home Office recommended that 'a specific grant designed to target resources at tackling racial disadvantage, administered by the Home Office, should be retained. But there must be a new clarity of direction and urgency about achieving results' (Home Office 1988, sec. a (1), 21). In its final recommendations, the 1988 Report also referred to the wording of the Section 11 text, in particular the term 'Commonwealth immigrant' was criticised for excluding non-Commonwealth immigrant groups with similar needs, such as the Vietnamese and the Somalis (Home Office 1988, 11). It therefore advocated that 'the concept of Commonwealth immigrant should be removed from the legislation and the grant should be payable in respect of ethnic minorities suffering racial disadvantage' (Home Office 1988, sec. b (36), 25). Although the original drafting of Section 11 had referred to the 'immigrants from the [New] Commonwealth' for purely historical reasons, the subsequent *Local government (Amendment) Act 1993* eventually changed its wording to include all ethnic minorities, hence:

> Subject to the provisions of this section, the Secretary of State may pay to local authorities, who in his opinion are required to make special provision in the exercise of any of their functions in consequence of the presence within their areas of persons belonging to ethnic minorities whose language or customs differ from those of the rest of the community, grants of such amounts as he may with the consent of the Treasury determined on account of expenditure of such description (being expenditure in respect of the employment of staff) as he may so determine (*Local Government (Amendment) Act* 1993, chp. 27, sec. 1 (1) (11), 1).

The main recommendations of the 1988 Home Office Report *A Scrutiny of Grants Under Section 11 of the Local Government Act 1966* were taken up by the government, and in 1990 the *Home Office Circular no. 78/1990* set out the new arrangements for the administration of Section 11 grants (Home Office 1990).[48] They accordingly introduced a number of changes including: the establishment of a regular annual timetable according to which applications had to be made, compared with the earlier rolling programmes of bids that could be submitted at any time; the formation of bids in the shape of projects rather than on a post by post basis; the creation of a policy criteria under which provisions must fall; and the regular monitoring of projects against recognisable performance targets (LARRIE 1992, 1).[49]

Above all, these Home Office guidelines illustrated the extent to which public perceptions about ESL education had now changed. In contrast to the intention behind

---

48 Home Office (1990), *The Home Office Circular no. 78/1990: Section 11 of the Local Government Act 1966,* (London: HMSO).

49 Local Authorities Race Relations Information Exchange (LARRIE) (1992), *Guide to Section 11 Funding: the 1992/93 Section 11 Allocation, LARRIE Research Report, no. 3* (London: LARRIE), 1.

the original statute, by 1990, Section 11 funding was being understood as addressing 'issues particular to ethnic minority groups that prevent them from entering fully into mainstream activities' (Home Office 1990, para. 12, 4–5). As the *Home Office Circular no. 78/1990* indicated:

> The government's fundamental objective is to enable everyone, irrespective of ethnic origin, to participate fully and freely in the life of the nation while having the freedom to maintain their own cultural identity. The achievement of this objective involves central and local government; the private and voluntary sectors; and the ethnic minority communities themselves. The government believes that at present there is a continuing need for specific grant to meet needs particular to ethnic minorities of Commonwealth origin that prevent full participation in the mainstream of national life. Barriers to opportunities arise in a number of areas, particularly through differences of language, in educational attainment and through economic, social and cultural differences (Home Office 1990, para. 6, 2–3).

In a further policy document entitled the *Grant Administration and Policy Criteria*, the government set out its vision of Section 11 grant likewise:

> The government believes that Section 11 has an important role to play in assisting ethnic minority communities to enter fully and benefit from the mainstream of national life. The government's aim is to help the members of such communities to benefit fully from opportunities for educational, economic and social development. To this end the grant has provided and will continue to provide support in the teaching of English, in strategies aimed at improving educational performance and in tackling particular needs which arise where economic, social or cultural differences impede access to opportunities or services (Home Office 1990, para. 9, 3).[50]

In November 1996, Timothy Kirkhope, Home Office Minister, in an additional press release, *A Way Ahead for Ethnic Minority Community Funding,* similarly declared that:

> Ethnic minority communities bring diversity and cultural enrichment to our society. I am determined that they, like everyone else, should have every opportunity to play a full part in the social and economic life of this country. Projects funded under section 11 have played an important part in this (Home Office 1996, 1).[51]

In November 1998, the government finally announced the introduction of an altogether new ESL funding allocation programme under the title Ethnic Minority Achievement Grant (EMAG). This new scheme, administered by the Department for Education and Employment, was designed to replace the ailing 33 year old Section 11 grant with an overall more inclusive ESL financial support package (Baker and Eversley 2000, 62).[52] The introduction of EMAG took place against the

---

50 Home Office (1990), *Section 11 of the Local Government Act 1966: Grant Administration: Policy Criteria,* (London: HMSO), para. 9, 3.

51 Home Office (1996), *News Release no. 350/96: A Way Ahead for Ethnic Minority Community Funding,* (London: Home Office), 1.

52 Baker, P. and J. Eversley (eds) (2000), *Multilingual Capital: the Languages of London's School Children and their Relevance to Economic, Social and Educational Policies,*

backdrop of the *Macpherson Report* into the murder of Afro-Caribbean teenager Stephen Lawrence (*The Stephen Lawrence Inquiry* 1999).[53] The Report, which had conceptualised the notion of 'institutional racism', recommended that the National Curriculum be amended so as to include in its ethos 'valuing cultural diversity and preventing racism, in order to better reflect the needs of a diverse society' (*The Stephen Lawrence Inquiry* 1999, 334). In welcoming the Report's suggestions, Charles Clark, Schools Minister, declared:

> We agree with the view of the Macpherson Report that it is important that the National Curriculum properly reflects the needs of a diverse society. As part of the National Curriculum review, we are seeking ways to ensure that all pupils gain an understanding of citizenship and democracy. An important part of this will be fostering an understanding of the diversity of cultures, which exist in Britain today. I believe that this is the best way in which we can reflect these issues in the curriculum, but of course, we are looking at a range of ways of ensuring that the curriculum responds fully to the needs of all pupils (DfES Press Office 1999a, 1).[54]

In line with the *Stephen Lawrence Inquiry*'s recommendations, the new EMAG was expected to provide 'equality of opportunity for all minority ethnic groups' (DfEE 1999, 1). As Jacqui Smith, Schools Minister, pointed out, there still remained a wide educational gap between English-speaking white students and their non-English-speaking coloured peers, thus:

> Children from ethnic minorities are an important and vibrant part of today's society, and it is vital that we ensure they have the same opportunities to succeed as everyone else. Many Asian children achieve very good results – better than average. But too many children from ethnic minority backgrounds are under-performing. If you are Pakistani, Bangladeshi or of African-Caribbean origin, your chance of gaining five good GCSE is half that of white pupils (DfES Press Office 1999b, 1).[55]

According to the DfES' *Ethnic Minority Achievement Grant: Consultation Paper*, the new EMAG subsidy was specifically aimed 'to meet the particular needs of pupils for whom English is an additional language (EAL); and to raise standards of achievement for those minority ethnic groups who are particularly at risk of under-achieving' (DfEE Ethnic Minorities Pupils Team 1999, paras. (a) and (b), 1).[56] In the words of David Blunkett, Education and Employment Secretary, 'there is no reason why underachievement should be tolerated' (DfES Press Office 2001, 1).[57]

(London: Battlebridge), 62.

53 *The Stephen Lawrence Inquiry: Report of an Inquiry by Sir William Macpherson of Cluny* (1999) (London: HMSO).

54 DfES Press Office (1999a), *Press Notice no. 1999/0110: Improved Standards for Ethnic Pupils will be our Lasting Response to the Lawrence Inquiry,* (London: DfES), 1.

55 DfES Press Office (1999b), *Press Notice no. 1999/0405: Ethnic Minority Pupil Grant will boost Achievement,* (London: DfES), 1.

56 DfEE, Ethnic Minorities Pupils Team (1999), *Ethnic Minority Achievement Grant: Consultation Paper* (London: DfEE), paras. (a) and (b), 1.

57 DfES Press Office (2001), *Press Notice no. 2001/0212: Raising the Achievement of Ethnic Minority Pupils* (London: DfES), 1.

By including additional marginal communities, such as Travellers, which Section 11 had failed to fund, the EMAG scheme hoped to achieve those objectives (Baker and Eversley 2000, 62). In establishing the grant, Charles Clark indicated that 'the new Ethnic Minority Grant replacing Section 11 is providing £430 million over the next three years, as part of a new drive to improve the education of ethnic minority pupils and children of refugees'(DfEE Press Office 1999, 1).[58] Eversley pointed out, however, that the impact of the EMAG would be actually restricted both by the size of the total available resources and the need for authorities to find additional funding to supplement their allocation (Baker and Eversley 2000, 62).

The EMAG nevertheless broadened considerably the scope of Section 11, by aiming to provide ESL services, as well as improving the academic achievement of all ethnic minority students. The DfES' guidelines on EMAG went on to explain the dual nature of this grant. On the one hand, it 'provides an opportunity to build on Section 11 work and to ensure that schools and LEAs work together to provide genuine equality of opportunity for all pupils'; while on the other hand, EMAG 'links with the LEA's Education Development Plan and the Literacy Strategy, and contributes to the national priority to raise standards for under-achieving groups, including those for whom English is an additional language' (DfES 1999, 1).[59]

Under the EMAG schools were ultimately expected to establish a whole set of policies to help raise the attainment of ethnic minority pupils, who are at risk of under-performing. It also required LEAs to monitor the achievement of ethnic minority pupils and set targets for year on year improvement (DfES Press Office 1999b, 1). On the whole, the replacement of Section 11 with the new EMAG epitomises a long process of ESL policy reframing in which a multicultural discourse based on the notion of equality of access had come to dominate the public policy arena.

Conclusion

The turbulent two decades of 1960s–1980s witnessed the demographic and ideological transformation of British society in fundamental ways. Faced, for the first time, with mass influxes of New Commonwealth migrants, the government of the day was forced to confront the overall impact of such arrivals into their host society. As competition for scarce resources intensified, hostile public attitudes to immigrants surfaced. In an attempt to deal with this escalating situation, successive administrations presided over a muddled policy strategy featuring on the one hand, tight immigration controls, while at the same time enacting far-reaching equality and diversity legislation.

Throughout this time, public awareness of the impoverished living conditions experienced by these migrants was mostly scanty. But as research progressively filled knowledge gaps, attitudes to the newcomers started to change. A spate of urban riots during the early and mid-1980s focused the public mind on prevailing social

---

58 DfEE Press Office (1999), *Press Notice no. 1999/0191: Clarke Reinforces Commitment to Educating Refugee Children,* (London: DfEE), 1.

59 DfES (1999), 'Guidance on Ethnic Minority Achievement Grant', 1 <http://www.dfee.gov.uk/ethnic/guide.htm> (accessed 9 June 2002).

and economic inequalities disproportionally affecting minority ethnic communities. Now an integral part of the British nation, society could no longer afford to ignore the needs of these immigrants, particularly those of their non-English speaking children. As the next generation of British citizens, the education of migrant pupils became a central piece of the government's diversity strategy. One which has progressively come to embrace a vision of an inclusive, multiethnic and multicultural British society.

Chapter 6

1990s–2000s: A Discourse of Integration – Sharing Common Values

Towards Social and Linguistic Cohesion

The closing years of the twentieth century witnessed a continuation of governmental efforts to cater for the needs of the country's ever growing minority ethnic school population. This trend, which was very much in line with the multicultural discourse prevailing during the preceding decade, involved an increase in ESL funding as well as granting of additional services to the country's non-English-speaking school pupils. A glance at language education policy provision suggests that by 2002, some £480 million of general resources provided to schools through Standard Spending Assessment (SSAs) took account of ethnicity, and EMAG alone was worth up to £145 million a year. Other Standards Fund Programmes such as Excellence in Cities, KS3 and the Literacy and Numeracy strategies also were aimed at narrowing attainment gaps between different school populations. At the time, the government seemed to view ESL education programmes as providing the most effective way to allow non-English-speaking students access to the National Curriculum. Within this context, the DfES published *Removing the Barriers: Raising Achievement Level of Minority Ethnic Pupils: Key Points for Schools*, a school guide which focused on raising teachers and practitioners' awareness of good practice in support of minority ethnic pupils (DfES 2002).[1] Successful schools were therefore those deemed to be sensitive to the diverse identities of their pupils by allowing these children's cultural, linguistic and religious heritage to become an integral part of the school curriculum.

Despite such efforts to foster a multicultural ethos within Britain's educational establishment, a combination of socio-economic and political developments, both at home and abroad, saw a steady decline in public support for the country's official multicultural model. During the spring and early summer of 2001, a number of disturbances reminiscent of the urban riots of the 1980s took place across northern towns and cities in England such as Bradford, Oldham and Burnley. Almost two decades after the original troubles mainly involving the Afro-Caribbean community, these new instances of civic unrest saw clashes between predominantly disaffected inner-city white and Muslim youths, amid attacks on the police and scenes of chaos and destruction to property. Hailed as 'the worst racial violence in Britain for more than 15 years', this episode revisited some of the familiar social themes

---

1 DfES (2002), *Removing the Barriers: Raising Achievement Levels of Minority Ethnic Pupils – Key Points for Schools* <http://www.standards.dfes.gov.uk/ethnicminorities> (accessed 9 June 2002).

of its predecessors, namely decaying communities with large impoverished ethnic populations, racial ghettoisation with visibly segregated housing and schooling, endemic educational underachievement as well as high levels of school dropouts and youth unemployment (Bunyan and Sparrow 2001; Travis 2006).[2] As in previous occasions, the tensions not only highlighted the plight of a minority urban underclass; they focused attention on the wider challenge of living with diversity and the growing danger of Britain's civic fragmentation along ethnic and cultural lines.

Unprecedented influxes of non-English-speaking illegal immigrants and refugees into the UK furthermore led to widespread anxiety about the financial and cultural impact that the significant presence of these particular migrants may have. The newcomers' continuous arrival and the challenges they presented to Britain's educational system, labour market and welfare services precipitated adverse public reactions towards refugees themselves as well as drawing attention to the policies and resources aimed at them. Such climate was exacerbated by the terrorist atrocities perpetrated in New York City's World Trade Centre by Islamic extremists, in 2001. Given the perpetrators' alleged links with UK-based operatives, the attacks no only put under the spotlight the British Muslim community, but their Islamic values and customs as distinct from Britain's dominant western, liberal Christian tradition. The subsequent bombings in London by UK-born radicalised Muslims four years later only compounded this situation. The concatenation of these social, economic and political factors saw the country's prevailing multiculturalist discourse being challenged by an emerging integrationist ideology intent on protecting the dominant English-speaking Anglo-Saxon *status quo*, which was increasingly perceived to have come under threat.

Estimates from the Refugee Council indicate that by 2001, 71,700 new asylum applications had been made, of which 30,470 were successfully processed; this compared with 1996 figures in which 29,640 applications were made, of which only 7,295 had been granted some kind of refugee status (Refugee Council 2002).[3] Such figures and the public anxiety accompanying them were further aggravated by a particularly well-publicised episode involving a wave of illegal immigrants entering the UK from northern France. During May 2002, hundreds of illegal immigrants based in Sangatte, a Red Cross refugee camp controversially located in the vicinity of Calais, arrived in Britain via the Channel Tunnel linking both countries. Dramatic images depicting groups of immigrants attempting to flee into Britain by cutting through barbed wire fences or stowed away in vehicles crossing the Tunnel were widely relayed in the national media. Alarmist headlines in the press heighten the sense of crisis as it was reported that 'more than 200 illegal immigrants reached England

---

2　　Bunyan, N. and N. Sparrow 'Race Riot Town on a Knife-Edge', *Telegraph*, 5 June 2001 <http://www.telegraph.co.uk/news/main.jhtml?xml=/news/2001/05/28/noldh28.xml>(accessed 12 May 2007); Travis, A. "Summer of Race Riots' feared after Clashes in 2001', *The Guardian*, 28 December 2006 <http://www.guardian.co.uk/guardianpolitics/story/0,,1979152,00.html> (accessed 12 May 2007).

3　　Refugee Council (2002), *Annual UK Asylum Statistics* <http://www.refugeecouncil. org.uk/infocentre/stats/stats001.htm> (checked 9 June 2002).

in May through the Channel Tunnel' (Cullinan and Noble 2002, 23).[4] Government's reaction to the rapidly escalating situation saw further headlines such as 'Blair's Secret Plan to crack down on Asylum Seekers' (Milne and Travis 2002).[5] The Prime Minister was accordingly deemed to have taken 'personal control of asylum policy' and was 'considering proposals to mobilise Royal Navy warships to intercept people traffickers in the Mediterranean and carry out bulk deportations in RAF transport planes' (Milne and Travis 2002). In the event, no such actions materialised as the French refugee camp was eventually closed following an agreement between the UK and French governments, in December 2002. While the political controversy seemed to ebb away though, public feelings of hostility towards the immigrant community all but decreased.

Derogatory comments regarding asylum seekers made by David Blunkett, Home Secretary, around the time of the controversy are symptomatic of the changes in public perceptions taking place. Speaking on BBC Radio Four's Today Programme, Blunkett suggested that children of asylum seekers should be educated separately while their applications were being dealt with; as he put it: 'whilst they're [asylum seekers] going through the process, the children will be educated on the site, which will be open. People will be able to come and go, but importantly not swamping the local school' (*The Guardian* 2002).[6] Blunkett's comments are the more significant, since they were made in the context of the *Asylum Bill*, then going through Parliament (Hansard 2002).[7] The latter included proposals preventing non-English-speaking refugee children living in accommodation centres from attending mainstream classes at local schools. Not surprisingly, his suggestions for segregated education met with criticism from a variety of stakeholders, including educational institutions, migrant-led community organisations and lobby groups. Peter Smith, General Secretary of the Association of Teachers and Lectures(ATL), for instance, wrote a letter to the Home Secretary in which he indicated that 'it was disturbing to hear of your suggestions that the educational needs of young asylum seekers can be met by what sounds like a form of apartheid' (ATL 2002).[8] Gil Stainthorpe, ATL's Equal Opportunities Coordinator, furthermore argued that 'the proposal is deeply flawed. Teaching children in accommodation centres will deny them the educational opportunities they would get in mainstream schools – in English language and across the curriculum … Educating non-English speakers in isolation simply pools ignorance. Children require good models of language in order to learn' (ATL 2002).

---

4   Cullinan, S. and K. Noble 'Sangatte', *Time*, 27 May 2002, 23.

5   Milne S. and A. Travis 'Blair's Secret Plan to crack down on Asylum Seekers', *The Guardian*, 23 May 2002 <http://www.guardian.co.uk/uk_news/story/0,3604,720608,00.html> (9 June 2002).

6   'Row erupts over Blunkett's "swamped" Comment', *The Guardian,* 24 April 2002 <http://politics.guardian.co.uk/homeaffairs/story/0,11026,689919,00.html> (accessed 9 June 2002).

7   Hansard (2002), *House of Commons, Nationality, Immigration and Asylum Bill*, (London: HMSO).

8   Association of Teachers and Lecturers (ATL) (2002), 'ATL urges the Home Secretary to withdraw Segregation Clause from the Immigration and Asylum Bill' <http://www.askatl. org.uk/news/press_releases/pn100602.htm> (accessed 12 June 2002).

Perhaps, the reaction of Bill Morris, General Secretary of the Transport and General Workers' Union, to the government's proposals best illustrates the strength of feelings such issue aroused:

> We cannot preach a socially inclusive society on the one hand, and on the other hand argue that the children of asylum seekers should be educated in some sort of detention camps. The two do not mix (Travis 2002, 10).[9]

Significantly, Blunkett's off-the-cuff remarks were indirectly condoned by Downing Street, which merely clarified his comments as 'reflecting a particular context', rather than describing immigration as an issue (*The Guardian* 2002). Nevertheless, during the subsequent five years, the government was to preside over a series of social, immigration and educational policies as well as legislative measures seemingly designed to move away from the prevailing multicultural model and towards an integrationist discourse with underlying nationalistic overtones. The following instances of government's social, immigration and nationality as well as language education initiatives serve to illustrate this trend.

Community Cohesion – The Cantle Report, 2001

In the aftermath of the urban disturbances in England's northern towns during 2001, a Ministerial Group on Public Order and Community Cohesion was set up in order to explore 'how national policies might be used to promote better community cohesion, based upon shared values and a celebration of diversity' (Home Office 2001a, foreword).[10] As part of this process, a newly formed Community Cohesion Review Team (CCRT), chaired by Ted Cantle, Associate Director of the Improvement and Development Agency (IdeA) for Local Government, was charged with the task of gathering and analysing evidence from the communities affected by the riots, so as to ascertain the roots of the problem and identifying good practice. As a starting point, the Review Team explored the actual concept of 'community cohesion' and the various socio-economic, civic and cultural 'domains' through which it may be construed. The ensuing *Community Cohesion* Report provided various definitions of this multifaceted notion, including 'common moral principles and codes of behaviour', 'absence of general conflict and threats to the existing order', 'tolerance; respect for differences; inter-group co-operation', and a 'high degree of social interaction within communities and families' (Home Office 2001, 13). Having heard submissions from those affected by the disturbances, the Report concluded that community cohesion had all but collapsed in the hotspots that experienced civic unrest:

> Whilst the physical segregation of housing estates and inner city areas came as no surprise, the [CCRT] team was particularly struck by the depth of polarisation of our towns and cities. The extent to which these physical divisions were compounded by so many other aspects

9   Travis, A. 'Charities and Union Leader attach Asylum Plans', *The Guardian*, 11 June 2002, 10.

10   Home Office (2001a) *Community Cohesion: A Report of the Independent Review Team Chaired by Ted Cantle* (London: TSO), foreword.

of our daily lives, was very evident. Separate educational arrangements, community and voluntary bodies, employment, places of worship, language, social and cultural networks, means that many communities operate on the basis of a series of parallel lives. These lives often do not seem to touch at any point, let alone overlap and promote any meaningful interchanges (Home Office 2001, 9).

Among the factors that contributed to this state of affairs, the Report identified widespread ignorance about each other's communities that could easily grow into fear, ultimately leading to divisions and hostilities between different groups; lack of community leadership, which was mostly unwilling to confront the issues and unable to engage in open and honest dialogue in order to find solutions; as well as institutional inertia, prevalent throughout Local Authorities, political parties and even voluntary organisations, which compounded the situation. As a result, there was little appetite to promote common values and a sense of collective British citizenship among those living next to each other, yet worlds apart. Within this context, it was hardly surprising that the development of social capital and the promotion of community cohesion were neither seen as a priority nor an end in themselves; with the often worthy but overtly bureaucratic grassroots initiatives already in place mainly perpetuating rather than alleviating the problem (Home Office 2001, 9–10).

The 67 recommendations included in the Report sought to tackle the underlying causes of the existing breakdown in community cohesion through a combination of civic education, diversity awareness and conflict resolution initiatives, the fostering of community and institutional leadership and dialogue as well as the development local collaborative partnerships and regenerational programmes (Home Office 2001, 46–52). Overall, the proposals strived to bring divided communities together by disregarding the differences that pull them apart, while emphasising instead those traits they share in common, namely their membership of the British nation, their national identity and citizenship together with the rights and responsibilities that come with them.

Secure Borders, Safe Haven: Integration with Diversity in Great Britain, 2001

Aimed at ensuring 'social integration and cohesion in the UK', this White Paper set out the government's key objectives for the development of a comprehensive citizenship and nationality policy. In welcoming the publication of the Paper, the Home Secretary summed up the values behind this document by stating that 'a nationality, immigration and asylum policy that secures … sustainable growth and social inclusion … are an essential part of our core principles' (Home Office 2001b, 32).[11] *Secure Borders, Safe Haven* envisaged Britain's changing approach to nationality, immigration and asylum policy as a 'two-way street' requiring 'commitment and action from the host community, asylum seekers and long-term immigrants alike' (Home Office 2001b, foreword). As the Home Secretary explained in his foreword to the Paper:

---

11 Home Office (2001b), *Secure Borders, Safe Haven: Integration with Diversity in Modern Britain* (London: HMSO), chp. 2, para. 2.14, 32.

We have fundamental moral obligations which will always honour. We must uphold basic human rights, tackling the racism and prejudice which people still face too often. At the same time, those coming into our country have duties that they need to understand and which facilitate their acceptance and integration (Home Office 2001b, foreword).

The Paper dealt with a wide range of social policy issues relating to nationality and citizenship, migration and asylum seeking, including the UK and EU labour markets, trafficking of people, fraud, border controls, marriage and family visits. A key aspect of *Secure Borders, Safe Haven* was its treatment of the question of British nationality and its relationship with the English language, which were deemed inseparable. Not only was British identity understood to embody an English-speaking ideal, but any immigrant intending to become naturalised in Britain would be required to learn the English language:

> Becoming British through registration or naturalisation is – or should be – a significant life event. It can be seen as an act of commitment to Britain and an important step in the process of achieving integration into our society. Yet, in spite of this, some applicants for naturalisation do not have much practical knowledge about British life or [English] language, possibly leaving them vulnerable and ill-equipped to take an active role in society. This can lead to social exclusion and may contribute to problems of polarisation between communities. We need a sense of civic identity and shared values; and knowledge of the English language … can undoubtedly support this objective (Home Office 2001b, 32).

The government therefore considered essential that those peoples living permanently in the UK should be able 'through adequate command of the [English] language and an appreciation of our democratic processes', to take their full place in our civic society' (Home Office 2001b, 32). In order to promote the importance of an adequate command of English and an understanding of British society, the government would require applicants for naturalisation to demonstrate that the have achieved 'a certain standard' of English proficiency. The Paper indicated that 'subject to certain limited exceptions', applicants would need to produce certificates showing that they have passed a language test, if necessary after having taken part in a suitable course (Home Office 2001b, chp. 2, para. 2.14, 32). In other words, the government was prescribing that in order to become a British citizen, one should be able to speak the language of the land; thus establishing a direct link between British citizenship and the English language. To the question: is the English language an integral part of our national identity? Our elected representatives' answer was an incontrovertible 'yes'.

Nationality, Immigration and Asylum Act 2002

In line with the *Secure Borders, Safe Heaven* White Paper, the ensuing *Nationality, Immigration and Asylum Act 2002* clearly set out the government's blueprint for Britain's citizenship and immigration policy. This comprehensive piece of legislation dealt with every aspect of a migrant's entry into the country, including: nationality and naturalisation, immigration controls and services, asylum-seeking, unlawful entry and human trafficking, dependants and visitors, accommodation centres, provision of support and assistance by Local Authorities, detention and removals, immigration and asylum appeals, work permits and immigration procedures and offences, to name a few. As the Act explains, its main purpose was 'to make provision about nationality, immigration and asylum; to create offences in connection with international traffic in prostitution; to make provision about international projects connected with migration; and for connected purposes' (*Nationality Act 2002*, c. 41).[12]

The significance of the Act lies in a number of key modifications made to the *British Nationality Act 1981* regarding the criteria for obtaining citizenship (*British Nationality Act 1981*).[13] Accordingly, individuals seeking British citizenship would now be required to meet the following prerequisites: firstly, 'sufficient knowledge of a language [i.e. English, Welsh or Scottish Gaelic] for the purpose of naturalisation'; secondly, 'sufficient knowledge of life in the United Kingdom'; and thirdly taking up a Citizenship Oath and a Pledge at a civil ceremony (*Nationality Act 2002*, c. 45, part 1 (1)). As the Act puts it 'A person of full age shall not be registered under this Act as a British citizen unless he made the relevant citizenship oath and pledge … at a citizenship ceremony' (*Nationality Act 2002*, c. 41, sch. 1, sec. 3 (1)). The form of citizenship oath and pledge envisaged in the Act is as follows:

OATH

'I, *[mane]*, swear by Almighty God that, on becoming a British citizen, I will be faithful and bear true allegiance to Her Majesty Queen Elizabeth the Second, Her Heirs and Successors according to law'.

PLEDGE

'I will give my loyalty to the United Kingdom and respect its rights and freedoms. I will uphold its democratic values. I will observe its laws faithfully and fulfil my duties and obligations as a British citizen' (*Nationality Act 2002*, c.45, sch. 5).

The making of such criteria a condition for attainting naturalisation can be seen as the strongest indication yet of the paradigm shift taking place within government. Requiring would-be British citizens to demonstrate knowledge of the English language, acquiescence with Britain's way of life as well as the making of a public commitment to our common values and democratic principles indeed reflects a concerted move towards integration and away from multiculturalism. Of particular consequence is the establishment of US-style civil ceremonies, as it appears specifically designed to raise the status of becoming a British citizen, while emphasizing the significance of British naturalisation as a life-changing event. An event which ultimately witnesses the rebirth of unconnected and non-descriptive migrants into fully-fledged British citizens, irretrievably linked by a common bond.

---

12 *Nationality, Immigration and Asylum Act 2002* (2002) (London: TSO), c. 41.
13 *British Nationality Act 1981* (1981) (London: HMSO).

Life in the United Kingdom – A Journey to Citizenship, 2004

In order to implement the policy initiatives and provisions contained in the *Secure Borders, Safe Haven* White Paper and the subsequent *Immigration, Nationality and Asylum Act 2002*, the government appointed an independent advisory group chaired by Professor Sir Bernard Crick, in September 2002. The group's remit was to advise the Home Secretary 'on the method, conduct and implementation of a 'Life in the United Kingdom' naturalisation test', which implied defining what should be meant by 'sufficient' in both the cases of ability in language and knowledge of society and civic institutions (Home Office 2003, 3).[14] The following year, *The New and the Old – The report of the 'Life in the United Kingdom' Advisory Group* was produced, detailing suggestions for furthering the government's plans to promote language skills and practical knowledge of Britain among those seeking to become naturalised (Home Office 2003). The report's main recommendations – which dealt with issues such as citizenship and English language testing methods, language support and training, naturalisation ceremonies, volunteering and mentoring, and the role of employers, among others – comprised four key proposals: firstly, the publication of a 'Living in the United Kingdom' handbook, both in English and in bilingual versions, which *'should be given free'* to all those United Kingdom residents applying for naturalisation or those who apply at posts abroad for work permits and entry clearance (Home Office 2003, 17). Secondly, making of 'the assessment of applicant's *progress* in developing language skills' a major component of naturalisation, as opposed to requiring a common language standard for all applicants. Here, the Advisory Group disregarded a 'one-size-fits-all' approach to evaluating English language proficiency in favour of individual attention to each applicant's particular levels of fluency. To this end, attainment in language tests for naturalisation would be linked to the levels set out in the National Standards for Adult Literacy and the Adult ESOL Core Curriculum. Fourthly, the holding of 'a periodic civic [naturalisation] ceremony in which the Mayor or Provost should make a speech of welcome to the new citizens and their families stressing the rights and duties of citizenship'; such events would take place in the presence of invited local dignitaries such as Members of Parliament, candidates, councillors and leaders of community and religious groups (Home Office 2003, 30). At the ceremonies, as the applicants took the Citizenship Oath and Pledge, they would be presented with their newly designed certificates of naturalisation, intended to be 'far more impressive and suitable to be framed' than their predecessors (Home Office 2003, 30). Finally, the Advisory Group suggested the establishment of an 'Advisory Board on Education for Naturalisation' as an independent implementation and assessment authority, chaired by a leading public figure appointed by the Home Secretary (Home Office 2003, 35).

In 2004, the Advisory Group's recommendation regarding the production of a handbook for prospective British citizens materialised in the shape of a guide entitled *Life in the United Kingdom – A Journey to Citizenship*. Published on behalf

---

14 Home Office (2003), *The New and the Old – A Report on the 'Life in the United Kingdom' Advisory Group* (Croydon: Home Office Communications Directorate).

of the Life in the United Kingdom Advisory Group, it was aimed primarily to assist teachers of English as a Second Language, mentors and others helping immigrants, new or old, who had workable English already and who were required to take a citizenship test (Home Office 2004, 9).[15] This all-encompassing manual for aspiring British citizens contains practical information on every aspect of daily life in Britain, including: a historical overview of the British nation, an insight into the country's demographic, cultural and religious makeup; our civic and political institutions; UK laws and the criminal justice system; as well as information on basic needs such as housing, health, education and employment; and details of available sources of help and advice, including the public libraries, the Police and the Citizens Advice Bureau. In welcoming the publication of *Life in the United Kingdom* and the running of the first ever British naturalisation ceremony in Brent, the Home Secretary, who attended the event, recalled how 'like all those who were present, I came away with a real sense that this was a powerful way of boosting personal, civic and national pride, challenging society to offer a welcome to those who have positively chosen to take our nationality' (Home Office 2004, 4).

Against this background, the government's immigration and nationality policies seemed to reflect a concerted effort to ensure the integration of newcomers into British society. This developing trend in the direction of integration also became apparent in the government's changing approach to language education policy. While would-be immigrants were expected to embrace the country's Anglo-Saxon traditions and master the English language, native school children were being instructed through an English-dominant curriculum that discouraged them from learning Modern Foreign Languages. In a move, seen by many as driven by Anglocentric and nationalistic tendencies, the government began to steer the British education system away from its commitment to a multicultural, multilingual syllabus and in the direction of English mono-lingual tuition. The following educational initiatives provide a case in point.

14–19: Extending Opportunities, Raising Standards, 2002

This education Green Paper described the government's strategy for the modernisation of the Secondary school curriculum (DfES 2002).[16] Introducing the Paper, Estelle Morris, Secretary of State for Education and Skills, remarked that 'no society can tolerate under-achievement ... School must engage every young person. Social inclusion as well as economic prosperity remains a key objective of our 14–19 proposals'. She argued that if Britain is to match the needs of the 'global knowledge economy' it must be able to 'quickly respond to this demand for new skills', otherwise 'the damage to national economic performance will be considerable' (DfES 2002, 1–2).

With the purpose of attaining this educational goal, the government proposed a new structure for the National Curriculum at Key Stage 4, which established a

---

15 Home Office (2004), *Life in the United Kingdom – A Journey to Citizenship*, Published on behalf of the Life in the United Kingdom Advisory Group (Norwich: TSO), 9.

16 DfES (2002), *14–19: Extending the Opportunities, Raising Standards*, (London: HMSO) <http://www.dfes.gov.uk/14–19greenpaper/foreword.shtml> (accessed 9 June 2002).

criterion for mandatory subjects. Subjects should become compulsory at this stage only if they met one of the two following stated prerequisites:

> They [subjects] provide an essential basis for progression, across all areas of learning and for keeping young people's options open; or they are essential for personal development, contributing to young people's spiritual, cultural, social and moral development as they begin to take their place in society and in the world of work (DfES 2002, ch. 3, para. 9, 2).

Only English, Mathematics, Science and ICT were deemed to meet the first criterion of being 'essential for progression'; therefore they would remain as a statutory requirement for all schools. In contrast, students would not be obliged to study either Modern Foreign Languages or Design and Technology (DfES 2002, ch. 3, paras. 10 and 16, 2–4). The government believed that the study of Foreign Modern Languages, in particular, would be 'too constraining' and would not 'preserve access to a broad and balanced curriculum for all' (DfES 2002, ch. 3, para. 16, 3–4). It consequently suggested the introduction of a new statutory entitlement to access that would require schools to make the study of Modern Foreign Languages available but not obligatory. As the Green Paper indicated:

> We would expect all schools to make Modern Foreign Languages, Design and Technology, the Arts and the Humanities available, but how schools provide such entitlement to access in these subjects is a matter for local decision (DfES 2002, ch. 3, para. 17, 4).

While recognising that the teaching of Modern Foreign Languages 'needs to reflect the reality of the world in which we live', the government explained the scale of disapplication from Modern Foreign Languages at Key Stage 4 by arguing that 'for some young people aged 14–16, language learning presents serious problems', which would be ameliorated by allowing them 'to choose from a wider range of options' (DfES 2002, ch. 3, paras. 20 and 21, 4).

The detrimental effect of these proposals for the long-term learning and teaching of Modern Foreign Languages in British schools was soon to be felt, as headlines such as 'School ditch language learning' and 'Schools jump gun in ditching language services' reflect (Garner 2002, 1; Henry and Shaw 2002, 1).[17] At the time, a national survey of language tuition in schools conducted by the Association of Language Learning (ALL) showed that nearly 30 per cent of schools were planning to abandon the teaching of compulsory Modern Foreign Languages; while those planning to offer the subject were likely to only provide 'a token hour per week' (Garner 2002, 1; Henry and M. Shaw 2002, 1). The survey, which included comprehensive and independent schools as well as specialist language colleges, found that more than 1,000 schools would drop Modern Foreign Languages as a compulsory subject at the level of 14 year-olds. The schools inspected gave two main reasons for their decision to abandon language tuition: on the one hand, the difficulty in attracting

---

17 Garner, R. 'Schools ditch Language Learning', *The Independent*, 25 May 2002, 1; and Henry, J. and M. Shaw 'Schools jump gun in ditching Languages', *The Times Education Supplement*, 24 May 2002, 1.

qualified staff to teach Modern Foreign Languages; on the other hand, the fact that Language GCSEs were viewed as difficult subjects for some pupils. This would make it improbable for the students to obtain high grades and thus contributing to enhance individual schools' exam performance results (Garner 2002, 1). Within this context, Terry Lamb, President of the Association of Language Learning, warned that:

> We are talking about getting on for half of the schools that are not independent or language colleges making it optional. I suspect there will be parental pressure in middle-class areas where people recognise languages will be a key skill for better jobs to continue to make it compulsory. In areas where languages are not particularly valued and parents don't travel abroad much, it will be decimated. It will become an elitist subject (Garner 2002, 1).

Sir Trevor MacDonald, Chairman of the Nuffield Foundation's Language Team, furthermore contended that the implementation of the Green Paper's proposals would be 'a retrograde step and a major setback to foreign language learning in this country'. He reasoned that making the learning of languages optional would have 'a seriously damaging effect on national competitiveness and on the overall educational levels of our children as they seek employment. The UK would fall even further behind our European and international competitors' (Nuffield Foundation 2002).[18]

Sir Trevor's comments are particularly relevant as they were made against the background of the Nuffield Foundation's own inquiry into the state of language teaching in Britain, published two years earlier. Set up in the spring of 1998, the Nuffield Languages Inquiry was established in response to the concerns of an independent Working Group of representatives from the language teaching, business and employment sectors regarding the state of language education in Britain. The Inquiry aimed at providing 'an independent view of the UK's future needs for capability in languages and the nation's readiness to meet them' (Nuffield Foundation 2000, 10).[19] As part of the Inquiry, major surveys were conducted by the National Institute of Adult Continuing Education (NIACE) and the Further Education Development Agency (FEDA), one thousand contributions were gathered by the Foundation as well as carrying out an intensive programme of interviews with individual employers in the private and public sectors. The resulting *Languages: The Next Generation* report made for uncomfortable reading. As the Chairmen of the Inquiry put it:

> The scale of what needs to be done has become ever more striking as our work has gone on. At the moment, by any reliable measure, we are doing badly. We talk about communications but don't always communicate. There is enthusiasm for languages but it is patchy. Educational provision is fragmented, achievement poorly measured, continuity

---

18 Nuffield Foundation (2002), 'Nuffield Languages Team Responds to the 14–19 Green Paper' <http://www.nuffieldfoundation.org/languages/news/nw0000000202.asp> (accessed 9 June 2002).

19 Nuffield Foundation (2000), *Languages: the Next Generation – The Final Report and Recommendations of the Nuffield* Inquiry (London: Nuffield Foundation), 10.

not very evident. In the language of our time, there is a lack of joined-up thinking (Nuffield Foundation 2000, 5).

The Inquiry suggested a number of recommendations designed to address such challenges, including recognition of languages as a key skill, the establishment of a national strategy for the development of capability in languages in the UK, the appointment of a 'languages supremo' to ensure the implementation of the national languages strategy, raising the profile and quality of language learning provision across the curriculum and beyond, and developing strategic partnerships between the education and business sectors (Nuffield Foundation 2000, 84–98). Despite the modern phenomenon of English language globalisation, the Inquiry recognised the need to develop British children's language skills, so as to enable them to compete on equal terms with their far more linguistically adept European and East Asian counterparts:

> In a competitive world we cannot afford to be without strong and complete skills: no skills – no jobs. The need to strengthen our children's literacy, numeracy and technology skills are clear and we support this. Side by side with these should go the ability to communicate across cultures. It too is a key skill (Nuffield Foundation 2000, 4).

Against this background, the British government's approach to language education policy appeared to stand in stark contrast with the multilingual ideology in which Europe's vision for its citizenry was based. Not only did the European Union celebrate the linguistic diversity of its Member States, but actively sought to produce polyglot European citizens through its educational and social policy initiatives (Julios 2002, 184–201).[20] Having designated the year 2001 as the 'European Year of Languages', the European Commission recommended that all EU pupils should master at least two European languages in addition to their mother tongue by the end of compulsory education (European Commission 1997, 1: 2–3; EUROPA 1999).[21] The UK government's proposals regarding the teaching of Foreign Modern Languages seemed, on the contrary, be heading in the opposite direction. The Nuffield Foundation concluded that the Green Paper's proposals were not only 'wholly incompatible with the government's stated commitment to developing a coherent strategy for language learning from Primary school through to university and adult life', but they were equally incompatible with a vision of a world-class education system (Nuffield Foundation 2002, 1).

On the whole, the Green Paper can be said to signal an ideological shift from a multilingual educational approach to a predominantly Anglocentric model. By placing a premium on the English language as opposed to the lesser value attributed to its Foreign Modern counterparts, the government was effectively abandoning its

---

20 Julios, C. (2002), 'Towards a European Language Policy', in M. Farrell, S. Fella and M. Newman (eds), *European Integration in the 21st Century*, (London: Sage Publications), 184–201.

21 European Commission (1997), 'Council Resolution of 16 December 1997 on the Early Teaching of European Union Languages', *Official Journal of the European Union*, vol. 1, 2–3; EUROPA (1999), 'Languages' <http://www.europa.eu.int> (accessed 12 June 2002).

previous commitment to multicultural education in favour of an English-dominant curriculum. As the Nuffield Foundation put it, 'the government has sent out the message loud and clear to young people – and those who run their schools and teach in them – that language learning is a frill, an optional extra to education' (Nuffield Foundation 2002, 1).

Languages for All: Languages for Life, 2002

Following the publication of the Nuffield Foundation's *Languages: the Next Generation* report, the DfES set up a Languages National Steering Group so as to develop a national strategy for languages, in July 2001. The resulting *Languages for All: Languages for Life* report was published in December 2002 (DfES 2002).[22] Underlying the government's language strategy was the recognition that in a globalised twentieth-first century world economy, the ability to effectively operate in different multicultural and multilingual settings was an essential skill mostly lacking within the UK workforce. As the report indicated:

> For too long we have failed to value language skills or recognise the contribution they make to society, to the economy and to raising standards in schools. This has led to a cycle of national underperformance in languages, a shortage of teachers, low take up of languages beyond schooling and a workforce unable to meet the demands of a globalised economy. We need to challenge these attitudes and inspire people of all ages to learn languages through life (DfES, 2002, 10).

The strategy had three overarching objectives: firstly, improving teaching and learning of languages; secondly, introducing a recognition system to complement existing qualification frameworks; and thirdly, increasing the number of people studying languages in Further and Higher Education as well as work-based training (DfES 2002, 5). In order to meet these targets, the *Languages for All* report suggested a number of educational and outreach strategies, including the development of early language opportunities and language pathfinders, maximising ICT and e-learning technologies as well as the establishment of innovative partnerships with schools in other countries. As a sign of the government's commitment to language learning, it moreover announced Britain's joining of the Council of Europe's European Centre for Modern Languages (ECML); an institution at the forefront of the development of innovative approaches to Modern Foreign Language teaching and learning based in Graz, Austria. Membership of the Centre would allow the UK to make a contribution to the work of the Common European Framework and European Languages Portfolio.

In spite of the government's apparent efforts to remedy the effects of its own language education policy, Foreign Modern Languages became an optional rather than a compulsory subject at Key Stage 4, in 2004. On the first year when languages were no longer compulsory, the overall number of young people studying languages

---

22 DfES (2002), *Languages for All: Languages for Life – Strategy for England* (London: DfES).

at GCSE, A-level and degree level fell; with GCSE participation rates across all languages, in particular, falling by 15.1 per cent (DfES 2006).[23]

The continuing decline in the popularity of language learning across the curriculum was, in turn, to be felt in an increasingly linguistically challenged UK labour market. In 2004, the British Chambers of Commerce (BCC) published a language survey, sponsored by the Learning and Skills Council (LSC), exploring the impact of lack of Foreign Modern Languages skills on British businesses. On the occasion, Isabella Moore, President of the BCC, explained how:

> The declining number of young people studying modern languages in recent years continues to cause concern both within and outside the educational establishment. Statistics this year show further reductions in the number of young people at all academic levels opting to study languages. This is therefore an important time for the BCC to understand clearly the medium and long term effects this is likely to have on the competitiveness of British business (BCC 2004, foreword).[24]

The BCC survey, which mostly focused on the language experiences of UK exporters, found that 80 per cent of English exporters could not competently conduct business dealings overseas in even one foreign language; and although one half of English exporters had a formal qualification in a foreign language, nearly two-thirds (63 per cent) had 'no formal strategy to maintain or instigate trade with foreign speaking businesses' (BCC 2004, ii). The survey clearly identified the importance of language skills as a key business performance tool, with businesses featuring multilingual proficient staff consistently outperforming their Anglocentric counterparts. As the survey indicated 'There is a direct correlation between the value an exporter places on language skills within their business and their annual turnover' (BCC 2004, ii). Most significantly, the survey established a link between language learning across the school curriculum and British business workforce's multilingual ability. In particular, children's experiences of multilingualism during their formative years were deemed a significant factor in determining their linguistic abilities and outlook in adulthood:

> The ability to speak at least one foreign language is greatest amongst exporters who have had the opportunity to both study a modern language in their early years at primary school and follow on with a GSCE or O'level qualification at secondary school. Compared to others, a greater proportion of these exporters are also able to speak a foreign language sufficiently fluently that they can negotiate business deals, reducing their reliance on English. They also consider it important to employ UK based staff with language skills (BCC 2004, 1).

Overall, the results of the survey provided further corroboration of the detrimental, far-reaching implications of the government's approach to Foreign Modern Languages learning.

---

23 DfES (2006), 'Language Lessons' <http://findoutmore.dfes.gov.uk/2006/10/language_lesson.html> (accessed 20 April 2007).

24 British Chambers of Commerce (2004), *BCC Language Survey – The Impact of Foreign Languages on British Business – Part 2: The Qualitative Results* (London: BCC), foreword.

14-19: Education and Skills, 2005

On February 2005, the government published the *14-19: Education and Skills* White Paper detailing its proposed changes to the schools curriculum and assessment system (DfES 2005a).[25] This Paper was a response to the proposals put forward by the Working Group on 14–19 Reform, established two years earlier (Working Group on 14–19 Reform 2004).[26] Chaired by Sir Mike Tomlinson, the Group aimed to address key challenges facing Britain's school population such as low post-sixteen participation and achievement, an overtaxing curriculum and appraisals structure, and a disjointed approach to vocational qualifications. As Sir Mike explained:

> It is our view that the status quo is not an option. Nor do we believe further piecemeal changes are desirable. Too many young people leave education lacking basic and personal skills; our vocational provision is too fragmented; the burden of external assessment on learners, teachers and lecturers is too great; and our system is not providing the stretch and challenge needed, particularly for higher attainers. The results are a low staying-on rate post-16; employers having to spend large amounts of money teaching the 'basics'; HE struggling to differentiate between top performers; and young people's motivation and engagement with education reducing as they go through the system (Working Group 2004, 1).

In order to raise pupils' achievement and 'get the basics right', the Group's recommendation's focused on ways to enhance depth and breadth of learning within the curriculum, strengthening vocational programmes and reducing the assessment burden. Given the importance attached to English, Maths and Sciences as core subjects, the Group's report placed the strongest emphasis on their mastery.

Within the context of a competitive global labour market though, the role of Foreign Modern Languages was deemed an important socio-economic tool:

> Modern languages skills have a particular importance to economic success in the increasingly internationalised business environment. Alongside the specific skills which it delivers, the teaching and learning of a foreign language is an effective way of fostering the understanding of other countries and other cultures which we have identified as an element of CKSA [Common Knowledge, Skills and Attributes]. Within the overall 14–19 framework, we are concerned to ensure that all young people have access to flexible teaching and learning in foreign modern languages, building upon the developments already in hand through the Government's national languages strategy, and that community languages are given the respect they deserve and recognised as a valuable access for the future (Working Group 2004, 43).

Notwithstanding recognition of the intrinsic value of multilingual fluency and the desirability of a linguistically proficient workforce, the Group did not consider it necessary to either reinstate Foreign Modern Languages as a compulsory subject at

---

25 DfES (2005a), *14–19 Education and Skills*, Presented to Parliament by the Secretary of State for Education and Skills by Command of Her Majesty, cm. 6476 (Norwich: TSO).

26 Working Group on 14–19 Reform (2004), *14–19 Curriculum and Assessment Reform – Final Report of the Working Group on 14–19 Reform* (Nottinghamshire: DfES Publications).

Key Stage 4 or confer it altogether compulsory status across the school curriculum. It suggested, instead, extending current statutory entitlement to language learning throughout:

> We also support the current statutory entitlement of all 14–16 year olds to study at least one modern foreign language. To ensure consistency across the 14–19 framework, we believe this entitlement should be extended to 16–19 year olds (Working Group 2004, 43).

In addition to lengthening the statutory entitlement to language learning, the Group suggested the use of vocational courses, in the shape of Diplomas, as a way of enabling continuity of Modern Foreign Language education, as well as other discretionary subjects, beyond the schooling years:

> For those who whish to focus on language learning after compulsory schooling, there should be within the diploma lines options to specialise in foreign modern languages. Within other specialisations, languages may also have a role in supporting the main area of specialisation either as an elective or compulsory component of main learning. Such options may well be tailored to support the main 'named' area of learning (Working Group 2004, 43).

In line with the Working Group's suggestions, the subsequent *14–19 Education and Skills* White Paper focused on raising school children's standards of achievement through their mastery of basic skills and the study of the three core subjects: English, Maths and Sciences. The teaching and learning of these key disciplines across the curriculum would arguably take place at the expense of 'lesser' optional subjects such as Foreign Modern Languages. The Paper reasoned that 'A good level of knowledge and skill in English, Maths, ICT and Sciences are the most essential preparation for the 14–19 phase' (DfES 2005a, 25). Seen as 'the basics' of modern life, without knowledge of these subjects 'no young person can consider themselves truly educated', 'no-one can make the most of everyday life' neither can they 'better themselves at work' nor 'progress to learn as much as they otherwise could' (DfES 2005, 24). It is precisely to ensure that young people achieve a good grounding in these key fields of study, the government argued, that 'we have already reduced the amount of prescription in the Key Stage 4 curriculum, providing more scope for schools to support catch-up in English and Maths' (DfES 2005, 5). Existing statutory entitlement to study Foreign Modern Languages was therefore deemed appropriate to enable students to develop their linguistic skills throughout the schooling years. Beyond that, students would have the option of accessing the newly proposed system of employer-designed specialised Diplomas, as part of the more flexible, tailor-made 14–19 phase.

Shortly after the publication of the *14–19 Education and Skills* White Paper, Ruth Kelly, Secretary of State for Education, announced a major investment in Foreign Modern Languages learning including a £115 million boost to support language learning and teaching over the next three years, the recruitment of 6,000 specialist language teachers to teach in primary schools, 9,000 teaching assistants to be given training to teach Modern Foreign Languages to their pupils as well as an increase in the number of specialist language schools (DfES 2005b). To mark the occasion, Kelly said:

Languages are vital for children in today's world. They open doors to new experiences, increase employment opportunities and break down cultural barriers. They also boost community cohesion and our economy's competitiveness. This investment will fund a major increase in language teachers to ensure that every child aged 7–11 will have the opportunity to study another language and develop their interest in the culture of other nations. This is crucial if more young people are to continue studying languages at secondary school level and beyond (DfES 2005b).[27]

Despite the government's seemingly remedial efforts to encourage language learning across the board, evidence continued to point to a decline in the take up of Foreign Modern Languages among the school population; with the Qualifications and Curriculum Authority having warned that A-level French and German were now in 'chronic decline' (BBC 2005).[28] Additional proof of the long-term impact of this trend was provided by the House of Lords' European Union Committee, whose Report on the *Proposed EU Integrated Action Programme for Life-long Learning* provided a devastating verdict on the government's approach to language education policy (House of Lords, European Union Committee 2005, report, HL paper 104–I).[29] Charged with the task of considering plans for the development of the European Union's Europe-wide education schemes, including schools and Higher Education exchange, vocational training and adult education schemes such as the *Socrates* (i.e. *Erasmus, Grundtvig, Lingua,* etc.) and *Leonardo da Vinci*; the Committee heard evidence from a wide range of stakeholders, academics and experts (House of Lords, European Union Committee 2005, volume 2: evidence, HL Paper 104–II). The results of the inquiry left Peers with little doubt as to the extent and protracted consequences of the government's Anglocentric approach to language learning. They described how:

We are deeply disturbed by the evidence we have been given about the declining capacity for language learning in this country. The consequences go well beyond the scope of this Inquiry and the programmes we are considering cannot do much to redress the balance unless urgent and effective action is taken nationally to invest more in language-learning at all levels. It is to our national advantaged that English is the generally-accepted international medium for communication. But that must not be seen as a substitute for the ability to communicate effectively in one or more other mainstream European languages which is essential if this country is to do business successfully in the widest sense with our other European neighbours and with other countries where other languages are spoken (House of Lords, European Union Committee 2005, report, HL paper 104–I, para. 318, 64).

---

27 DfES (2005b), Press Release 'Major Investment for Foreign Language Learning – Kelly' (Ref. 2005/0034) 11 March 2005 <http://www.gnn.gov.uk/Content/Detail.asp?ReleaseID=151443&NewsAreaID=2> (accessed 22 March 2005).

28 BBC (2005), 'Fear over Poor UK Language Skills', BBC News: Education <http://news.bbc.co.uk/1/hi/education/4442223.stm> (accessed 6 May 2007).

29 House of Lords, European Union Committee (2005), *17th Report of Session 2004–2005: Proposed EU Integrated Action Programme for Life-long Learning,* Report, HL paper 104–I (London: TSO).

Among those submitting evidence to the Committee was the University Council of Modern Languages (UCML) who stressed the importance of 'developing citizenship in an international context, and supporting the acquisition of skills and cultural competences which will prepare our young people to operate in a globalised and competitive economy' (House of Lords, European Union Committee, 2005, volume 2: evidence, HL paper 104–II, sec. 1, para. 1.2, 290). Here, language skills were seen as crucial, for they enhance 'employability' and the ability of students to fully contribute to the EU project as fully-fledged European citizens. Another witness to the Inquiry, Dr Annette Kratz, Head of the Centre for International Exchange and Languages at Keele University, spelt out the difficulties involved in realising such a multilingual European vision. A linguist by training, she pointed out that:

> Language learning does not happen overnight. It is hard work and it takes a long time. So I welcome the proposition from the Government to start language learning in primary school. It is much easier to learn a language at primary school. But it will take an awful long time to filter through. By the time this programme is finished, the integrated programme, in 2013, we, in HE, will not have seen the first of those primary school kids benefiting from that language training … If young people stop learning a language at age fifteen, or the school can no longer provide that teaching because there are no language teachers, we have to catch up at university … We can help but we cannot remedy … those [overseas language taster] courses cost money … So unless there are incentives for the students to go and undertake that language learning, only the rich kids are going to do it. So again we come back to the inequality in the whole system. If there is no funding to support it, we are going to be the poor man in Europe … Our young people are going to be disadvantaged in the job market. There is evidence in the City that employers are employing young Continental Europeans with already more than one language and perfect English at the expense of British graduates (House of Lords, European Union Committee 2005, volume 2: evidence, HL paper 104–II, q147, 86).

The Committee heard a wealth of similar evidence regarding the academic, cultural and linguistic competencies needed to success in a competitive and highly-skilled twentieth-first century global economy; an economy where Britain's Anglocentrism appeared at odds with the multilingual approach of her European counterparts. In its closing remarks, the Committee stated:

> We conclude that the United Kingdom is already falling badly behind in language-learning capability. This will seriously limit British ability to take part fully in and benefit from the new EU programmes, especially *Erasmus*. But it has far wider implications for the employability and cultural awareness of the coming generation and will severely hamper the country's ability to protect and promote our interests abroad and to compete successfully in the Single Market and elsewhere (House of Lords, European Union Committee 2005, report, HL paper 104–I, para. 619, 64).

While acknowledging the difficulties faced by a linguistically challenged UK workforce, Dr Kim Howells, Minister of State for Life-long Learning, Further and Higher Education, went on to reaffirm the government's position on Modern Foreign Language teaching:

We have a problem with the teaching of languages in this country, there is no question about that, and there are so many derogations to the compulsory teaching of languages at the secondary level that they would basically suspended it. We said "No, you don't have to teach these foreign languages up to GCSE, or whatever". Instead, what we have done is we have decided now to concentrate on 7 year-olds. Now that is going to take time to work through but I will bet you that there are as many local authorities that are doubtful about this or feel rather indifferently about it as there are local authorities that are enthusiastic about it … I do think, however, that we have to be very careful about the way in which we judge the recent decisions on language teaching in this country because all too often I fear we have tried to force kids to learn languages and we have put them off rather than encouraged them. There is only a certain pot of money there and I am very glad that we have decided to concentrate on early years rather than trying to get some enthusiasm moving later (House of Lords, European Union Committee 2005, volume 2: evidence, HL paper 104–II, q479–480, 197–198).

The Committee generally welcomed the government's emphasis on early-years language learning, but pointed to the time-gap that would elapse before such tuition had an effect on the linguistic capacity of young British adults; stretching well beyond the termination of the proposed EU education programmes. It consequently predicted a shortfall in the number of language teachers needed to provide early language teaching in schools; a situation which would only be aggravated by the reduction of compulsory language learning at secondary level. The Committee criticised the government for failing to address the deep-seated language deficiency afflicting Britain, which would require a strategic approach involving long-term commitment and investment in sustained improvement. It therefore recommended that the government should carry out 'an urgent reappraisal of language teaching policy, not only for the implications it will have for the United Kingdom participation in the new EU programmes but much more widely' (House of Lords, European Union Committee 2005, report, HL paper 104–I, para. 322, 64).

Languages Review – The Dearing Report, 2007

In October 2006, Alan Johnson, Secretary of State for Education and Skills, appointed Lord Dearing and Dr Lid King, National Director for Languages at the DfES, to advise the government on 'what action should be taken about the severe fall in the numbers continuing with the study of modern foreign languages … at Key Stage 4 in secondary schools' (DfES 2006, 1).[30] Following a consultative process and the drafting of an interim report, the *Languages Review* was published in February 2007 (DfES 2007).[31] The *Review* proposed a packaged of measures aimed at ensuring a 'renaissance' of language learning in secondary schools, including establishing an Open Languages School together, an increase in specialist language colleges, enhancing retention, training and professional development of language teachers,

---

30 DfES (2006), *Languages Review – Consultation Report: Short Text* (Nottingham: DfES Publications), 1.

31 DfES (2007), *Languages Review*, (Nottingham: DfES Publications).

improving funding and support structures as well as seeking international links with overseas educational and cultural institutions.

In accordance with the National Languages Strategy's original objective of enabling all primary schools to offer a language by 2010, the *Review* recommended making language learning a standard part of the National Curriculum for Key Stage 2 in primary schools (DfES 2007, 9). Despite the emphasis on early-years learning, the *Review* recognised that 'the fall in the study of languages at Key Stage 4 has gone further than the Government might have expected or wished' (DfES 2007, 24). Given that since 2000, the take up of languages has consistently been on a downward trajectory, the *Review* reflected on the possibility of returning to the original mandatory requirement for Modern Foreign Languages at Key Stage 4. The issue had already been considered at the consultative stage, with the interim report concluding this was not a preferred course of action:

> A qualified return to a mandatory requirement ... would have to be weighed against the reasons that led to the decision in 2004 to remove them: the need for a curriculum that motivates many more of our people to stay in education and training to eighteen. The present curriculum for languages works against that and any return would have to be preceded by a new curriculum. We are not at this stage recommending a return to languages as part of the required/compulsory curriculum ... it would be wrong to make students return to a curriculum which for may is inappropriate or, as they see it, not relevant (DfES 2006, 7).

In spite of such reservations, the *Review* sought assurances from government that a return to the compulsory element of language learning in the curriculum – though in a modified mandatory form – would be pursued, if the continuing decline in the take up was not reversed. In a direct appeal to the Secretary of State for Education and Skills, Lord Dearing and Dr King stated 'We further recommend you make clear that you are prepared, if the decline is not halted and turned around within a reasonable timeframe, to return languages to the statutory curriculum' (DfES 2007, 2). At the time of writing though, Modern Foreign Languages continues to have a discretionary rather than compulsory status at Key Stage 4.

Conclusion

The arrival of the New Millennium in Britain has been accompanied by a paradigm shift, away from the multicultural public discourse prevailing in the late twentieth century and towards an emerging Anglocentric ideology. The result of a combination of social, political and economic factors, such transition has seen Britain's immigration, citizenship and education policies moving in the direction of an integrationist model; one which emphasises Britishness, common values and socio-linguistic cohesion over difference and separateness.

Within the context of an increasingly diverse British society, instances of civic unrest together with the growing problem of illegal migration and the advent of international terrorism triggered a backlash against migrant communities both at home and abroad, old and new. Sensationalist headlines, pandering to prejudicial attitudes and deep-seated fears of cultural and linguistic fragmentation, have given way to official pronouncements on the need to reassert our sense of Britishness and national identity. Immigration and citizenship legislation was to follow, specifically aimed at ensuring social integration, national unity and ultimately the preservation of the *status quo*. The *Nationality, Immigration and Asylum Act 2002*, in particular, which provided a blueprint for the future shape of the country's citizenship and immigration policy, spelt out the government's vision of a British nation inhabited by British citizens committed to the British way of life. Newcomers, whose distinct ethnic makeup and traditions had until recently been celebrated as contributing to the UK's multicultural brand, are now required to integrate into mainstream society. Not only do prospective British citizens need to display sufficient knowledge of life in Britain, its culture and civic institutions; they are expected to take a citizenship oath and make a pledge of allegiance at a public ceremony. Most significantly, those wishing to take up British nationality will have to be able to speak English.

In so establishing a direct link between our national identity and the English language, the government has gone further than ever before by unequivocally defining British citizenship as an English-speaking Anglo-Saxon model. This Anglocentric trend in turn has translated into a series of education policy initiatives purposely aimed at strengthening an English-dominant school curriculum; a curriculum ultimately tailored to the needs of the country's English-speaking student population. As part of the government's previous commitment to diversity, the past decade witnessed the deployment of considerable educational energy and resources into preserving the linguistic and cultural heritage of Britain's migrant school children. In contrast, our education system is now firmly focused on ensuring mastery of the three core subjects: English, Maths and Science. Deemed to be the basic tools needed to operate in modern life, they take precedent over any other field of study at school level; space within the curriculum has therefore been made for them.

In 2004, the government performed a policy U-turn by abandoning the former compulsion to study Foreign Modern Languages at Key Stage 4 in favour of an entitlement to do so. The pernicious consequences of this strategy were soon to be felt; with a substantial drop in the take up of languages across the board having consistently continued to this day. In the face of overwhelming evidence regarding the long-term implications of such an unrelenting loss of linguistic ability among the UK's workforce, the government has opted for a number of remedial measures including channelling language resources into early-years education. It has fallen short, however, of extending the compulsory element of language teaching throughout the school curriculum as well as devising a sustainable and far-reaching policy strategy for the future learning of Foreign Modern Languages in Britain. Despite political rhetoric to the contrary, the UK government's Anglocentric stand on language policy has been shown to be at odds with the multicultural and multilingual approached championed by its European counterparts. Within the wider context of Britain's public debate on the national identity question, current social, immigration and language education policy trends provide yet the clearest illustration of a now prevailing integrationist discourse.

PART 3
Conclusion

Chapter 7

Contemporary British Identity – Over a Hundred Years in the Making

The Challenge of Migration

In the same way as inquisitiveness is an innate quality of human nature, migration is an essential feature of our planet's history. From ancient civilisations to the Industrial Revolution and modern times, people have travelled the world in search of knowledge, new frontiers and opportunities. There is nothing more controversial and yet more natural, Blunkett reminds us, than 'men and women from across the world seeking a better life for themselves and their families' (Home Office 2002, cm 5387).[1]

Leaving aside the deplorable practice of human trafficking, voluntary migration has long brought considerable benefits both to host societies and the migrants entering their shores, with higher levels of economic activity, enhanced educational and skills base as well as increased cultural diversity, to name a few. For those fleeing war-torn countries and political and/or religious persecution, migration has moreover provided them with the prospect of a peaceful existence free from oppression. Despite the undeniable merits of migration – domestic and international, population movements invariably present challenges to those affected by them. Whether native communities or the migrants themselves, the arrival of foreigners upon home soil – particularly in large numbers – is frequently accompanied by tensions at the grassroots. Not only do newcomers place a burden on existing social, educational and welfare services; the inevitable economic and cultural impact on their adopted countries often breeds resentment. As part of a minority population, migrants easily become prime targets for deep-seated xenophobic and racist attitudes ever present within our midst.

One particular area of friction brought about by migration is that of nationality and citizenship. As the demographic makeup of nations is constantly altered by successive waves of immigrants, and their offspring in turn grow into fully-fledged citizens; traditional notions of national identity and citizenship are rapidly becoming obsolete. In recent years, the accelerated transformation of societies across the world into diverse, multicultural, multiethnic and multilingual states together with the advent of globalisation and the changes associated with it have led to greater complexity in pattens of migration. As a result, peoples' perceptions of their individual and national identities are being altered in fundamental ways. The government's *Secure Borders,*

---

1 Home Office (2002), *Secure Borders, Safe Haven: Integration with Diversity in Modern Britain*, Presented to Parliament by the Secretary of Sate for the Home Department by Command of Her Majesty, foreword (London: TSO).

Safe Haven White Paper already recognised the challenge posed by contemporary migration to societies everywhere and their citizens' sense of belonging:

> The first challenge migration poses is to our concepts of nationality and citizenship. Migration has increased the diversity of advanced democracies, leading to changes in national culture and identity. Many of us already have overlapping identities based on our cultural and ethnic backgrounds. More than half of the countries of the world now accept dual citizenship. At the same time, globalisation of communication media and information technology has opened up national cultures to diverse influences, and provided channels of mutual interaction between different parts of the world that literally know no boundaries. Social changes such as the decline of old certainties of class or place, and the emergence of new political institutions alongside the nation state, have also contributed to these changes in identity and political belonging (Home Office 2002, 9–10).

How societies deal with diversity can be said to reflect their particular perceptions of themselves, their national identity and that of their citizens. Through immigration, welfare and educational policies as well as legislative measures different countries delineate the boundaries between the rights of their majority and minority populations, between individual and collective responsibilities, between personal choice and the rule of law, between living with difference and sharing common values, and between linguistic uniformity and multilingual fragmentation. It is in this manner, that nations' public narratives are constructed and deconstructed over time.

In the case of Britain, the closing years of the twentieth century witnessed a gradual ideological shift away from multiculturalism and towards integration; away from the individual right to be different and towards the collective duty to integrate. The past decade has indeed been characterised by a combination of legislative and policy initiatives mainly aimed at promoting national unity, social cohesion and a sense of Britishness. Stretching into the new millennium, this trend has now culminated in an unprecedented public debate about the state of multiculturalism in Britain.

Changing Public Narratives – From Multiculturalism to Integration

As a country built on migration, multiculturalism is an integral part of Britain's national fabric. Debate on the subject, however has only surfaced in modern times; with some scholars tracing its origins back to the Post-War period, when the *British Nationality Act 1948* provided 'the legal framework within which a multicultural Britain emerged' (Hansen 2000, 35).[2] As Hansen explains, the United Kingdom began the Post-War years with a non-white population of some 300,000 people; in contrast, it approached the end of the century with over three million people 'whose origins extend from Africa, the Pacific Rim, the Caribbean and the Indian Subcontinent. Together with France and Germany it has among the largest ethnic populations in Europe and it shares with France the largest ethnic minority citizenry' (Hansen 2000, 3). The accelerated transformation of Britain into a multiethnic,

---

2   Hansen, R. (2000), *Citizenship and Immigration in Post-War Britain: The Institutional Origins of a Multicultural Nation* (Oxford: Oxford University Press).

multicultural and multifaith society, during the second half of the twentieth century, has been accompanied by a growing body of scholarly work on the subject of multiculturalism and nationhood (Modood 2005a,b,c; Parekh 2000; Taylor 1994; Joppke 2004; Hall 2000; Hansen 2000).[3] In the same way as related issues such as 'ethnicity', 'race', 'identity' and 'Diaspora' have long been analysed and discussed; multiculturalism is nowadays regularly examined, constructed and deconstructed. While the term 'multiculturalism' has become a familiar part of our vocabulary, there continues to be a lack of consensus regarding its semantics. Among the myriad of existing definitions, Hall's suggested distinction between 'multi-cultural' and 'multiculturalism' can be said to succeed in clearly conceptualising this rather elusive notion. Accordingly, the term 'multicultural' describes 'the social characteristics and problems of governance posed by any society in which different cultural communities live together and attempt to build a common life while retaining something of their own 'original' identity'. By contrast, 'multiculturalism' refers to 'the strategies and policies adopted to govern or manage the problems of diversity and multiplicity which multi-cultural societies throw up' (Hall 2000, 209).

Over the past five years, a combination of socio-political developments, including increased illegal migration and the recent urban disturbances in England's northern towns has raised questions about the effectiveness and long-term sustainability of Britain's particular brand of multiculturalism. Following the New York City's World Trade Centre atrocities on September 2001; the subsequent London bombings on July 2005 by home-grown Islamic extremists focused attention on the dangers of social fragmentation when difference is allowed to go unchecked. While at the time, the spotlight fell on the UK's Muslim community; it was as much their perceived inability as unwillingness – to the point of overt rejection in some instances – to integrate into mainstream British society that was seen as posing the biggest threat to our national security, civic values and way of life. During the last twelve months, ensuing controversies over the state of race relations and community cohesion in Britain, including the so-called 'veil and Big Brother rows' have cast further doubts over the way in which we deal with diversity and the implications for the future of the British nation. As the public debate on multiculturalism gathered momentum, the health of our seemingly abating social fabric has been exhaustively studied by a succession of academic experts, stakeholders and policy-makers. Controversial at the best of times, the

---

3   Modood, T. (2005a), 'Multiculturalism or Britishness: A False Debate', *Connections*, Winter 2004/05 <http://www.cre.gov.uk/publs/connections/articles/04wi_falsedebate.html> (accessed 28 February 2007); Modood, T. (2005b), *Multicultural Politics: Racism, Ethnicity and Muslims in Britain* (Edinburgh: Edinburgh University Press); Modood, T. (2005c), 'Remaking Multiculturalism after 7/7', Open Democracy, <http://www.opendemocracy.net/conflict-terrorism/multiculturalism_2879.jsp> (accessed 13 March 2007); Parekh, B. (2000) *Rethinking Multiculturalism: Cultural Diversity and Political Theory* (London: Palgrave); Taylor, C. (1994), *Multiculturalism – Examining the Politics of Recognition* (Princeton: Princeton University Press); Joppke, C. (2004) 'The Retreat of Multiculturalism in the Liberal State: Theory and Policy', *The British Journal of Sociology*, 55:2, 237–57; Hall, S. (2000), 'The Multicultural Question', in B. Hesse (ed.) *Un/Settled Multiculturalisms: Diasporas, Entanglements, 'Transruptions'* (London: Zed Books).

debate over multiculturalism has attracted unprecedented mass media interest as well as featuring strong views and contrasting opinions; frequently provoking virulent reactions that have polarised public opinion. Overall, it has signalled the realisation of a gradual, yet unwavering, shift in our national consciousness towards integration. Recent headlines such as 'Labour loose Faith in Multiculturalism', 'Multiculturalism drives Young Muslims to shun British Values', 'I feel British, but I don't want Enforced Patriotism' and 'Misunderstanding Multiculturalism' reflect the wide-ranging nature of the ongoing debate (*Telegraph* 2006, *Daily Mail* 2007; Alibhai-Brown 2007; Giddens 2006).[4] A closer look at the latest press coverage generated by this process provides an insight into the complexity of the issues involved and the momentum now gathered by our unravelling public discourse.

The Multiculturalism Debate

Background Heighten media attention on multiculturalism has taken place against a backdrop of interest in various social policy related matters competing to grab the headlines. On the one hand, a seemingly innocuous incident at the local constituency of Jack Straw, Leader of House of Commons, involving a Muslim female resident removing her veil while at a surgery visit, resulted in a full-blown national 'veil row' over the desirability of Muslim women wearing the veil or niqab in modern day Britain. This particular episode served to highlight once more the distinct values espoused by the country's Islamic community as opposed to those of Britain's dominant liberal Christian tradition; in particular, the apparent anachronistic treatment of women by the former. The 'veil row' thus saw editorials such as 'Debate on the Veil Shows how West is turning into Islam, Scholar warns', 'Surge in Racism in Schools blamed for 7/7 and Veil Row' and 'Muslim Women are the Key to Change' (Akbar 2006; Daily Mail 2006; Ali 2006).[5] On the other hand,

---

    4   'Labour loose Faith in Multiculturalism', *Telegraph*, 19 October 2006 <http://www. telegraph.co.uk/opinion/main.jhtml;jsessionid=BVMECJ0ZEEPRRQFIQMGSFGGAVCBQ WIV0?xml=/opinion/2006/10/18/dl18101.xml> (accessed 1 March 2007); 'Multiculturalism Drives Young Muslims to shun British Values'*, The Daily Mail*, 28 January 2007 <http:// wwww.dailymail.co.uk/pages/live/artilces/news/thml?in_article_id=432075&in_page_id=1770&ct=5> (accessed 1 March 2007); Alibhai-Brown, J. 'I feel British, but I don't want Enforced Patriotism', *The Independent*, 29 January 2007 <http://comment.independent. co.uk/columnists_a_l/yasmin_alibhai_brown/article2193730.ece> (accessed 1 March 2007); Giddens, A. 'Misunderstanding Multiculturalism', *The Guardian*, 16 October 2006 <http:// commentisfree.guardian.co.uk/anthony_giddens/2006/10/tony_giddens.html> (accessed 1 March 2007).
    5   Akbar, A. 'Debate on the Veil shows how West is turning on Islam, Scholar Warns', *The Independent*, 27 October 2006 <http://news.independent.co.uk/uk/this_britain/article1932752. ece.> (accessed 1 March 2007); 'Surge in Racism in Schools blamed for 7/7 and Veil Row', *Daily Mail*, 20 November 2006 <http://www.dailymail.co.uk/pages/live/articles/news/news. html?in_article_id=417454&in_page_id=1770> (accessed 1 March 2007); Ali, A.H. 'Muslim Women and the Key to Change', *Sunday Times*, 29 October 2006 <http://www.timesonline. co.uk/article/0,,2092-2426413,00.html> (accessed 1 March 2007).

media attention has focused on the ever present issue of migration, racial tensions and strained community relations. With memories of Sandgate and Bradford still fresh in the public mind and unremitting influxes of new immigrants entering the UK, the prickly matter of community cohesion has continued to make it onto the front pages. On this occasion, the press produced a familiar motley assortment of pieces on the subject including, 'Violence flares between Youths in Windsor over Plan to build Mosque', 'Schools told to promote Integration of Communities' and the alarmist 'Immigrants swell the Population at a Rate of 500 a Day', to name but a few (Beard 2006; Russell 2006; Johnston 2006).[6] At the beginning of 2007, however, a single story came to briefly dominate the headlines, namely the 'Big Brother row'. What started as the misguided exploitation of racist bullying as a form of mass entertainment by a British broadcaster, escalated into a media-led national crisis of sorts with international repercussions. The decision of Channel Four's *Celebrity Big Brother* reality-TV show to allow the protracted racial and psychological abuse of an Indian contestant by three fellow white British participants to go unchallenged caused unprecedented national and international outrage. The incident drew attention to the existing gap between the ideal of a modern multicultural British nation and the reality of everyday life in Britain, where overtly racist and prejudicial attitudes still run deep within some sections of our society. The backlash triggered by the broadcast was caused as much by revulsion over the actual contemptible behaviour displayed as by the affront it represented to our nation's cherished values of tolerance and civility. Newspapers headlines at the time captured this sentiment: 'Racism gets a Reality Check', 'A Vote of No Confidence' and 'Cameron blast Crude bullying on 'British Values'' (Verkaik et al. 2007; Graef 2007; Hinsliff and Doward 2007).[7] A final issue coming under the media spotlight is the recurring question of British identity and citizenship. Against a background of general uneasy regarding the state of our social order, coverage of this topic has tended to reflect the emerging integrationist public narrative that seeks to reassert the *status quo*. Here, we have been treated to headlines of a rather nationalistic nature such as 'Accept British Way of Life or Stay Away, Blair tells Immigrants', 'Citizenship, Schools and the Imposition of National

---

6   Beard, M. 'Violence flares between Youths in Windsor over Plan to build Mosque', *The Independent*, 6 October 2006 <http://news.independent.co.uk/uk/this_britain/article1813595. ece> (accessed 1 March 2007); Russell, B. 'Schools told to promote Integration of Communities', *The Independent*, 31 October 2006 <http://education/independent.co.uk/news/ article1943293> (accessed 1 March 2007); Johnston, P. 'Immigrants swell the Population at a Rate of 500 a Day', *Telegraph*, 3 November 2006 <http://www.telegraph.co.uk/news/main. jhtml?xml=/news/2006/11/03/nmigrant03.xml> (accessed 1 March 2007).

7   Verkaik, R., B. Russell and J. Huggler 'Racism gets a Reality Check', *The Independent*, 18 January 2007 <http://news.independent.co.uk/media/article2162868.ece> (accessed 1 March 2007); Graef, R. 'A Vote of No Confidence', *The Guardian*, 23 January 2007 <http:// www.guardian.co.uk/comment/story/0,,1996482,00.html> (accessed 1 March 2007); Hinsliff, G. and J. Doward 'Cameron blasts at Crude Bullying on 'British Values'', *The Observer*, 28 January 2007 <http://observer.guardian.co.uk/politics/story/0,,2000512,html> (accessed 1 March 2007).

Values' and 'Britishness and the Class System' (Yeoman 2007; *The Independent* 2007; Henry 2007).[8]

The Evidence   The past few years have seen the publication of a wealth of conflicting evidence regarding the state of diversity and multiculturalism in Britain. On the one hand, official figures continue to show the accelerated transformation of Britain into a diverse multi-ethnic society, with about eight per cent of the UK population now belonging to an ethnic minority other than white. Between 1991 and 2001, the number of people ascribing to this category grew by 53 per cent, from 3.0 million in 1991 to 4.6 million in 2001 (National Statistics 2004a).[9] Those of mixed parentage, in particular, have consistently increased their share of the UK population. By 1997, already half of black men and a fifth of Asian men in relationships in Britain had a white partner, conversely a third of black women and ten per cent of Asian women had also opted for a white partner (Modood et al. 1997; John 2002).[10] Over the past decade, the number of inter-ethnic couples and children of mixed parentage has ostensibly risen by 20 per cent, there now being four times more children than adults of mixed ethnicity. There is also evidence that British society is becoming more mixed, with the numbers of mixed neighbourhoods increasing from 864 to 1,070 in the decade to 2001 (Livingstone 2006).[11]

While in 1951, 2.1 million (4.2 per cent) of the UK population were born overseas, by 2001, this had more than doubled, with 4.9 million (8.3 per cent) born overseas (National Statistics 2005).[12] The increase in absolute numbers of the foreign-born population between 1991 and 2001 was greater than in any of the preceding post-war decades and is in line with the general trend of rising international migration over the same period. The recent arrival in Britain of nationals from the new EU accession states has only accentuated this demographic drive.

---

8   Yeoman, F. 'Accept British Way of Life or Stay Away, Blair tells Immigrants', *The Times*, 11 December 2007 <http://www.timesonline.co.uk/article/0,,17129-2494782,00.html> (accessed 1 March 2007); 'Citizenship, Schools and the Imposition of National Values', *The Independent*, 26 January 2007 <http://coment.independent.co.uk/leading_articles/article2186492.ece> (accessed 1 March 2007); Henry, J. 'Britishness and the Class System', *Sunday Telegraph*, 22 January 2007 <http://www.telegraph.co.uk/news/main.jhtml?xml=/news/2007/01/21/nedu121.xml> (accessed 1 March 2007).

9   National Statistics (2004a), *People and Migration – Ethnicity*, National Statistics <http://www.statistics.gov.uk/CCI/nugget.asp?ID=764&Pos=4&ColRank=1&Rank=176> (accessed 22 May 2007).

10   Modood, T., R. Berthoud, J. Lakey, J. Nazroo, P. Smith, S. Virdee and S. Beishon (1997), *Ethnic Minorities in Britain – Diversity and Disadvantage*, Fourth National Survey of Ethnic Minorities (London: Policy Studies Institute); John, C. (2002), 'Changing Face of Britain', BBC News <http://news.bbc.co.uk/hi/english/static/in_depth/uk/2002/race/changing_face_of_britain.stm> (accessed 22 May 2007).

11   Livingstone, K. 'To defend Multiculturalism is to defend Liberty', *The Independent*, 28 November 2006 <http://comment.independent.co.uk/commetators/article2021228.ece> (accessed 28 February 2007).

12   National Statistics (2005), *Focus on People and Migration – Foreign – Born,* National Statistics <www.statistics.gov.uk/cci/nugget.asp?id=1312> (accessed 26 February 2007).

It is estimated that over the next two decades, ethnic minorities will account for half the growth in the working age population, with cities like Leicester and Birmingham set to become 'minority majority cities' (EOC 2006; *The Guardian* 2006).[13] In London alone, where about a third of the population belongs to an ethnic minority other than white and over 300 languages are spoken, one in three Londoners is born overseas, bringing the foreign-born population of the Capital to a total of 2.2 million people (Frith 2006).[14] Despite their different ethnic and religious backgrounds though, the majority of people in Britain seem to have a strong sense of national identity, describing themselves as either British, English, Scottish or Welsh. Around 95 per cent of Christians and those with no religion, 80 per cent of Sikhs, 70 per cent of Muslims and 69 of Hindus describe themselves in this manner (National Statistics 2006a).[15]

On the other hand, evidence reveals that fewer than one in ten (seven per cent) Local Authority areas in England and Wales has high levels of ethnic diversity and just three per cent has high religious diversity – defined as a 50 per cent chance that two people at random will belong to different groups. This is perhaps not surprising when considering that across England and Wales, 87 per cent of the population is white British and 72 per cent Christian (National Statistics 2006). Over the past ten years, changes in demographics, household and labour market differentials among ethno-religious groups have resulted in wide variations among different regions, with the London borough of Brent having been identified as the most religiously diverse area in England and Wales – with an 85 per cent chance that two people at random would be from different religious groups; this compares with Harrow, where the likelihood of this happening is 62 per cent and Easington, with a two per cent likelihood (National Statistics 2006b).[16]

In spite of having a presence in the country spanning over half a century, there is ample evidence of persistent socio-economic inequalities disproportionally affecting Britain's minority ethnic communities, particularly women belonging to these groups. Recent research by the Equal Opportunities Commission (EOC) paints a bleak picture of the labour market prospects of Pakistani, Bangladeshi and black Caribbean women in modern Britain, regardless of their increasing attainment at school and high aspirations. *Moving on Up? Bangladeshi, Pakistani and Black Caribbean Women and Work* shows how over half of Pakistanis and Bangladeshi girls

---

13 Equal Opportunities Commission (EOC) (2006), Press Release: Launch of Interim Report in to BME Women in the Work Place, *Moving on Up? Bangladeshi, Pakistani and Black Caribbean Women and Work*, EOC <http://www.eoc.org.uk?Default.aspz?page=1944 3&theme=print> (accessed 26 February 2007); 'Mixed Responses', *The Guardian*, Society Guardian, 13 December 2006, 3.

14 Frith, M. 'The World City: One in Three Londoners was born Overseas', *The Independent*, 14 November 2006.

15 National Statistics (2006a) *Focus on Religion – Country of Birth and National Identity*, National Statistics <http://www.statistics.gov.uk/cci/nugget.asp?id=958> (accessed 28 February 2007).

16 National Statistics (2006b) News Release – 'Brent is The Most Ethnically Diverse Area', National Statistics <http://www.statistics.gov.uk/pdfdir/eth1006.pdf> (accessed 26 February 2007).

and nearly half of black Caribbean girls aspire to jobs requiring a degree education and long periods of study and training, compared with only a third of their white counterparts in the same age category (EOC 2006). Despite being overwhelmingly supported by their families, these girls remain mostly outside the labour market, facing major barriers to progress such as racism, sexism and pejorative stereotyping. Within British society at large, the situation for women remains far from ideal, with a recurrent gender gap pervading throughout the labour market. The EOC has calculated that at the current rate of progress, it will take another 20 years to achieve equality in the country's civil service top management tier, 40 years to achieve an equal number of senior women in the judiciary, 60 years to achieve an equal number of female directors at FTSE 100 companies and up to 200 years – another 40 elections – to achieve an equal number of women in Parliament (EOC 2007).[17]

Official statistics furthermore continue to show disproportionally high unemployment rates among UK-born minority ethnic groups compared with the general white population. In 2004, for instance, Pakistani women had the highest unemployment rates (20 per cent) of any population group in Britain. They were followed by women from black African and mixed ethnic groups (12 per cent each); these figures were around three times the unemployment rates for white British women (four per cent each). Among men, those from black Afro-Caribbean, Bangladeshi and mixed ethnic groups recorded the highest unemployment rates (between 13 and 14 per cent each) among the male population, around three times the unemployment rates for white British men (five per cent) (National Statistics 2004b).[18] A series of recent studies on poverty and ethnicity by the Joseph Rowntree Foundation has furthermore revealed the extent of disadvantage experienced by certain communities in the UK and the 'ethnic penalties' they encounter as a result of their continuing discrimination across the board (Platt 2007; Palmer and Kenway 2007; Salway et al. 2007; Clarke and Drinkwater 2007).[19] Overall, it is estimated that the 'racial gap' in employment between white Britons and the minority ethnic population will take up to 45 years to be closed; this is notwithstanding research showing that most people favour increased diversity within the workforce (Branigan 2006; Fuller 2007).[20]

---

17 EOC (2007), Press Release: Where are the Women missing from Scotland's Top Spots? EOC, 5 January 2007 <http://www.eoc.org.uk/Default.aspx?page=19843&theme=pr int> (accessed 28 February 2007).

18 National Statistics (2004b), *Ethnicity and Identity – Labour Market* (London: TSO).

19 Platt, L. (2007), *Poverty and Ethnicity in the UK* (Bristol: Policy Press in association with the Joseph Rowntree Foundation); Palmer, G. and P. Kenway (2007), *Poverty among Ethnic Groups: How and Why does it differ?* (York: Joseph Rowntree Foundation); Salway, S., L. Platt, P. Chowbey, K. Harriss and E. Bayliss (2007), *Long-term Ill-health, Poverty and Ethnicity* (York: Joseph Rowntree Foundation); Clarke K. and S. Drinkwater (2007), *Ethnic Minorities in the Labour Market: Dynamics and Diveristy* (York: Joseph Rowntree Foundation).

20 Branigan, T. 'Racial Gap in Employment 'will take 45 Years to close'', *The Guardian*, 9 November 2006 <http://www.guardian.co.uk/print/0,,329622585–110414,00.html>. (accessed 27 February 2007); Fuller, G. (2007), 'Most People favour Increased Diversity in the Work Force', *Personnel Today*, 3 January 2007 <http://www.personneltoday.com/

The Case for Multiculturalism   While the subject of multiculturalism is by no means new among the scholarly community, it is a relatively young and rapidly growing academic discipline. Given the multiplicity of issues involved and the wealth of theoretical and empirical knowledge already in existence, only a brief acquaintance with an otherwise complex debate can be anticipated here. Any exploration of recent thinking on the question of multiculturalism must be made with reference to the Runnymede Trust's seminal report *The Future of Multi-ethnic Britain* (Runnymede Trust 2000).[21] Published in 2000, the so-called Parekh Report, after the Chair of the Commission on the Future of Multi-ethnic Britain that oversaw the work, is arguably the most far-reaching investigation into the state of multiculturalism in Britain to date. Set up in 1998 by the Runnymede Trust, the Commission comprised 23 public figures with distinguished track records of engagement in race-related issues at home and abroad. Its specific remit was 'to analyse the current state of multi-ethnic Britain and to propose ways of countering racial discrimination and disadvantage and making Britain a confident and vibrant multicultural society at ease with its rich diversity' (Runnymede Trust 2000, Preface). In order to achieve this objective, the Commission started by revisiting the 'national story' of Britain, its steady progression into a modern multicultural nation and the challenges it faces, both present and future, in its efforts to deal with growing diversity while fostering social cohesion. The role of national institutions such as government, the police and the criminal justice system was considered as well as key areas of social policy such as education, health, welfare and employment. The picture emerging from this analysis was one of a diverse, yet deeply unequal British society where an underclass of minority ethnic and disadvantaged communities remained firmly stranded at the margins. Here, both individual prejudices and organisational mind-sets played a central role in perpetuating the *status quo*. Against this backdrop, the Commission articulated a vision of a multicultural Britain as 'a community of communities' each containing many identities and affiliations, each at different stages of development and each with its own internal tensions and contradictions; but nonetheless all part of the wider British nation (Runnymede 2000, 105). If this vision of Britain was to be realised, the Commission suggested combining the values of equality and diversity, liberty and solidarity as well as pursuing the ideals and principles of liberalism and communitarianism (Runnymede 2000, 105).

The *Future of Multi-ethnic Britain* contains many recommendations of good practice relating to core foundations of our social fabric such as state institutions, political representation and law enforcement together with an array of policy interventions critical to everyday life in Britain. The recommendations were framed within the context of seven fundamental principles: firstly, the *Three central concepts: cohesion, equality and difference*: 'People must be treated equally, but also with regard to real difference of experience, background and

---

Articles/2007/01/03/38737/most-people-favour-increased-diversity-in-the-workforce-research.html> (accessed 28 February 2007).

21 Runnymede Trust (2000), *The Future of Multi-ethnic Britain – The Parekh Report*, Report of the Commission on the Future of Multi-ethnic Britain (London: Profile Books Ltd.).

perception'. Secondly, *Demonstrable change at all levels*: 'The concepts of equality and diversity must be driven through the government machinery at national and regional levels'. Thirdly, *Addressing racisms*: 'there must be a sustained and fearless attack on all forms of racial injustice. Such injustice threatens the very basis of citizenship'. Fourthly, *Tackling Disadvantage*: 'Street racism and violent racism arise and flourish in situations of economic disadvantage and inequality'. Fifthly, *Colour-blind approaches do not work*: 'There must be a commitment to go beyond the racism- and culture-blind strategies of social inclusion currently under way'. Sixthly, *Empowering and enfranchising*: 'There must be vigorous commitment to recognising cultural diversity through, for example, the systematic representation of black, Asian and Irish communities to public bodies'. Finally, *A pluralistic culture of human rights*: 'Human rights standards provide both an ethical and a legal basis for the changes required' (Runnymede 2000, 296–97).

In line with the findings and recommendations of the Commission, academic exponents of multicultural models such as Parekh, Modood and Taylor, among others, have wrestled with a seemingly intractable dichotomy facing civic society everywhere: on the one hand, the need to nurture diversity by accommodating different cultural traditions within the wider nation-state; whilst simultaneously ensuring social cohesion by fostering a shared sense of belonging and national identity. Key to resolving this conundrum is the notion of 'equality'. Since every society needs to be both respectful of diversity as well as cohesive, 'equality' must be defined in a culturally sensitive way and ultimately applied in a discerning rather than discriminatory fashion. As Parekh explains 'When equality ignores relevant differences and insists on uniformity of treatment, it leads to injustice and inequality; when differences ignore the demands of equality, they result in discrimination' (Runnymede Trust 2000, ix). Within this context, Modood has argued that multiculturalism and Britishness are not exclusive choices and therefore the multicultural circle can be squared by 'renegotiating the terms of integration' of minority communities rather than resorting to all-out separatism. It is 'commitment to equal respect'; he points out, what distinguishes 'multiculturalism from non-multiculturalism'. The former, Modood concludes, interprets equality as meaning that non-assimilation is acceptable and that minority identities and traditions ought to be included in the public sphere (Modood 2005a; Taylor 1994; Parekh 2000).

Multiculturalism – A Critique Despite the reasoned arguments put forward by those advocating multicultural approaches, similarly persuasive views have been expressed by critics of such models; often pointing to the seemingly unsurmountable gulf between the ideology and the reality of multiculturalism in Britain. Inside the academic community, a number of scholars have come to question both the desirability of a multicultural British model and its long-term feasibility. Various social theory critiques have consequently emerged to counteract perceived flawed assumptions of group dynamics upon which notions of multiculturalism have been built. Proponents of alternative approaches such as Bauman, Joppke and Hewitt, to name but a few, suggest revisiting multiculturalism to take into account often overlooked contextual factors, including multiple and fluid identities, 'transnationalisms' and globalisation

(Bauman 1999; Joppke 2004; Hewitt 2005).[22] In the midst of a post-9/11 – 7/7 discourse, the ultimate worth and viability of multiculturalism as a civic model has moreover come under scrutiny, with some calls being made for it to be replaced by a new strain of 'politics of integration' (Kivisto 2005).[23]

Within the wider national policy debate, a number of public figures have similarly added their voices to the growing choir of those expressing concerns with the direction of Britain's multicultural project. Significantly, a former member of the Commission on the Future of Multi-ethnic Britain, Trevor Phillips, has become one of the most outspoken critics of the country's particular brand of multiculturalism. Now Chairman of the newly established Commission for Equality and Human Rights, he has repeatedly claimed that community relations in Britain are progressively deteriorating. As a result, an increasingly polarised society appears to be threatening our national stability together with the values and traditions that binds us together as British citizens. Following the terrorist atrocities in London in July 2005, Phillips's controversial speech titled 'After 7/7: Sleepwalking to Segregation' described the state of our British nation as one where 'time is becoming our enemy in the fight for an integrated society'. The fact is – he argued – that 'we are a society, which almost without noticing it, is becoming more divided by race and religion. We are becoming more unequal by ethnicity'. Phillips went as far as to say that 'Our universities have started to become colour-coded, with virtual 'whites keep-out' signs in some urban institutions; and if you look closely at the campuses of some of our most distinguished universities, you can pick up the invisible 'no blacks need apply' messages … some districts are on their way to become fully fledged ghettoes' (Phillips 2005).[24] Such contentions remarks have not only made newspapers headlines, but seen Phillips at odds with Professor Crick, former Chair of the government's Advisory Board on Naturalisation and Integration (ABNI). Professor Crick has argued that one of the main problems for immigrant communities is residual white racism amid poverty as well as wider xenophobia; any attempts to promote Britishness in place of multiculturalism risks alienating marginalised groups even further, as he put it:

> I don't regard the debate which has broken out as phoney. Yes, Trevor Phillips is half right to say that we need more stress on 'Britishness'; but he is half wrong – and could cause confusion and fear – to set out to junk 'multiculturalism' … Yes, integration is neither assimilation nor cultural separatism; but to rubbish multiculturalism is to create greater insecurity among the communities. Integration is a two-way process. The new must understand the old, but the older communities must also understand them better. If attacking multiculturalism is an attempt by New Labour and its supporters to placate rather

---

22 Bauman, G. (1999) *The Multicultural Riddle* (London: Routledge); Joppke, C. (2004) 'The Retreat of Multiculturalism in the Liberal State: Theory and Policy', *The British Journal of Sociology,* 55:2, 237–57; Hewitt, R. (2005) *White Backlash and the Politics of Multiculturalism* (Cambridge: Cambridge University Press).

23 Kivisto, P. (2005) *Incorporating Diversity – Rethinking Assimilation in a Multicultural Age* (Colorado: Paradigm Publishers).

24 Phillips, T. (2005) 'After 7/7: Sleepwalking to Segregation', Commission for Racial Equality (CRE) <http://www.cre.gov.uk/Default.aspx?LocID=Ohgnew07s&RefLocID=0hg0 0900c002&Lang=EN&> (accessed 28 February 2007).

than confront the anti-immigrant fervour of the tabloid editors, I fear that in reassuring some it may lose many (Crick 2004).[25]

Ken Livingstone, Mayor of London, has also publicly refuted Phillip's assertions regarding the state of multiculturalism in British society, while accusing him of harming community relations and using inflammatory language for the sake of 'alarmist headlines' (Muir 2006).[26] The Mayor has likened advocating multiculturalism to 'a long struggle between liberty and its opponents'; it is not, he explains 'about personal differences of opinion, but between the values of an open and closed society' (Livingstone 2006). Livingstone has charged Phillips, who is of Caribbean descent, with 'pandering to the right' so much that 'soon he'll be joining the BNP'; and refused to attend the two-day Race Convention 2006 event organised by Phillips, accusing him of 'peddling falsehoods and failing victims of racism' (Hinsliff 2006; BBC 2006b).[27] Phillips, on the other hand, has purportedly dismissed Livingstone's criticism as a distraction from his unwillingness to engage in honest debate; with Phillips' supporters, in turn, allegedly condemning the Mayor for being 'stuck in a 1980s time warp' (Millward 2006).[28] On this occasion, Phillips used his opening speech at the Convention to warn that 'As a nation we are becoming more ethnically segregated by residence, and inequality is being amplified by our separate lives'. He reflected on how 'bigotry still remains a strong feature of British life' together with the 'phenomenon of stealth racism – the racism that smiles to your face just as it's dumping your job application in the bin marked 'Not White Enough'. He concluded by saying that 'Britain is by far – I mean by far – the best place in Europe to live if you are not white' (CRE 2006).[29]

Besides Phillips' views on the subject, other public and political figures have voiced their misgivings regarding Britain's multiculturalism; most notably, David Cameron, Leader of the Conservative Opposition, who believes it has damaged Britain. Cameron argues that the doctrine of multiculturalism has undermined our

25 Crick, B. 'All this Talk of Britain is so … English', *The Guardian*, 12 April 2004 <http://society.guardian.co.uk/raceequality/comment/0,,1190252,00.html> (accessed 17 June 2007); Crawford, A. (2005), 'Crick hits out at Call for Britishness', *The Sunday Herald*, 31 July 2005 <http://findarticles.com/p/articles/mi_qn4156/is_20050731/ai_n14827389> (accessed 17 June 2007).

26 Muir, H. 'Mayor's New onslaught on 'Alarmist' Race Watchdog', *The Guardian*, 27 November 2006 <http://www.guardian.co.uk/print/0,,329644262-103685,00.html> (accessed 28 February 2007).

27 Hinsliff, G. 'Livingstone declares War on Race Equality Watchdog', *The Observer*, 26 November 2006 <http://observer.guardian.co.uk/print/0,,329643832-102279,00.html> (accessed 28 February 2007); BBC (2006b) 'Top Racism Event faces Boycott' BBC News <http://newsvote.bbc.co.uk/mpapps/pagetools/print/news.bbc.co.uk/1/hi/uk_politics/61> (accessed 28 February 2007).

28 Millward, D. 'Livingstone boycotts Phillips's Race Debate', *Telegraph*, 28 November 2006 <http://www.telegraph.co.uk/news/main.jhtml?xml=/news/2006/11/27/nslave127.xml> (accessed 15 March 2007).

29 Commission for Racial Equality (CRE) (2006) 'Race Convention 2006: Trevor Phillips' Opening Speech', CRE <http://www.cre.gov.uk/Default.aspx.LocID-0hgnew0nu. RefLocID-0hb00900c002.Lang-EN.htm> (accessed 1 March 2007).

nation's sense of cohesion because it emphasises what divides us rather than what brings us together. The tenets of multiculturalism have been manipulated 'to favour a divisive idea – the right to difference … instead of promoting a unifying idea – the right of everyone to be treated equally despite their differences'. In a direct reference to John Reid, Home Secretary, and Gordon Brown, Chancellor of the Exchequer, both of which have actively championed the notion of Britishness, Cameron has asserted that 'We can't bully people into feeling British – we have to inspire them' (Cameron 2007; Hinsliff and Doward 2007).[30] In the same vein, David Davis, Shadow Home Secretary, has branded the country's traditional approach to multiculturalism as being 'outdated'. Britain, he explains, 'has pursued a policy of multiculturalism – allowing people of different cultures to settle without expecting them to integrate into society … Often the authorities have seemed more concerned with encouraging distinctive identities than with promoting common values of nationhood' (ePolitix 2005).[31]

The leadership of the Church of England has similarly raised concerns about the pernicious effects of multiculturalism on British society: a society built on Christian values and traditions and whose citizenships remain overwhelmingly so. Here, multiculturalism is seen as diluting the fundamental character of our nation and the Christian morality which is integral to it. Notably, it is the Church of England's only Asian Bishop who has become the most prominent critic of multiculturalism. The Rt Rev Dr Michael Nazir-Ali, Bishop of Rochester, has publicly expressed his reservations regarding the emphasis on minority ethnic cultures and traditions at the expense of the majority Christian heritage and faith. He is particularly alarmed at the Prince of Wales' assertion that on his coronation, he hopes to be known as 'Defender of Faith' as opposed to 'Defender of the [Protestant] Faith'; as well as the failure of Ruth Kelly, Communities Secretary, to allow representation of Christian churches on the newly formed Commission on Integration and Social Cohesion (Gledhill, 2006).[32] During the course of the 'veil row', Dr Nazir-Ali stated that 'I can see nothing in Islam that prescribes the wearing of a full-face veil' (Gledhill, 2006). As the Church's acknowledged authority on Islam – and a convert from Islam himself, the Bishop has furthermore denounced what he perceives as the displaying of double standards by the Muslim community – the largest non-Christian faith group in Britain. British Muslims, he argues, actively promote the idea of 'victimhood' as a persecuted minority within the UK, while at the same time seeking ideological domination by turning a blind eye to their own role in the rise of home-grown Islamic extremism. He has gone as far as to say that 'Their [Muslims] complaint often boils down to the position that it is always right to intervene when Muslims are victims, as in Bosnia

---

30 Cameron, D., MP (2007), Speech by the Leader of the Opposition, 'Bringing Down the Barriers to Cohesion', Conservatives, <http://www.conservatives.com/tile.do?def=news.story.page&obj_id=134759> (accessed 19 March 2007).

31 ePolitix (2005), 'Davis warns on "Outdated Multiculturalism"', ePolitix, <http://www.epolitix.com/EN/Bulletins/PressReview/Items/200508/604f7c4c-64f8-478> (accessed 28 February 2007).

32 Gledhill, R. 'Bishop accuses Muslims of having Victim Complex', *The Times*, 6 November 2006 <http://www.timesonline.co.uk/tol/news/uk/article626214.ece> (accessed on 28 March 2007).

or Kosovo, and always wrong when the Muslims are the oppressors or terrorists, as with the Taleban or in Iraq' (Gledhill, 2006).

Towards Integration   Against a background of shitting public attitudes regarding the state of multiculturalism and nationhood in Britain, a recent bespoke study for the Commission for Racial Equality (CRE) threw some light into the changes taking place. The 'Britishness' in the Last Three General Elections: from Ethnic to Civic Nationalism report charts the way in which UK politicians and the press depicted the issue of 'Britishness' during the country's past three national electoral polls (i.e. 1997 to 2005) (Billig et al. 2006a).[33] Given an increased public focus on issues such as race, religion, asylum and migration; political parties across the board were found to have used the language of nationhood as a campaign tool. As the authors of the report remind us, such language matters, for it reveals much about evolving public perceptions of our own sense of identity and the kind of society we ultimately whish to live in (Billig et al. 2006a, 6).

The last election in particular threw up a seemingly bewildering situation regarding the national question, with both main party leaders keen to portray themselves as being tough on migration, while at the same time, stressing the value of multiculturalism. Such combination of softness and toughness was arguably designed to appeal simultaneously to 'xenophobic fears and tolerant inclinations' (Billig et al. 2006b).[34] As Labour appropriated the language of patriotism, there has been a noticeable move from so-called ethnic nationalism to civic nationalism. According to the report:

> Civic nationalism contains a number of features: it embraces the idea of multiculturalism; it distances itself from old-style racism; it depicts the nation as based on shared values, not shared ethnicity. However, the discourse of civic nationalism is not straightforward. It allows the behaviour of ethnic groups to be criticised on the basis of the values the members supposedly have rather than on the basis of their ethnicity (Billig et al. 2006a, 4).

Despite its seemingly multicultural and inclusive credentials, civic nationalism fundamentally remains a form of nationalism; one that ultimately gives priority to 'us' and our values over those of 'others' (Billig et al. 2006a, 95). This ambiguous mixture of tolerance and jingoism has allowed the civic nationalist discourse to create 'new outsiders', that is, those who do not share 'our' values as opposed to 'our' ethnicity. Treatment of the Muslim question at the last election clearly illustrates this point:

---

33 Billig, M., J. Downey, J. Richardson, D. Deacon and P. Golding (2006a), *'Britishness' in the Last Three General Elections: from Ethnic to Civic Nationalism*, Report for the Commission for Racial Equality from Loughborough Centre for Communication Research (Loughborough: Loughborough University).

34 Billig, M., D. Deacon, J. Downey, J. Richardson and P. Golding (2006b), 'Chilly Britannia', *Catalyst* <http://www.catalystmagazine.org/Default.aspx.LocID-0hgnew0ed. RefLocID-0hg01b001006002.Lang-EN.htm> (accessed 23 June 2007).

During the 2005 election, scares about migration and asylum seekers were more prominent than during the two previous elections. So were fears about 'Muslim extremists'. One of our most dramatic findings was based on a simple word count. The terms 'Muslim' and 'Islam' hardly appeared in press reports in 1997 and 2001, but were frequently used in 2005. The riots in Oldham and other Lancashire towns occurred at the same time as the 2001 campaign. The press invariably called the rioters 'young Asians', making no mention of their religious affiliation. Four years on, it was clear that there had been a huge discursive shift. Were the riots to occur now, it would be unthinkable that the rioters would not be labelled 'young Muslims', and that the press would not worry about the role of 'Islamic fundamentalism' in fomenting civil strife (Billig 2006b).

It is against this backdrop that Prime Minister Tony Blair recently articulated his government's vision of a diverse, multicultural, yet socially cohesive British society in a speech ominously entitled 'The Duty to Integrate: Shared British Values' (Blair 2006).[35] Delivered in December 2006, the lecture saw the Prime Minister tread a difficult path between expressing his government's commitment to the realisation of a modern British multicultural ideal, while at the same time stating its unqualified belief in the need to achieve community integration and social cohesion. In an impassioned defence of our civic society's 'essential values' – namely, the rule of law, tolerance, equal treatment for all and respect for this country and its shared heritage, the Prime Minister referred to these key principles shared by all British citizens as 'the glue that binds our nation together'. As he put it, they are 'what gives us the right to call ourselves British' and at that point, 'no distinctive culture or religion supersedes our duty to be part of an integrated United Kingdom' (Blair 2006). Blair justified his call to 'go back to what a multicultural Britain is all about' by allusion to the threat posed to our national unity from international terrorism and home-grown Islamic extremism as well as the challenges accompanying increased migration within a globalised world.

To those who argue for the need to dispense with multicultural Britain, the Prime Minister's response is, on the contrary, to 'continue celebrating it'; but in the face of the challenge to our values, he suggests 'to reassert also the duty to integrate, to stress what we hold in common and to say: these are the shared boundaries within which we are all obliged to live, precisely in order to preserve our right to our own different faiths, races and creeds' (Blair 2006). Blair went on to list six main areas of public policy in which intervention is needed in order to transform this vision into reality including: firstly, the provision of grants to communities promoting integration and cultural diversity; secondly, a firm public standing on equality, respect and equal treatment for all citizens at all times; thirdly, universal allegiance to the rule of law; fourthly, nurturing of home-grown community preachers and monitoring of their overseas visiting fellows; fifthly, establishing a set of rights and responsibilities inherent to British citizenship and inculcating them to the younger generation through the school curriculum; and sixthly, setting the use of English language as a condition of citizenship.

---

35 Blair, T., PM (2006) Speech by the Prime Minister, 'The Duty to Integrate: Shared British Values', Number – 10 <http://www.number-10.gov.uk/output/Page10563.asp> (accessed 27 February 2007).

The Prime Minister's words were echoed both by the Chancellor of the Exchequer and the Home Secretary, among other Cabinet members. Brown, in particular, has repeatedly made the case for 'Britishness' by alluding to our shared values, a belief in liberty and civil duty, and an internationalism founded on these values (Brown 2006a).[36] Speaking recently at the Fabian Society, the Chancellor reflected on the importance of promoting those civic values that bind us together, while also recognising the need to reconcile the individual and collective spheres of our social life:

> I would argue that if we are clear about what underlies our Britishness and if we are clear that shared values – not colour, nor unchanging and unchangeable institutions – define what it means to be British in the modern world, we can be far more ambitious in defining for our time the responsibilities of citizenship; far more ambitious in forging a new and contemporary settlement of the relationship between state, community and individual; and it is also easier too to address difficult issues that sometimes come under the heading 'multiculturalism' – essentially how diverse cultures, which inevitably contain differences, can find the essential common purpose without which no society can flourish (Brown 2006b).

Straw, whose comments regarding the wearing of the veil by Muslim women – as a 'visible statement of separation and of difference' – sparked the wider public discussion on community integration, has called for a 'frank debate' on the state of our society to be had. In line with his Cabinet colleagues, he has stressed the need for a 'stronger sense of shared British identity' among ethnic groups and a commitment to fully embracing 'common values' and a 'common language'. As he indicated, 'Simply breathing the same air as other members of society isn't integration' (BBC 2006a).[37]

This orchestrated governmental push towards integration, which has recently seen calls for a national 'Britain Day' as a way of strengthening our collective sense of Britishness (Kelly and Byrne 2007),[38] has now culminated in the publication of the eagerly awaited final report of the Commission on Integration and Cohesion. A body originally set up by Ruth Kelly, Communities and Local Government Secretary, in the aftermath of the London bombings of July 2005. At the time, the Commission was charged with exploring existing barriers to integration and cohesion at community level, whilst suggesting local and practical interventions that would allow for such obstacles to be overcome; in particular the prevention

---

36 Brown, G., MP (2006a) Speech by the Chancellor of the Exchequer, 'Stronger Together, Weaker Apart', Scottish Labour <http://www.scottishlabour.org.uk/brownspeechsept2006/?print=friendly&searchword=> (accessed 28 February 2007). Brown, G., MP (2006b) Speech by the Chancellor of the Exchequer, 'The Future of Britishness', Fabian Society <http://fabians.org.uk/events/new-year-conference-06/brown-britishness/speech>(accessed 23 February 2007).

37 BBC (2006a) 'Muslims must feel British – Straw', BBC News <http://newsvote.bbc.co.uk/mpapps/pagetools/print/news.bbc.co.uk/1/hi/uk_politics/61> (accessed 28 February 2007).

38 Kelly, R. and L. Bryne (2007), 'A Common Place' – Fabian Society Pamphlet (London: Fabian Society).

of tensions resulting from segregation and the dissemination of radical ideologies. On the occasion of the Commission's launch, the Communities Secretary reiterated the urgency of promoting national unity in an increasingly diverse and seemingly fragmented British society:

> I believe that Britain's diversity is a huge asset to our country – economically, culturally and socially ... And I believe that we should celebrate and clearly articulate the benefits that migration and diversity have brought – but while celebrating that diversity we should also recognise that the landscape is changing, changing rapidly. And we should not shy away from asking – and trying to respond to – some of the more difficult questions that arise. I believe it is time now to engage in a new and honest debate about integration and cohesion in the UK. If we are to have an effective, progressive response to these issues, then we must be honest about the challenges we face and be prepared to meet these head on with renewed energy and impetus (Communities and Local Government 2006).[39]

In response to Kelly's call for a new approach to integration and cohesion, Darra Singh, Chair of the Commission, reflected on the scale of the task ahead:

> A past built on difference, a future which is shared. As a Commission our vision of society is one where people are committed to what we have in common rather than obsessing with those things that makes us different ... Integration and cohesion is no longer as special programme or project. It is also not about race, faith or other forms of group status or identity. It is simple about how we all get on and secure benefits that are mutually desirable for our communities and ourselves (Commission on Integration and Cohesion 2006, 3–5).[40]

The Commission's final report, *Our Shared Future*, goes on to provide a blueprint for the implementation of the government's integration strategy. It therefore contains a wide-ranging set of recommendations aimed at addressing the challenges to cohesion and integration faced by the country both at local level and within the context of an overarching national framework (Commission on Integration and Cohesion 2007). As a starting point, *Our Shared Future* suggests a definition of social cohesion and integration as two interlinked, yet distinct processes:

> Cohesion is principally the process that must happen in all communities to ensure different groups of people get on well together; while integration is principally the process that ensures new residents and existing residents adapt to one another (Commission on Integration and Cohesion 2007, 38).

Understanding cohesion and integration as two interlocking concepts, appears here as a prerequisite to developing effective local interventions that would enable communities to peacefully coexist and thrive as part of the wider British nation.

---

39 Communities and Local Government (2006), 'Launch of the Commission on Integration and Cohesion', Speech by Ruth Kelly MP at the launch on the new Commission on Integration and Cohesion on 24 August 2006 <http://www.communities.gov.uk/index.asp?id=1502280> (accessed 16 June 2007).

40 Commission on Integration and Cohesion (2007), *Our Shared Future* (West Yorkshire: Commission on Integration and Cohesion), 3–5.

To this end, the report considers a number of key areas of intervention including, a stronger focus on citizenship, a revitalised role for Local Authorities with support from national government and an overhaul of English language training and translation services. Among the many recommendations to emerge, the following eight are particularly central to the government's overall strategy: firstly, the development of a 'shared national vision' including a clear statement from central government of integration and cohesion policy. Secondly, crucial to that vision is a 'commitment to a shared language as being fundamental to integration and cohesion – for settled communities, new communities and future generations of immigrants' (Commission on Integration and Cohesion 2007, 72). The Commission consequently proposes a review of English language learning and training schemes, so as to maximise its use among non-English speaking migrants. Here, mastery of English is understood as a key socio-economic tool and thus to be considered and promoted as such both by educationalists and employers alike. Within this context, readily available translations of official informative materials into community languages are to be discouraged in favour of English-only formats:

> English is both an important part of our shared heritage, and a key access factor for new communities to the labour market and wider society. It binds us together as a single group in a way that a multiplicity of community languages cannot – hence our proposal ... that translation into those community languages should not always be first approach (Commission on Integration and Cohesion 2007, 73).

The report indeed recommends that Local Authorities and their partners move from a position of 'automatic translation' of all documents into community languages, towards a more selective, needs-driven approach set within the context of their overall communications strategy for the entire resident population. In addition to a change in mindsets, the report suggests transferring the monies saved from translation of written materials into the funding pot available for English lessons.

Thirdly, the Commission also proposes the implementation of a 'national shared futures campaign' to enable government to make an open case for the sort of integrated society we want to live in. Fourthly, stressing further the need to inculcate respect for individual rights and responsibilities among the country's population; as the report indicates:

> Our proposal is that we use integration and cohesion policy to generate a working sense of citizenship that is based on a set of rights and responsibilities appropriate for the changing UK of the 21st century, and one that chimes at a national as well as local level (Commission on Integration and Cohesion 2007, 62).

Fifthly, the promotion of strong local leadership together with the revival of local democracy; both of which are seen as central to achieving positive change at the grassroots level. Sixthly, the provision of access to information and guidance to newcomers, in the shape of 'welcome packs for all new immigrants'; too often lacking in such support mechanisms on arrival. Seventhly, the development of working partnerships between Local Authorities, voluntary, community and faith groups who are to play a central role in delivering a 'cultural debriefing' to new migrants

– including, information on how local communities operate, in particular, their unwritten social rules, etiquette and protocols; welcoming and helping communities in transition by addressing isolation and alienation; as well as providing reassurance and mediation at times of conflict and crisis. Employers are also called upon to take responsibility for addressing the needs of their migrant workers and facilitating their absorption into society. It is within this context that a 'new integration and cohesion forum for employers' to be coordinated by the Confederation of British Industries (CBI) and the new Commission for Equality and Human Rights (CEHR) is being put forward. Finally, underlying the reports' recommendations is the proposed creation of a national body to manage the integration of new migrants, sponsored by Communities and Local Government, but independent from government. The later may perhaps be modelled on the existing Advisory Board on Naturalisation and Integration (ABNI), supported by the Home Office.

Against a backdrop of escalating government interventions designed to reassert our collective sense of Britishness and nationhood, *Our Shared Future* must undoubtedly be seen as a milestone. A far-reaching blueprint for government action, which clearly sets out the strategic direction to follow and the practical steps to be taken in order to realise its vision of a socially cohesive and integrated British society. As part of this process though, our previous commitment to multiculturalism seems to have been all but abandoned. The Communities Secretary indeed reminds us that 'we have moved from a period of uniform consensus on the value of multiculturalism, to one where we can encourage that debate by questioning whether it is encouraging separateness' (Communities and Local Government 2006). Such observation together with the actions of the British government seem to reaffirm Isin and Turner's belief that 'multiculturalism is crisis, because most liberal governments are retreating from open commitment to cultural diversity, emphasising instead security, cohesion and integration (Isin and Turner 2007, 11).[41]

International Multicultural Perspectives The current move away from multiculturalism and towards integration in Britain must be understood against the backdrop of other multicultural models elsewhere. The perceived failures of our particular brand of multiculturalism are often arrived at by comparison to other country's multicultural strategies, in particular, those of the former British settler societies of Canada, the USA, Australia and New Zealand. While in all of these countries, including Britain herself, there have been countless commissions, task forces and ad hoc committees on multiculturalism, Canada's has gone further than any of them by actually enacting a Multiculturalism Act, thus enshrining into law the Canadian nation's dominant multicultural ideology (Department of Justice Canada 2007).[42] In 1971, Canada indeed became the first country in the world to adopt an official Multiculturalism Policy. This policy provided for programs and

---

41 Isin, E.F. and B.S. Turner (2007), 'Investigating Citizenship: An Agenda for Citizenship Studies', *Citizenship Studies*, 11:1, 5–17.

42 Department of Justice Canada (2007), *Canadian Multiculturalism Act, 1985*, Department of Justice Canada <http://laws.justice.gc.ca/en/ShowFullDoc/cs/c-18.7///en> (accessed 14 March 2007).

services to support ethno-cultural associations, while helping individuals overcome barriers to their full participation in Canadian society. In 1982, the multicultural character of Canada gained constitutional recognition in Section 27 of the newly adopted Canadian Charter of Rights and Freedoms. This postulate specified that the courts were to interpret the Charter 'in a manner consistent with the preservation and enhancement of the multicultural heritage of Canada'. By virtue of this section of the Charter, Canada became a constitutional multicultural state (Canadian Heritage 2007).[43] Given the multi-ethnic nature of Canadian society, the country's approach to diversity is frequently seen as an aspirational multicultural model; one that has already achieved a shift in institutional mindsets, while delivering enhanced social cohesion on the ground. Banton has argued that the presence of such an official Multiculturalism Act has worked well in the Canadian context, providing both 'an official endorsement of the need for this sort of institutional rethinking' as well as some 'financial and intellectual support for institutions to do so' (Banton 2000, 727).[44]

In contrast with the Canadian experience, a single national vision of multiculturalism has so far eluded the decentralised North American federal system. As a result, the process of institutional reform has mostly been carried out arbitrarily, with some institutions having gone through intensive rethinking and change, whereas others have barely started (Banton 2000, 727). In its long march towards multiculturalism though, US civil society seems largely committed to achieving the ideal of a diverse and inclusive state. Whereas in the past Americans sought to assimilate migrant communities into the US collective, they have now turned to multiculturalism; as Glazer has put it 'we are all multiculturalists now' (Glazer 1997).[45]

As a relatively new nation made up of settlers from all over the world as well as indigenous people, the North American experience provides some similarities with another young multicultural state, namely: Australia. This southerner country, however, has arguably encountered special problems in defining its identity and culture, and thus devising appropriate political institutions to deal with them. Castles points out that Australian society, where large scale migration since 1945 led to profound demographic and cultural changes, is still fundamentally based on the model of the 'nation-state' as it emerged in Western Europe and North American from the eighteenth century onwards. This model implies ethno-cultural homogenisation of the population (Castles 2000).[46] As a result, notwithstanding Australian social policies underlining a wider notion of 'multicultural citizenship'; they appear mostly

43 Canadian Heritage (2007) 'Multiculturalism – Canadian Diversity, Respecting our Differences', Canadian Heritage <http://www.pch.gc.ca/progs/multi/respect_e.cfm> (accessed 14 March 2007).

44 Banton, M. (2000) 'A UK Perspective', *Journal of Ethnic and Migration Studies*, 26: 4, 719–38.

45 Glazer, N. (1997), *We are All Multiculturalists Now* (London: Harvard University Press).

46 Castles, S. (2000), *Ethnicity and Globalisation: From Migrant Worker to Transnational Citizen* (Oxford: Sage Publications).

concerned with facilitating migrant settlements whilst avoiding community tensions (Castles 2000).

The European Union, which by its very nature epitomises a multicultural ideal, has long pursued socio-economic and educational policies aimed at transforming such an aspiration into tangible results on the ground. The reality of multiculturalism for individual member states however, has not followed progress at the supra-national European level. This unresolved dichotomy between the central European state and its individual constituent members is at the core of the inevitably flawed European multicultural model. Steenbergen et al. have argued that at both the European and individual society level 'we find tendencies towards *fusion*, convergence or integration, and *fission*, divergence or differentiation' (Steenbergen et al. 1999, 1).[47] These two seemingly contradictory tendencies of integration and disintegration occur simultaneously within the ever growing European family. While the process of European integration can mostly be found at the federal system level, the process of differentiation or disintegration is dominated by the individual social level. As Steenbergen et al. explain, 'these disintegrative tendencies are specially pronounced around ethnic conflict, racism and nationalism, on the one hand, and around social exclusion derived from unemployment and poverty, on the other hand'. (Steenbergen et al. 1999, 1). Sweden provides a case in point. While state institutions here proclaim to seek a multicultural ideology, multi-ethnic neighborhoods are increasingly becoming segregated from those almost exclusively inhabited by white indigenous Swedes. Living in a multi-ethnic neighborhood, Bjurström explains, becomes associated with low socio-economic status, welfare dependency and high rates of crimes. Consequently, differences in terms of ethnicity in the Swedish population tend to equate with differences in terms of social class (Bjurström 2004).[48]

A final instance of emerging multicultural models is to be found in the young post-colonial nations of South East Asia. Following independence, most newly formed states focused their efforts in consolidating themselves as 'unitary and homogenising nation-states'; multicultural institutional models were therefore largely discouraged. Such nationalistic tendencies often resulted in armed ethnic minority-led resistance and secession movements across the region, notably in countries such as India, Pakistan, China, Burma, Indonesia and the Philippines to name a few. Today, South East Asian states have come to recognise the need to accommodate their increasingly diverse populations, if their civil societies are to endure. Through South East Asia, Kymlicka and He observe, countries are now developing multicultural policy models, 'from the recognition of indigenous rights in the Philippines to regional autonomy in Indonesia and China, to multinational federalism in Sri Lanka and

---

47 Steenbergen, B.V, B.V. Steenderen, T.P. Boje and S. Walby (eds) (1999), *European Societies: Fusion or Fission?* (London: Routledge).

48 Bjurström, E. (2004), 'Multiculturalism and Youth Culture: The Construction of Ethnic Identity in Youth Styles', paper presented at the Youth, Ethnic Identity and the Future of Multiculturalism in Europe Seminar held at the Centre for Research on Nationalism, Ethnicity and Multiculturalism (CRONEM), University of Surrey, 21 July 2004 <http://www.surrey.ac.uk/Arts/CRONEM/seminar-04-07-21-CRONEM-BSA-abstracts.htm#Bjurström> (accessed 15 March 2007).

India' (Kymlicka and He 2005, 1).[49] Multiculturalism is now widely seen as a key ingredient in any process of democratisation and state development in the region. The Malaysian experience, which like many of its regional counterparts 'exhibits and interesting and unique mix of Western influences and local accommodations', is one such cases (Ganesan 2005, 136).[50] A former British colony, the federal state of Malaysia nowadays practices a form of 'consociational democracy', which involves the 'elite accommodation of minority ethnic groups within the framework of political parties and coalition governments'; as a result, minority rights at individual level are constitutionally guaranteed (Ganesan 2005, 136). In the last three decades, political and economic developments have significantly empowered the Malay-Muslim community, which comprises almost two-thirds of the entire population. Despite the presence of such an ethno-religious dominant group though, the ruling coalition government has consistently articulated its desire to protect the country's minority groups (Ganesan 2005, 136).

Conclusion

During the past hundred years, the notion of Britishness has been endlessly debated, constructed and deconstructed; with scholars, stakeholders and policy-makers seeking to unravel the meaning of this complex idea and the values underlying it. As part of this process, successive generations of British citizens have gone on to articulate their particular interpretations of our national identity through a series of evolving and often contrasting public narratives.

Like a pendulum swinging under the influence of gravity, public perceptions of British identity and the values they espouse have fluctuated over time. They have evolved from a discourse of *Laissez-faire* at the beginning of the twentieth century that took for granted the prevailing white Anglo-Saxon *status quo*, to one of multiculturalism in later years, which aimed to accommodate the socio-economic and linguistic needs of our rapidly growing minority ethnic population. Nowadays, in the midst of unprecedented migration influxes, fears of cultural fragmentation, the threat of international terrorism and the advent of English language globalisation, we seem to have come full circle. The current integrationist discourse is intent on reasserting our national identity by rediscovering those common values and traits that so came to define Britishness at the turn of the twentieth century, namely: the English language, Britain's national institutions and cultural heritage as well as our country's long tradition of democratic and civil liberties. Echoes from the past do indeed reverberate today.

Speaking in the summer of 1896, The Right Rev. Mandel Creighton, Lord Bishop of Peterborough, reflected on how a nation's character essentially remains the abiding product of its past, traditions and the spirit which moulded the country over time.

---

49 Kymlicka, W. and B. He (eds) (2005), *Multiculturalism in Asia* (Oxford: Oxford University Press).

50 Ganesan, N. (2005), 'Liberal and Structural Ethnic Political Accommodation, in Malaysia', W. Kymlicka and B. He (eds) *Multiculturalism in Asia* (Oxford: Oxford University Press).

Here, the individual citizen becomes the embodiment of all those influences 'as if the ultimate test of their value'. Key to a nation's identity, he explained, are those common traits shared by its citizenry that set them, and their homeland, apart from other nation-states; as the Bishop put it:

> In fact, nations, as we conceive them, are founded upon a consciousness of common interests and ideas, which are the result of a long and complicated experience. That consciousness separates them from other nations who do not share those interests, and are consequently termed as foreigners (Creighton 1896, 8–9).[51]

In December 2006, Prime Minister Blair outlined in similar terms his government's understanding of our country's unique character as well as the nature of those common interests and fundamental values that so define the British nation and its citizens:

> when it comes to our essential values – belief in democracy, the rule of law, tolerance, equal treatment of all, respect for this country and its shared heritage – then that is where we come together, it is what we hold in common; it is what gives us the right to call ourselves British. At that point, no distinctive culture or religion supersedes our duty to be part of an integrated United Kingdom (Blair 2006).[52]

At the dawn of the twentieth first century, the accelerated transformation of Britain into a modern multicultural, multiethnic and multifaith society has brought into sharp focus the difficulties inherent in living with diversity and difference at an individual level, while at the same time nurturing a collective sense of citizenship and nationhood. In trying to square this particular circle, the government of the day has articulated a contemporary vision of British citizenship, which paradoxically has striking similarities to that in vogue over a hundred years ago. Despite socio-economic and ethno-linguistic projections pointing towards a continuation of this trend, the future shape of our national identity is ultimately anybody's guess. One certainty remains though: in a hundred years from now, our descendants will still be grappling with this fascinating, yet elusive concept. Defining British identity will long continue to be the subject of much debate. Questions such as what does it mean to be British? Which values does Britishness enshrine? Is the English language an integral part of our national identity? will invariably generate strong views and lengthy academic discussions. It is nevertheless unlikely that they will yield many satisfying answers.

---

51 Creighton, M.D.D., The Right Rev., Lord Bishop of Peterborough and Honorary Fellow of Merton College, Oxford, 'The English National Character', The Romanes Lecture, delivered in the Sheldonian Theatre, 17 June 1896, (London: Henry Frowde, Amen Corner, E.C.), 8–9.

52 Blair, T., PM (2006), Speech by Prime Minister Tony Blair, 'The Duty to Integrate: Shared British Values', 8 December 2006 <http://www.pm.gov.uk/output/Page10563.asp> (accessed 4 January 2007).

Bibliography

Books

Aldrich, R. and P. Leighton (1985), *Education: Time for a New Act* (London: Institute of Education).

Allen, I.L. (1983), *The Language of Ethnic Conflict: Social Classifications and Lexical Culture* (New York: Columbia University Press).

Andersson, T. and M. Boyer (1970), *Bilingual Education Learning in the United States,* Vol. 2 (Austin, Texas: Southwest Educational Development Laboratory).

Andrian, C. (1989), *Children and Civic Awareness: A Study in Political Education* (Columbus, Ohio: Merrill).

Arditis, Solon (ed.) (1994), *The Politics of East-West Migration* (New York: St. Martin's Press).

Armitage, D. (2000), *The Ideological Origins of the British Empire* (Cambridge: Cambridge University Press).

Ashmore, H. (1954), *The Negro and The Schools* (Chapel Hill: University of North Carolina Press).

August, D., K. Hakuta and Board on Children, Youth and Families (U.S.), Committee on Developing a Research Agenda on the Education of Limited-English-Proficient and Bilingual Students (1998), *Educating Language-minority Children: A Research Agenda* (Washington, DC: National Academy Press).

Baker, C. (1985), *Aspects of Bilingualism in Wales* (Clevendon, PA: Multilingual Matters).

Baker, C. (1988), *Key Issues in Bilingualism and Bilingual Education* (Clevendon, PA: Multilingual Matters).

Baker, C. (2001), *Foundations of Bilingual Education and Bilingualism* (Clevendon, PA: Multilingual Matters).

Baker, C. and N. Hornberger (eds) (2001), *An Introductory Reader to the Writings of Jim Cummins* (Clevendon, PA: Multilingual Matters).

Baker, C. and S.P. Jones (eds) (1998), *Encyclopedia of Bilingualism and Bilingual Education* (Clevendon, PA: Multilingual Matters).

Baker, P. and J. Eversley (eds) (2000), *Multilingual Capital: the Languages of London's School Children and their Relevance to Economic, Social and Educational Policies* (London: Battlebridge).

Baldwin-Edwards, M. and M.A. Schain (eds) (1994), *The Politics of Immigration in Western Europe* (Essex: Frank Cass).

Banton, M. (1972), *Racial Minorities* (London: Collins).

Banton, M. (1997), *Ethnic and Racial Consciousness,* second edn. (Harlow: Longman).

Banton, M. (1998), *Racial Theories,* second edn. (Cambridge: Cambridge University Press).

Barth, F. (1969), *Ethnic Groups and Boundaries* (Boston: Little Brown).

Bartlett, R. (1993), *The Making of Europe* (Harmondsworth: Penguin).

Baugh A.C. and T. Cable (1978), *History of the English Language,* third edn. (London: Routledge and Paul Kegan).

Bauman, G. (1999), *The Multicultural Riddle* (London: Routledge).

Beauchamp, T.L., R.R. Faden, R.J. Wallance and L. Walters (eds) (1982), *Ethical Issues in Social Science Research* (Baltimore, MD: Johns Hopkins University Press).

Beider, F. (ed.) (1998), *Let's Go USA 1998* (London: Macmillan).

Bell, T.H. (1982), *The Condition of Bilingual Education in the Nation* (Washington, DC: Department for Education).

Berdichevsky, N. (2004), *Nations, Language and Citizenship* (London: McFarland and Company, Inc., Publishers).

Bernard, H.R. (2000), *Social Research Methods: Qualitative and Quantitative Approaches* (Thousand Oaks, CA: Sage Publications).

Bienstock, H. (1968), *Labour Force Experience of the Puerto Rican Worker* (New York: New York University School of Social Work).

Borjas, G.I. (1990), *Friends of Strangers? The Impact of Immigrants in the US Economy* (New York: Basic Books).

Bourne, J. (1989), *Moving into the Mainstream: LEA Provision for Bilingual Pupils* (Windsor: NFER-Nelson).

British Refugee Council (BRC) (1985), *Refugee Advisers' Handbook* (London: BRC).

Briggs, V. (1993), *Mass Immigration and the National Interest* (New York: Sharpe).

Brown, C. (1984), *Black and White Britain: the Third PSI Survey* (London: Heineman Educational).

Brutt-Griffler, J. (2002), *World English: A Study of its Development* (Clevendon: Multilingual Matters).

Bulmer, M. (ed.) (1982), *Social Research Ethics: an Examination of the Merits of Covert Participant Observation* (London: Macmillan).

Burnley, D. (1992), *The History of English Language: A Source Book* (London: Longman).

Butler, R.A. (1966), *The Education Act of 1944 and After* (London: Longman).

Byram, M. and J. Leman (1990), *Bicultural and Trilingual Education* (Clevendon, PA: Multilingual Matters).

Callaham, D. and B. Jennings (eds) (1983), *Ethnics, the Social Sciences and Policy Analysis* (London: Plenum).

Carr, R. (1984), *Puerto Rico: A Colonial Experiment* (New York: New York University Press).

Castellanos, D. and P. Leggio (1983), *The Best of Two Worlds: Bilingual-Bicultural Education in the US* (Trenton, NJ: New Jersey State Department for Education).

Castles, S. (2000), *Ethnicity and Globalisation: From Migrant Worker to Transnational Citizen* (Oxford: Sage Publications).

Castles, S. and M.J. Miller (1993), *The Age of Migration: International Population Movements in the Modern World* (Basingstoke: Macmillan Press Ltd.).

Chesire, J. (ed.) (1991), *English Around the World: Sociolinguistic Perspectives* (Cambridge: Cambridge University Press).

Chiswick, B. (ed.) (1992), *Immigration, Language and Ethnicity: Canada and the United States* (Washington, DC: AEI Press).

Churchill, S. (1986), *The Education of Linguistic and Cultural Minorities in the OECD Countries* (Clevendon: Multilingual Matters).

Cohen, R. (1987), *The New Helots: Migrants in the International Division of Labour*, Research in Ethnic Relations Series (London: Avebury).

Cohen, R. (1994), *Frontiers of Identity: the British and Others* (London: Longman).

Cohen, R. (ed.) (1995), *The Cambridge Survey of World Migration* (Cambridge: Cambridge University Press).

Coleman, D.A. (ed.) (1982), *Demography of Immigrants and Minority Groups in the United Kingdom* (London: Academic Press).

Coleman, D. and J. Salt (eds) (1996), *Ethnicity in the 1991 Census: Demographic Characteristics of the Ethnic Minority Populations*, Office of Population Censuses and Surveys, Vol. 1 (London: HMSO).

Colley, L. (1994), *Britons: Forging the Nation, 1707–1837* (London: Pimlico).

Collins Concise English Dictionary (1995), third edn. (Glasgow: Harper Collins Publishers).

Collinsom, S. (1993), *Europe and International Migration* (London: Royal Institute of International Affairs).

Connolloy, P. and B. Troyna (eds) (1998), *Researching Racism in Education: Politics, Theory and Practice* (Buckingham: Open University Press).

Cooper, J.E., R.E. Kendell, B.J. Gurland, L. Sharpe, J.R.M. Copeland and R. Simon (1972), *Psychiatric Diagnosis in New York and London: A Comparative Study of Mental Hospital Admissions* (London: Oxford University Press).

Cooper, R.L. (1989), *Language Planning and Social Change* (New York: Cambridge University Press).

Cox, B. (1991), *Cox on Cox: An English Curriculum for the 1990s* (London: Hodder and Soughton).

Coxall, B. and L. Robins (1998), *Contemporary British Politics,* third edn. (London: Macmillan Press Ltd.).

Crawford, J. (1992), *Hold Your Tongue: Bilingualism and the Politics of 'English Only'* (Teading, MA: Adison-Wesley).

Crawford, J. (ed.) (1992), *Language Loyalties: A Source Book on the Official English Controversy* (Chicago: The University of Chicago Press).

Crawford, J. (1995), *Bilingual Education: History, Politics, Theory and Practice* (Los Angeles: Bilingual Education Services).

Crawford, J. (2000), *At War with Diversity: US Language Policy in an Age of Anxiety* (Clevendon, PA: Multilingual Matters Ltd.).

Crystal, D. (1987), *Cambridge Encyclopaedia of Language* (Cambridge: Cambridge University Press).

Crystal, D. (1992), *An Encyclopaedic Dictionary of Language and Languages* (Oxford: Blackwell).

Crystal, D. (1997), *English as a Global Language* (Cambridge: Cambridge University Press).

Crystal, D. (2003), *English as a Global Language*, second edition (Cambridge: Cambridge University Press).

Cummins, J. (1986), *Bilingualism in Education: Aspects of Theory, Research and Practice* (London: Longman).

Cummins, J. (1996), *Negotiating Identities: Education for Empowerment in a Diverse Society* (Ontario, CA: California Association of Bilingual Education).

Cummins, J. (2000), *Language, Power and Pedagogy: Bilingual Children in the Crossfire* (Clevendon, PA: Multilingual Matters).

Cummins, J. and M. Danesi (1990), *Heritage Languages: the Development and Denial of Canada's Linguistic Resources* (Toronto: Garamond).

Davies, H., S. Nutley and P. Smith (2000), *What Works? Evidence-based Policy and Practice in Public Services* (London: Policy Press).

De Vaus, D.A. (1996), *Surveys in Social Research*, third edn. (London: Unwin Hyman).

Dent, H.C. (1955), *The Education Act 1944: Provisions, Regulations, Circulars and Later Acts*, fifth edn. (London: University of London Press Ltd.).

Denzin, N.K. and Y.S. Lincoln (eds) (1998), *The Landscape of Qualitative Research: Theories and Issues* (Thousand Oaks, CA: Sage Publications).

Denzin, N.K. and Y.S. Lincoln (eds) (2000), *Handbook of Qualitative Research*, second edn. (London: Sage).

Edmonston, B. and J.S. Passel (eds) (1994), *Immigration and Ethnicity: the Integration of America's Newest Arrivals* (Washington, DC: The Urban Institute Press).

Edwards, J. (1995), *Multilingualism* (London: Penguin Books).

Eggington, W. and H. Wren (eds) (1997), *Language Policy: Dominant English, Pluralistic Challenges* (Philadelphia: John Benjamins Publishing Company).

Encyclopaedia Britannica Year Book 1996 (1996), (Chicago: Encyclopaedia Britannica).

Engman, M. (ed.) (1992), *Ethnic Identity in Urban Europe: Comparative Studies on Governments and Non-dominant Ethnic Groups in Europe, 1850–1940*, Vol. 8 (New York: New York University Press).

Eriksen, T.H. (1993), *Ethnicity and Nationalism: Anthropological Perspectives* (London: Pluto Press).

Fainstein, S. (1994), *The City Builders: Property, Politics and Planning in London and New York City* (Oxford: Blackwell).

Farnen, R.F. (ed.) (1994), *Nationalism, Ethnicity and Identity: Cross National and Comparative Perspectives* (New Brunswick, U.S.A.: Transaction Publishers).

Ferguson, C.A. and S.B. Heath (eds) (1981), *Language in the USA* (London: Cambridge University Press).

Fine, G.A. and K.L. Sandstrom (1988), *Knowing Children: Participant Observation with Minors* (Beverly Hills, CA: Sage Publications).

Fisher, F. and J. Forrester (eds) (1993), *The Argumentative Turn in Policy Analysis and Planning* (London: UCL Press).

Fishman, J.A. (1976), *Bilingual Education: An International Sociological Perspective* (Rowley, Mass.: Newbury House).

Fishman, J.A. (1989), *Language and Ethnicity in Minority Sociolinguistic Perspective* (Clevedon: Multilingual Matters Ltd.).

Foddy, W. (1992), *Constructing Questions for Interviews and Questionnaires* (Cambridge: Cambridge University Press).

Fuchs, L.H. (1990), *The American Kaleidoscope: Race, Ethnicity and the Civic Culture* (Hanover: Wesleyan University Press).

Garcia, O. and C. Baker (1995), *Policy and Practice in Bilingual Education: Extending the Foundations* (Clevedon, PA: Multilingual Matters).

Gilbert, N. (ed.) (2001), *Researching Social Life,* second edn. (London: Sage Publications).

Gillborn, D. and H.S. Mirza (2000), *Educational Inequality: Mapping Race, Class and Gender – A synthesis of Research Evidence* (London: OFSTED).

Glazer, N. (1988), *The New Migration: A Challenge to American Society* (San Diego, CA: San Diego State University Press).

Glazer, N. (1997), *We are All Multiculturalists Now* (Cambridge, Mass.: Harvard University Press).

Gordon, P. (1985), *Policing Immigration: Britain's Internal Controls* (London: Pluto Press).

Gould, W.T.S. and A.M. Findlay (eds) (1994), *Population, Migration and the Changing World Order* (Chichester, New York: John Wiley and Sons).

Graddol, D., D. Leith and J. Swann (eds) (1996), *English: History, Diversity and Change,* The Open University (London: Routledge).

Graddol, D. (1997), *The Future of English?* (London: The British Council).

Grimes, B.R. (ed.) (1992), *Ethnologue: Languages of the World,* twelfth edn. (Dallas, Texas: The Summer Institute of Linguistics).

Guillherme, M. (2002), *Critical Citizens for an Intercultural World: Foreign Language Education as Cultural Politics* (Clevedon: Multilingual Matters).

Hajer, M.A. (1989), *City Politics: Hegemonic Project and Discourse* (Aldershot: Avebury).

Hakuta, K. (ed.) (1993), *Federal Education Programmes for Limited-English-Proficient Students: A Blueprint for the Second Generation* (Stanford, CA: Stanford Working Group).

Halpin, D. and B. Troyna (eds) (1994), *Researching Education Policy: Ethical and Methodological Issues* (London: Falmer Press).

Hansen, R.S. (2000), *Citizenship and Immigration in Post-War Britain: the Institutional Origins of a Multicultural Nation* (Oxford: Oxford University Press).

Hartmann, R. (1996), *The English Language in Europe,* European Studies Series (Oxford: Intellect).

Hewitt, R. (2005), *White Backlash and the Politics of Multiculturalism* (Cambridge: Cambridge University Press).

Hirsch, E. (1982), *The Concept of Identity* (New York: Oxford University Press).

Hollifield, J. (1992), *Immigrants, Markets and the States: the Political Economy of Immigration in Post-war Europe and the US* (Cambridge, Mass.: Harvard University Press).

Horowitz, D. (1985), *Ethnic Groups in Conflict* (Berkley, LA: University of California Press).

Ikin, A.E. (1944), *The Education Act 1944* (London: Sir Isaac Pitman and Sons Ltd).

Johnson, R.K. and M. Swain (eds) (1997), *Immersion Education: International Perspectives* (Cambridge: Cambridge University Press).

Jones, C. (1977), *Immigration and Social Policy in Britain* (Cambridge: Tavistock).

Jones, T. (1993), *Britain's Ethnic Minorities: An Analysis of the Labour Force Survey* (London: Policy Studies Institute).

Jorgensen, D.L. (1989), *Participant Observation: A Methodology for Human Studies* (London: Sage Publications).

Kachru, B. (1992), *The Other Tongue: English Across Cultures,* second edn. (Chicago: University of Illinois Press).

Katznelson, I. (1973), *Black Men, White Cities* (London: Oxford University Press).

Katzner, K. (1992), *The Languages of the World* (London: Routledge).

King, R. (ed.) (1993), *The New Geography of European Migrations* (London: Belhaven Press).

Kirk, J. and M.L. Miller (1986), *Reliability and Validity in Qualitative Research,* Qualitative Research Methods Series, Vol. 1 (London: Sage Publications).

Kirp, D.L. (1979), *Doing Good by Doing Little: Race and Schooling in Britain* (Berkeley, CA: University of California Press).

Kirp, D.L. (1982), *Just Schools: the Idea of Racial Equality in American Education* (Berkeley, CA: University of California Press).

Kirp, D.L. (1985), *Schools Days, Rule Days: the Legislation and Regulation of Education* (London: Falmer Press).

Kivisto, P. (2005), *Incorporating Diversity – Rethinking Assimilation in a Multicultural Age* (Colorado: Paradigm Publishers).

Kloss, H. (1977), *The American Bilingual Tradition* (Rowley, Mass.: Newbury House).

Kohn, H. (1955), *Nationalism, Its Meaning and History* (Princeton, NJ: D. Van Nostrand).

Krashen, S. (1981), *Second Language Acquisition and Second Language Learning* (Oxford: Pergamon Press).

Krashen, S. (1982), *Principles and Practice in Second Language Acquisition* (Oxford: Pergamon Press).

Kumar, R. (1999), *Research Methodology* (London: Sage).

Kymlicka, W. and B. He (eds) (2005), *Multiculturalism in Asia* (Oxford: Oxford University Press).

Lapkin, S. (ed.) (1998), *French Second Language Education in Canada: Empirical Studies* (Toronto: University of Toronto Press).

Layton-Henry, Z. (ed.) (1990), *The Political Rights of Migrant Workers in Western Europe* (London: Sage Publications Ltd.).

Layton-Henry, Z. (1992), *The Politics of Immigration* (Oxford: Blackwell).

Le Page, R.B. (1964), *The National Language Question: Linguistic Problems of Newly Independent States* (Oxford: Oxford University Press).

Le Page, R.G. and A. Tabouret-Keller (1985), *Acts of Identity: Creole-based Approaches to Language and Ethnicity* (Cambridge: Cambridge University Press).

Leung, C. (ed.) (2002), *Language and Additional/Second Language Issues for School Education: A Reader for Teachers* (Watford: National Association for Language Development in the Curriculum).

Local Economy Policy Unit (LEPU), South Bank University (1995), *Living in Bethnal Green: A Survey of Residents in the Bethnal Green City Challenge Area* (South Bank University: London).

Lorimer, W.L. (1988), *The New Testament in Scots* (Harmondsworth: Penguin).

Luciani, G. (ed.) (1993), *Migration Policies in Europe and the United States* (London: Kluwer Academic Publishers).

Machan T.W. and C.T. Scott (eds) (1992), *English in its Social Contexts: Essays in Historical Sociolinguistics* (Oxford: Oxford University Press).

Maclure, S. (1991), *Missing Links: Future Policies for Further Education* (London: Policy Studies Institute).

Maclure, S. (1992), *Education Reformed: A Guide to the Education Reform Act* third edn. (London: Hodder and Stoughton).

Maidment, R. and A. McGrew (1986), *The American Political Process* (London: Sage).

Marcus, S. (1999), *Apartment Stories: City and Home in Nineteenth-Century Paris and London* (Berkely: University of California Press).

Martinello, M. (1995), *Migration, Citizenship and Ethno-National Identities in the European Union* (Aldershot: Avebury).

Mason, D. (1995), *Race and Ethnicity in Modern Britain* (New York: Oxford University Press).

McClure, J.D. (1988), *Why Scots Matters: the Scots' Language is A Priceless National Possession* (Edinburgh: Saltire Society).

Michie, R.C. (1987), *The London and New York Stock Exchanges 1850–1914* (London: Allen and Unwin).

Miles, R. and D. Thranhardt (eds) (1995), *Migration and European Integration: the Dynamics of Inclusion and Exclusion* (London: Fairleig Dickinson University Press).

Miller, W.R. (1977), *Cops and Bobbies: Police Authority in New York and London: 1830–1870* (Chicago: The University of Chicago Press).

Modood, T., R. Berthoud, J. Lakey, J. Nazroo, P. Smith, S. Virdee and S. Beishon (1997), *Ethnic Minorities in Britain: Diversity and Disadvantage* (London: Policy Studies Institute).

Modood, T. (2005), *Multicultural Politics: Racism, Ethnicity and Muslims in Britain* (Edinburgh: Edinburgh University Press).

Mohan, B, C. Leung and C. Davison (eds) (2001), *English as a Second Language in the Mainstream: Teaching, Learning and Identity* (London: Longman).

Muller, T. and T. Espenshade (1985), *The Fourth Wave: Californian's Newest Immigrants* (Washington, DC: Urban Institute Press).

Nieto, S. (1992), *Affirming Diversity: the Socio-political Context of Multicultural Education* (New York: Longman).

Nimmi, H. (1991), *Ethnic Minority Identity: A Social Psychological Perspective* (Oxford: Clarendon Press).

Noin, D. and R. Woods (eds) (1993), *The Changing Population of Europe* (Oxford: Blackwell).

Orfield, G. (1993), *The Growth of Segregation in American Schools: Changing Patterns of Separation and Poverty Since 1968* (Alexandria, Virginia: National School Boards Association).

Ozolins, U. (1993), *The Politics of Language in Australia* (New York: Cambridge University Press).

Parekh, B. (2000), *Rethinking Multiculturalism: Cultural Diversity and Political Theory* (London: Palgrave).

Paul, K. (1997), *Whitewashing Britain: Race and Citizenship in the Postwar Era* (Cornell: Cornell University Press).

Peach, C. (ed.) (1996), *Ethnicity in the 1991 Census*, Vol. 2 (London: HMSO).

Pearsall, J. and B. Trumble (eds) (1995), *The Oxford English Reference Dictionary* (Oxford: Oxford University Press).

Pennycook, A. (1994), *The Cultural Politics of English as an International Language* (London: Longman).

Phillips, D.L. (1971), *Knowledge from What? Theories and Methods in Social Research* (Chicago: Rand McNally).

Piatt, B. (1990), *English Only? Law and Language Policy in the United States* (Albuquerque: University of New Mexico Press).

Potts, L. (1990), *The World Labour Market: A History of Migration* (London: Sez Books).

Procter, J. (2000), *Writing Black Britain, 1948–1998: An Interdisciplinary Anthology* (Manchester: Manchester University Press).

Rawkins, P.M. (1979), *The Implementation of Language Policy in the Schools of Wales* (Strathclyde: University of Strathclyde Centre for the Study of Public Policy).

Rex, J. and S. Tomlinson (1979), *Colonial Immigrants in a British City: A Class Analysis* (London: Routledge and Paul Kegan).

Richmond, A.H. (1988), *Immigration and Ethnic Conflict* (London: Macmillan Press).

Richmond, A.H. (1994), *Global Apartheid: Refugees, Racism and the New World Order* (Toronto: Oxford University Press).

Robson, C. (1994), *Real World Research: A Resource for Social Scientists and Practitioner-Researchers* (Oxford: Blackwell).

Rodriguez, C. (1989), *Puerto Ricans: Born in the USA* (Boston: Unwin Hyman).

Romanucci-Ross, L. and G.A. De Vos (eds) (1995), *Ethnic Identity: Creation, Conflict and Accommodation*, third edn. (London: Altamira Press).

Rubin, H. and I. Rubin (1995), *Qualitative Interviewing* (London: Sage).

Runnymede Trust (2000), *The Future of Multi-ethnic Britain – The Parekh Report*, Report of the Commission on the Future of Multi-ethnic Britain (London: Profile Books Ltd.).

Russell, S.S. (1993), *International Migration in North America, Europe, Central Asia, the Middle East and North Africa: Research and Research-Related Activities* (Geneva: United Nations Economic Commission for Europe).

Sanchez, G.J. (1993), *Becoming Mexican American: Identity in Chicano Los Angeles, 1900–1945* (New York: Oxford University Press).

Santiago, I. (1978), *A Community Struggle for Equal Educational Opportunity: ASPIRA v. Board of Education* (Princeton, NJ: Office for Minority Education Testing Service).

Schiffman, H.F. (1996), *Linguistic Culture and Language Policy* (London: Routledge).

Schlesinger, A.Jr. (1992), *The Disuniting of America* (New York: Norton).

Scmidt, R. (2000), *Language Policy and Identity Politics in the United States* (Philadelphia: Temple University Press).

Skutnabb-Kangas, T. (1984), *Bilingualism or Not: the Education of Minorities* (Clevendon, PA: Multilingual Matters).

Skutnabb-Kangas, T. and J. Cummins (eds) (1988), *Minority Education: From Shame to Struggle* (Clevendon, PA: Multilingual Matters).

Skutnabb-Kangas, T. (ed.) (1995), *Multilingualism for All*, European Studies on Multilingualism, Vol. 4 (Denmark: Swets and Zeitlinger).

Smith, A.D. (1986), *The Ethnic Origins of Nations* (Oxford: Blackwell).

Smith, A.D. (1991), *National Identity* (London: Penguin Books).

Smith, A.D. (1995), *Nations and Nationalism in a Global Era* (Cambridge, Mass.: Polity Press).

Solomos, J. (1989), *Race and Racism in Contemporary Britain* (London: Macmillan).

Spencer, I.R.G. (1997), *British Immigration Policy since 1939: the Making of Multi-Racial Britain* (London: Routledge).

Steenbergen, B.V, B.V. Steenderen, T.P. Boje and S. Walby (eds) (1999), *European Societies: Fusion or Fission?* (London: Routledge).

Strang, B. (1970), *A History of English* (London: Methuen).

Taylor, C. (1994), *Multiculturalism – Examining the Politics of Recognition* (Princeton: Princeton University Press).

Todd, L. (1984), *Modern Englishes: Pidgins and Creoles* (Oxford: Blackwell).

Troyna, B. (ed.) (1987), *Racial Inequality in Education* (London: Tavistock Publications).

Troyna, B. and B. Carrington (1990), *Education, Racism and Reform* (London: Routledge).

Troyna, B and V. Edwards (1993), *The Educational Needs of a Multiracial Society,* Occasional Papers in Ethnic Relations Series, no. 9 (Coventry: Centre for Research in Ethnic Relations, University of Warwick).

Trudgill, P. (1984), *Language in the British Isles* (Cambridge: Cambridge University Press).

Trudgill, P. (1986), *Dialects in Contact* (Oxford: Blackwell).

Verma, G.K. (ed.) (1989), *Education for All: a Landmark in Pluralism* (London: The Falmer Press).

Ward, P. (2004), *Britishness Since 1870* (London: Routledge).

Watkins-Goffman, L. (2001), *Lives in Two Languages: An Exploration of Identity and Culture* (Michigan: University of Michigan Press).

Williams, A. (1998), *Finding and Showing the Way: Teaching ESL in the Late 1990s* (Canberra: Australian Council of TESOL Associations).

Yanow, D. (1996), *How Does a Policy Mean? Interpreting Policy and Organisational Actions* (Washington, DC: Georgetown University Press).

Yanow, D. (2000), *Conducting Interpretive Policy Analysis*, Qualitative Research Methods Series, Vol. 47 (London: Sage Publications).

Yin, R. K. (1994), *Case Study Research: Design and Methods,* second edn. (London: Sage).

Yinger, J. Milton (1994), *Ethnicity: Source of Strength or Conflict?* (Albany, NY: State University of New York Press).

Young, K. and N. Rao (1997), *Local Government since 1945* (London: Blackwell).

Zentella, A.C. (1997), *Growing Up Bilingual: Puerto Rican Children in New York City* (New York: Blackwell).

Zimmermann, K.F. (ed.) (1992), *Migration and Economic Development* (Berlin: Springer-Verlag).

Journal Articles

Archdeacon, T.J. (1992), 'Reflections on Immigration to Europe in the Light of US Immigration History', *International Migration Review* 26:1, 525–48.

Asraf, R.M. (1997), 'The Cultural Implications of Teaching English as a Second or Foreign Language', *Muslim Education Quarterly* 14:4, 4–19.

Astill, B.R. and J.P. Keeves (1999), 'Assimilation, Absorption or Separatism in a Culturally and Linguistically Diverse Population', *International Journal of Bilingual Education and Bilingualism* 2:1, 1–12.

Banton, M. (2000) 'A UK Perspective', *Journal of Ethnic and Migration Studies*, 26: 4, 719–38.

Bassey, M. (1981), 'Pedagogic Research: on the Relative Merits of Search for Generalisation and Study of Single Events', *Oxford Review of Education* 7:1, 85.

Beardsmore, H.B. and J. Kohls (1985), 'Designing Bilingual Education: Aspects of Immersion and European School Models', *Journal of Multilingual and Multicultural Development* 6:1, 1–15.

Billig, M., D. Deacon, J. Downey, J. Richardson and P. Golding (2006b), 'Chilly Britannia', *Catalyst*, 17 May 2006 <http://www.catalystmagazine.org/Default. aspx.LocID-0hgnew0ed.RefLocID-0hg01b001006002.Lang-EN.htm> (accessed 23 June 2007).

Caldas, S.J. and S. Caron-Caldas (1999), 'Language Immersion and Cultural Identity: Conflicting Influences and Values', *Language, Culture and Curriculum* 12:1, 42–58.

Cavanaugh, M.P. (1996), 'History of Teaching English as a Second Language, *English Journal* 85:8, 40–44.

Clyne, M. (1988), 'Australia's National Policy on Language and its Implications', *Journal of Educational Policy* 3:3, 237–80.

Dudley, G. and J. Richardson (1999), 'Competing Advocacy Coalitions and the Process of 'Frame Reflection': A Longitudinal Analysis of European Steel Policy', *Journal of European Public Policy* 6:2, 225–48.

European Commission (1997), 'Council Resolution of 16 December 1997 on the Early Teaching of European Union Languages', *Official Journal of the European Union* 1, 2–3.

Franson, C. (1999), 'Mainstreaming Learners of English as an Additional Language: The Class Teacher's Perspective', *Language, Culture and Curriculum* 12:1, 59–71.

Fuller, G. (2007), 'Most People favour Increased Diversity in the Work Force', *Personnel Today*, 3 January 2007 <http://www.personneltoday.com/Articles/2007/01/03/38737/most–people–favour–increased–diversity–in–the–workforce–research.html> (accessed 28 February 2007).

Hattos, A. (2004), 'Promoting Diversity through Language-in-Education Policies: Focus on Australia and the European Union, *Current Issues in Language Planning*, 5:4, 438–54.

Hofmann, J. (1995), 'Implicit Theories in Policy Discourse: An Inquiry into the Interpretations of Reality in German Technology Policy', *Policy Sciences* 28, 127–48.

Isin, E.F. and B.S. Turner (2007), 'Investigating Citizenship: An Agenda for Citizenship Studies', *Citizenship Studies*, 11:1, 5-17.

Joppke, C. (2004), 'The Retreat of Multiculturalism in the Liberal State: Theory and Policy', *The British Journal of Sociology,* 55:2, 237–57.

Kolers, P. (1968), 'Bilingualism and Information Processing', *Scientific American* 218, 78–86.

Leung, C. (2001), 'English as an Additional Language: Distinctive Language Focus or Diffused Curriculum Concerns?' *Language and Education* 15:1, 33–55.

Lo Bianco, J. (1998), 'ESL: is it Migrant Literacy? Is it History? *Australian Language Matters* 6:2, 1–7.

Lopes, S. A. (2000), 'What is still needed in English as a Second Language K–12 Teaching? *Educational Research Quarterly* 23:4, 52–64.

Massey, D.S. (1995), 'The New Immigration and Ethnicity in the United States', *Population and Development Review* 21:3, 631–52.

McDowell, L. (2004), 'Narratives of Family, Community and Waged Work: Latvian European Volunteer Worker Women in Post-war Britain', *Women's History Review*, 13:1, 23–56.

Meakin, J. (1996), 'What Future for Section 11 Funding? *Municipal Review and AMA News* 766, 12.

Myhill, J. (1999), 'Identity, Territoriality and Minority Language Survival', *Journal of Multilingual and Multicultural Development* 20:1, 34–50.

Ortiz, V. (1985), 'Changes in the Characteristics of Puerto Rican Migrants from 1955 to 1980', *International Migration Review* 20:3, 612–28.

Pellew, J. (1989), 'The Home Office and the Aliens Act 1905', *The Historical Journal*, 32:2, 369–65.

Sargant, E.B. (1912), 'British Citizenship: A Discussion Initiated' Reprint of discussion on citizenship 'United Empire' by the *Journal of the Royal Colonial Institute*, November (London: Longmas, Green and Co.).

Skerry, P. (1996), 'Many American Dilemmas: the Statistical Politics of Counting by Race and Ethnicity', *The Brookings Review: Education in America* summer, 36–52.

Stephens, T.M. (1989), 'The Language of Ethnicity and Self-Identity in American Spanish and Brazilian Portuguese', *Ethnic and Racial Studies* summer, 138–40.

Tomlinson, S. (1989), 'The Strange Case of Section 11', *Local Government Review* 153:41, 803–06.

Unger, H. (1995), 'Bable Babble', *Education*, august, 9.

Varro, G. (1992), 'Immigrants' Languages in the French School', *Language Problems and Language Planning* 16:2, 137–62.

Verba, S. (1996), 'The Citizen Respondent: Sample Surveys and American Democracy', *American Political Science Review* 90:1, 1–7.

Verma, G.K. (1985), 'The Swann Report and Ethnic Achievement: a Comment', *New Community* 12:3, 470–75.

Chapters in Books

Artigal, J.M. (1995), 'Multiways Towards Multilingualism: the Catalan Immersion Programme Experience', in T. Skutnabb-Kangas (ed.), *Multilingualism for All*, European Studies on Multilingualism, Vol. 4 (Denmark: Swets and Zeitlinger).

Baker, C. (1995), 'Bilingual Education in Wales', in C. Baker and O. Garcia (eds), *Policy and Practice in Bilingual Education: Extending the Foundations* (Clevendon, PA: Multilingual Matters).

Beardsmore, H.B. (1994), 'An Overview of European Models of Bilingual Education', in R. Khoo, U. Kreher and R. Wong (eds), *Towards Global Multilingualism: European Models and Asian Realities* (Clevendon, PA: Multilingual Matters Ltd.).

Beardsmore, H. B. (1995), 'European Models of Bilingual Education: Practice, Theory and Development', in O. Garcia and C. Baker (eds), *Policy and Practice in Bilingual Education: Extending the Foundations* (Clevendon, PA: Multilingual Matters).

Bourne, J. (1997), 'The Grown-ups know Best: Language Policy-Making in Britain in the 1990s', in W. Eggington and H. Wren, *Language Policy: Dominant English, Pluralist Challenges* (Philadelphia: John Benjamin Publishing Company).

Bulmer, M. (2001), 'The Ethics of Social Research', in Nigel Gilbert (ed.), *Researching Social Life,* second edn. (London: Sage Publications).

Cameron, L. (2002), 'The Development of English as an Additional Language through Classroom Participation', in C. Leung (ed.), *Language and Additional/ Second Language Issues for School Education: A Reader for Teachers*, (Watford: National Association for Language Development in the Curriculum).

Clarke, A. (2001), 'Research and the Policy-making Process', in N. Gilbert (ed.), *Researching Social Life,* second edn. (London: Sage Publications).

Crick, B. (2001), 'The Sense of Identity of the Indigenous British', in B. Crick, *Crossing Borders – Political Essays* (London: Continuum).

Cummins, J. (1995), 'The European Schools Model in relation to French Immersion Programmes in Canada', in T. Skutnabb-Kangas (ed.), *Multilingualism for All, European Studies on Multilingualism*, Vol. 4, (Denmark: Swets and Zeitlinger).

Dicker, S.J. (2000), 'Official English and Bilingual Education: the Controversy over Language Pluralism in US Society', in J.K. Hall and W.G. Egginton (eds), *The Sociopolitics of English Language Teaching* (Clevendon: Multilingual Matters).

Edwards, D.G. (1994), 'Education and Welsh Language Planning', in R. Khoo, U. Kreher and R. Wong (eds), *Towards Global Multilingualism: European Models and Asian Realities,* (Clevendon, PA: Multilingual Matters Ltd).

Eversley, J. (2000), 'Section 11: A Brief History', in P. Baker and J. Eversley (eds), *Multilingual Capital* (London: Battlebridge Publications).

Fernandez, R.R. (1987), 'Legislation, Regulation and Litigation: the Origins and Evolution of Public Policy on Bilingual Education in the United States', in W.A. Van Horne (ed.), *Ethnicity and Language* (Milwaukee: the University of Wisconsin).

Fielding, N. and H. Thomas (2001), 'Qualitative Interviewing', in N. Gilbert (ed.), *Researching Social Life*, second edn. (London: Sage).

Ganesan, N. (2005), 'Liberal and Structural Ethnic Political Accommodation, in Malaysia', W. Kymlicka and B. He (eds) *Multiculturalism in Asia* (Oxford: Oxford University Press).

Garcia, O. (1997), 'New York's Multilingualism: World Languages and their Role in a US City', in O. Garcia and J.A. Fishman (eds), *The Multilingual Apple: Languages in New York City* (New York: Mouton de Gruyter).

Genesee, F. (1995), 'The Canadian Second Language Immersion Programme', in O. Garcia and C. Baker (eds), *Policy and Practice in Bilingual Education: Extending the Foundations* (Clevendon, PA: Multilingual Matters).

Gibbons, J. (1995), 'Multilingualism for Australians', in T. Skutnabb-Kangas (ed.), *Multilingualism for All*, European Studies on Multilingualism, Vol. 4 (Denmark: Swets and Zeitlinger).

Golini, A. (1993), 'A General Framework for the European Migration System in the 1990s', in R. King (ed.), *The Geography of European Migrations* (London: Belhave Press).

Hall, S. (2000), 'The Multicultural Question', in B. Hesse (ed.) *Un/Settled Multiculturalisms: Diasporas, Entanglements, 'Transruptions"* (London: Zed Books).

Hajer, M.A. (1993), 'Discourse Coalitions and the Institutionalisation of Practice: the Case of Acid Rain in Britain', in F. Fisher and J. Forrester (eds), *The Argumentative Turn in Policy Analysis and Planning* (London: UCL Press).

Harrison, T. (2001), 'Urban Policy: addressing wicked Problems', in H.T.O. Davies, S.M. Nutley and P.C. Smith (eds), *What Works? Evidence-based Policy and Practice in Public Services* (Bristol: The Policy Press).

Hernandez-Chavez, E. (1984), 'The Inadequacy of English Immersion Education as an Educational Approach for Language Minority Students in the United States', in US Department for Education, *Studies on Immersion Education: A Collection for US Educators* (Sacramento, CA: California State Department for Education).

Herriman, M. (1996), 'Language Policy in Australia', in M. Herriman and B. Brunaby (eds), *Language Policy in English-Dominant Countries: Six Case Studies* (Clevendon, PA: Multilingual Matters Ltd.).

Hoffman, C. (1996), 'Societal Individual Bilingualism with English in Europe', in R. Hartmann (ed.), *The English Language in Europe* (Oxford: Intellect).

Innes, M. (2001), 'Exemplar: Investigating the Investigators – Studying Detective Work', in N. Gilbert (ed.), *Researching Social Life*, second edn. (London: Sage Publications).

Julios, C. (1998), 'Bilingualism and the New American Identity', in A.J. Kershen (ed.), *A Question of Identity* (Aldershot: Ashgate).

Julios, C. (2002), 'Towards a European Language Policy', in M. Farrell, S. Fella and M. Newman (eds), *European Integration in the 21st Century* (London: Sage Publications).

King, R. (1993), 'Why Do People Migrate? The Geography of Departure', in R. King (ed.), *The Geography of European Migrations* (London: Belhave Press).

Lyons, J.J. (1992), 'Secretary Bennett versus Equal Opportunity', in J. Crawford (ed.), *Language Loyalties: A Source Book on the Official English Controversy* (Chicago: The University of Chicago Press).

Lyons, J.J. (1995), 'The Past and Future Directions of Federal Bilingual Education Policy', in O. Garcia and C. Baker (eds), *Policy and Practice in Bilingual Education: Extending the Foundations* (Clevendon, PA: Multilingual Matters).

Martin, P. (1993), 'The Migration Issue', in R. King (ed.), *The Geography of European Migrations* (London: Belhaven Press).

McArthur, T. (1996), 'English in the World and in Europe', in R. Hartmann (ed.), *The English Language in Europe* (Oxford: Intellect).

McGroarty, M. (1997), 'Language Policy in the USA: National Values, Local Loyalties, Pragmatic Pressures', in W. Egginton and H. Wren (eds), *Language Policy: Dominant English, Pluralists Challenges* (Canberra: John Benjamins Publishing Company/Language Australia).

McKay, P. (1998), *The Literacy Benchmarks and ESL* (Canberra: Australian Council of TESOL Associations).

Peach, C., V. Robinson, J. Maxted and J. Chance (1988), 'Immigration and Ethnicity', in A.H. Halsey (ed.) *British Social Trends since 1990 – A Guide to the Changing Social Structure of Britain* (London: Macmillan Press), 561–615.

Pakir, A. (1994), 'Making Bilingualism Work: Developments in Bilingual Education', in R. Khoo, et al. (eds), *Towards Global Multilingualism: European Models and Asian Realities* (Clevendon, PA: Multilingual Matters Ltd.).

Rein, M. and D. Schön (1993), 'Reframing Policy Discourse', in F. Fisher and J. Forrester (eds), *The Argumentative Turn in Policy Analysis and Planning* (London: UCL Press).

Ricento, T. (1996), 'Language Policy in the United States', in M. Herriman and B. Burnaby (eds), *Language Policies in English-Dominant Countries: Six Case Studies* (Clevendon, PA: Multilingual Matters).

Skutnabb-Kangas, T. and O. Garcia (1995), 'Multilingualism for All – General Principles?', in T. Skutnabb-Kangas (ed.), *Multilingualism for All,* European Studies on Multilingualism, Vol. 4 (Denmark: Swets and Zeitlinger Publishers).

Smolicz, J.J. and M.J. Secombe (2000), 'Language Resilience and Educational Empowerment: Philippines and Australia', in R. Phillipson (ed.), *Rights to Language: Equity, Power and Education: Celebrating the 60th Birthday of Tove Skutnabb-Kangas* (London: Lawrence Erlbaum Associates Publishers).

Stubbs, M. (1995), 'Educational Language Planning in England and Wales: Multicultural Rhetoric and Assimilationist Assumptions', in O. Garcia and C. Baker (eds), *Policy and Practice in Bilingual Education: Extending the Foundations* (Clevendon, PA: Multilingual Matters).

Watson-Gegeo, K.A. (1994), 'Language and Evaluation in Hawaii: Sociopolitical and Economic Implications of Hawaii Creole English', in M. Morgan (ed.), *Language and the Social Construction of Identity in Creole Situations* (Los Angeles, CA: University of California Centre for Afro-American Studies).

Williams, A. and E. Gregory (1999), 'Home and School Reading Practices in Two East End Communities', in A. Tosi and C. Leung (eds), *Rethinking Language Education: from a Monolingual to a Multilingual Perspective* (London: CILT).

Official Publications/Reports

Australian Institute of Multi-cultural Affairs (AIMA) (1980), *Review of Multi-cultural and Migrant Education* (Melbourne: AIMA).

Bailey, S.K. (1979), *Prejudice and Pride: the Brown Decision After Twenty-Five Years, May 17th 1954–May 17th 1979,* Report from the US National Academy of Education (Washington, DC: US Department of Health, Education and Welfare).

Billig, M., J. Downey, J. Richardson, D. Deacon and P. Golding (2006), *'Britishness' in the Last Three General Elections: from Ethnic to Civic Nationalism',* Report for the Commission for Racial Equality from Loughborough Centre for Communication Research (Loughborough: Loughborough University).

Board of Education of the City of New York (1995), *Curriculum Frameworks: Knowledge, Skills and Abilities, Grades Pre-K-12* (New York: NYC Board of Education).

British Chambers of Commerce (BCC) (2004), *BCC Language Survey – The Impact of Foreign Languages on British Business – Part 2: The Qualitative Results* (London: BCC).

British Nationality Act 1981 (1981) (London: HMSO).

California State Department of Education, Bilingual Education Office (1986), *Beyond Language: Social and Cultural Factors in Schooling Language Minority Students* (Los Angeles, CA: California State University).

Central Statistical Office (1996), *Social Trends*, Vol. 26 (London: HMSO).

Clarke K. and S. Drinkwater (2007), *Ethnic Minorities in the Labour Market: Dynamics and Diveristy* (York: Joseph Rowntree Foundation).

Coleman, D. and J. Salt (eds) (1996), *Ethnicity in the 1991 Census: Demographic Characteristics of the Ethnic Minority Populations*, Vol. 1 (London: HMSO).

Commission on Integration and Cohesion (2007), *Our Shared Future* (West Yorkshire: Commission on Integration and Cohesion).

Commonwealth Immigrants Act 1962 (1962) (London: HMSO).

Department of Employment, Education and Training (DEET) (1991), *The Australian Language: Australia's Language and Literacy Policy Companion* (Canberra: AGPS).

Department of City Planning of New York City (1994), *Puerto Rican New Yorkers in 1990* (New York City: Department of City Planning).

Department for Education and Sciences (DES) (1975), *A Language for Life: Report of the Committee of Inquiry into Reading and the use of English*, appointed by the Secretary of State for Education and Science under the Chairmanship of Sir Alan Bullock (London: HMSO).

DES (1985), *Education for All: Report of the Committee of Inquiry into the Education of Children from Ethnic Minority Groups*, appointed by the Secretary of State and Science under the Chairmanship of Lord Swann (London: HMSO).

DES (1988), *Draft Circular, the Education Reform Act 1988: the School Curriculum and Assessment* (London: HMSO).

DES (1988), *Report of the Committee of Inquiry into the Teaching of English Language,* appointed by the Secretary of State for Education and Science under the Chairmanship of Sir John Kingman (London: HMSO).

DES (1989), *Aspects of Primary Education: the Education of Children under Five* (London: HMSO).

DES (1989), *English for Ages 5 to 16* (London: HMSO).

DES (1989), *The Education Reform Act 1988: the School Curriculum and Assessment, Circular no. 5/89* (London: HMSO).

Department for Education and Employment (DfEE) (1995), *The National Curriculum* (London: HMSO).

DfEE Welsh Office (1995), *The National Curriculum* (London: HMSO).

DfEE (1997), *Excellence in Schools White Paper* (London: HMSO).

DfEE, Ethnic Minorities Pupils Team (1999), *Ethnic Minority Achievement Grant: Consultation Paper* (London: DfEE).

DfEE Press Office (1999), *Press Notice no. 1999/0191: Clarke Reinforces Commitment to Educating Refugee Children* (London: DfEE).

Department for Education and Skills (DfES) Press Office (1999), *Press Notice no. 1999/0110: Improved Standards for Ethnic Pupils will be our Lasting Response to the Lawrence Inquiry* (London: DfES).

DfES Press Office (1999), *Press Notice no. 1999/0405: Ethnic Minority Pupil Grant will boost Achievement* (London: DfES).

DfES Press Office (2001), *Press Notice no. 2001/0212: Raising the Achievement of Ethnic Minority Pupils* (London: DfES).

DfES (2002), *14–19: Extending the Opportunities, Raising Standards* (London: HMSO).

DfES (2002), *Languages for All: Languages for Life – Strategy for England* (London: DfES).

DfES (2005), *14–19 Education and Skills*, presented to Parliament by the Secretary of State for Education and Skills by Command of Her Majesty, cm. 6476 (Norwich, TSO).

DfES (2006), *Languages Review – Consultation Report: Short Text* (Nottingham: DfES Publications).

DfES (2007), *Languages Review* (Nottingham: DfES Publications).

Department of Justice Canada (2007) *Canadian Multiculturalism Act 1985*, Department of Justice Canada <http://laws.justice.gc.ca/en/ShowFullDoc/cs/c-18.7///en> (accessed 14 March 2007).

European Commission (2006), *Gateway to Education*, Socrates – European Community Action Programme in the Field of Education (2000–2006) (Brussels: European Commission).

General Register Office (1951), *Census 1951* (London: HMSO).

Hansard (1967), *House of Commons, Official Report, Session 1966–67*, comprising period from 17–28 April 1967 (London: HMSO).

Hansard (1981), *House of Commons, Fifth Report from the Home Affairs Committee, Session 1980–81, Racial Disadvantage* (London: HMSO).

Hansard (1985), *House of Commons, Official Report, Session 1984–85*, comprising period 11–22 March 1985, sixth series, Vol. 75 (London: HMSO).

Hansard (1986), *House of Commons, Home Affairs Committee First Report, Session 1986–87: Bangladeshis in Britain*, Vol. 3 (London: HMSO).

Hansard (1991), *House of Commons, Education (National Curriculum: Modern Foreign Languages) Order 1991* (London: HMSO).

Hansard (1995), *House of Commons, Education and Community Services Committee, Session 1994–1995: Third Report, Performance in City Schools*, Vol. 1 (London: HMSO).

Hansard (2002), *House of Commons, Nationality, Immigration and Asylum Bill* (London: HMSO).

Home Office (1977), *British Nationality and Citizenship of the United Kingdom and Colonies* booklet (London: Home Office).

Home Office (1988), A *Scrutiny of Grants under Section 11 of the Local Government Act 1966: Final Report* (London: HMSO).

Home Office (1990), *Section 11 of the Local Government Act 1966: Grant Administration: Policy Criteria* (London: HMSO).

Home Office (1990), *The Home Office Circular no. 78/1990: Section 11 of the Local Government Act 1966* (London: HMSO).

Home Office (1996), *Home Office Annual Report 1996* (London: HMSO).

Home Office (1996), *News Release no. 350/96: A Way Ahead for Ethnic Minority Community Funding* (London: Home Office).

Home Office (2001a), *Community Cohesion: A Report of the Independent Review Team Chaired by Ted Cantle* (London: TSO).

Home Office (2001b), *Secure Borders, Safe Haven: Integration with Diversity in Modern Britain* (London: HMSO).

Home Office (2003), *The New and the Old – A Report on the 'Life in the United Kingdom' Advisory Group* (Croydon: Home Office Communications Directorate).

Home Office (2004), *Life in the United Kingdom – A Journey to Citizenship*, published on behalf of the Life in the United Kingdom Advisory Group (Norwich: TSO).

Home Office (2007), *Life in the United Kingdom – A Journey to Citizenship* (Norwich: TSO).

House of Lords, European Union Committee (2005), *17th Report of Session 2004–2005: Proposed EU Integrated Action Programme for Life-long Learning,* report, HL paper 104–I and volume 2: evidence, HL paper 104–II (London: TSO).

Hussey, M.A. (1994), *Inspection under Section 9 of the Education (Schools) Acts 1992: Swanlea School (School no. 211/4297),* 28 February–4 March 1994 (London: HMSO).

International Labour Office (ILO) (1986), *Economically Active Population, 1950–2025* (Geneva: ILO).

ILO (1984), *World Labour Report,* Vol. 1 (Geneva: ILO).

Kelly, R. and L. Bryne (2007), 'A Common Place' – Fabian Society Pamphlet (London: Fabian Society).

Local Authorities Race Relations Information Exchange (LARRIE) (1992), *Guide to Section 11 Funding: the 1992/93 Section 11 Allocation, LARRIE Research Report, no. 3* (London: LARRIE).

Local Economy Policy Unit (LEPU) South Bank University (1995), *Living in Bethnal Green: a Survey of Residents in the Bethnal Green City Challenge Area* (South Bank University: London).

Lo Bianco, J. (1987), *National Policy on Languages,* Commonwealth Department for Education (Canberra: Australian Government Publishing Service).

Local Government (Amendment) Act 1993 (1993) (London: HMSO).

Modood, T., R. Berthoud, J. Lakey, J. Nazroo, P. Smith, S. Virdee and S. Beishon (1997), *Ethnic Minorities in Britain – Diversity and Disadvantage*, Fourth National Survey of Ethnic Minorities (London: Policy Studies Institute).

National Statistics (2004a), *People and Migration – Ethnicity*, National Statistics <http://www.statistics.gov.uk/CCI/nugget.asp?ID=764&Pos=4&ColRank=1&Rank=176> (accessed 22 May 2007).

National Statistics (2004b), *Ethnicity and Identity – Labour Market* (London: TSO).

National Statistics (2005), *Focus on People and Migration – Foreign-Born,* National Statistics <www.statistics.gov.uk/cci/nugget.asp?id=1312> (accessed 26 February 2007).

National Statistics (2006a), *Focus on Religion – Country of Birth and National Identity*, National Statistics <http://www.statistics.gov.uk/cci/nugget.asp?id=958> (accessed 28 February 2007).

National Statistics (2006b), News Release – 'Brent is The Most Ethnically Diverse Area', National Statistics <http://www.statistics.gov.uk/pdfdir/eth1006.pdf> (accessed 26 February 2007).

Nuffield Foundation (2000), *Languages: the Next Generation – The Final Report and Recommendations of The Nuffield Languages Inquiry* (London: Nuffield Foundation).

New York City Board of Education (NYCBOE) News Bureau (1974), *Press Release no. N–13–1974/75* (New York: Office of Public Affairs).

NYCBOE (1991), *Language Achievement Battery: Norms Booklet, Native Speakers of English, Forms A and B, Grades K-12, Fall and Spring* (New York: NYCBOE).

NYCBOE (1995), *Curriculum Frameworks: Knowledge, Skills and Abilities, Grades Pre-K-12* (New York: NCBOE).

NYCBOE (1995), *Seward Park High School Annual Report 1995–96* (New York: NYCBOE).

New York City Department of City Planning (NYCDCP) (1994), *Puerto Rican New Yorkers in 1990* (New York: NYCDCP).

NYCDCP (1996), *The Newest New Yorkers 1990–94: An Analysis of Immigration to New York City in the Early 1990s* (New York: NYCDCP).

Organisation for Economic Co-operation and Development (OECD) (1987), *The Future of Migration* (Paris: OECD).

Office for Standards in Education (OFSTED) (1994), *Educational Support for Minority Ethnic Communities: A Survey of Educational Provision Funded under Section 11 of the Local Government Act 1966* (London: HMSO).

OFSTED (1995), *English: A Review of Inspection Findings 1993/9, A Report from the Office of Her Majesty's Chief Inspector of Schools* (London: HMSO).

OFSTED (1996), *The Education of Travelling Children: A Survey of Educational Provision for Travelling Children* (London: HMSO).

Office for National Statistics (ONS) (1998), *Regional Trends 33: 1998 Edition* (London: HMSO).

ONS (1999), *Focus on London 99* (London: HMSO).

OPCS (Office of Population, Censuses and Surveys) (1991), *Census 1991* (London: HMSO).

Palmer, G. and P. Kenway (2007), *Poverty among Ethnic Groups: How and Why does it differ?* (York: Joseph Rowntree Foundation).

Platt, L. (2007), *Poverty and Ethnicity in the UK* (Bristol: Policy Press in association with the Joseph Rowntree Foundation).

Reyes, L.O. (1994), *Making the Vision a Reality: A Latino Action Agenda for Education Reform*, Final Report of the Latino Commission on Educational Reform submitted to the New York City Board of Education (NYCBOE) and Chancellor Ramon C. Cortines (New York: NYCBOE).

Runnymede Trust (2000), *The Future of Multi-ethnic Britain – The Parekh Report*, Report of the Commission on the Future of Multi-ethnic Britain (London: Profile Books Ltd.).

Salvo, J. and R. Ortiz (1992), *The Newest New Yorkers: An Analysis of Immigration into New York City During the 1980s* (New York: NYC Department of City Planning).

Salway, S., L. Platt, P. Chowbey, K. Harriss and E. Bayliss (2007), *Long-term Ill-health, Poverty and Ethnicity* (York: Joseph Rowntree Foundation).

Sinnott, J. (1995), *Living in Tower Hamlets: A Survey of the Attitudes of Secondary School Pupils* (London: Tower Hamlets Council).

Sinnott, J. (1997a), *An Analysis of the 1995 London Reading Test* (London: Tower Hamlets Council).

Sinnott, J. (1997b), *An Analysis of the 1996 GSCE Results by Pupil Background Factors* (London: Tower Hamlets Council).

Sinnott, J. (1997c), *Analysis of Key Stage One: SATs Results–1996* (London: Tower Hamlets Council).

Smith, D.J. (ed.) (1976), *The Facts of Racial Disadvantage*, Vol. XLII, broadsheet no. 560 (London: Political and Economic Planning).

Solesbury, W. and C. Julios (2001), *Social Exclusion: Current Policy and Practice, Queen Mary Papers on Public Policy*, no. 1 (London: Queen Mary University of London).

The British Nationality Act 1948 (1948), (London: HMSO).

The Education Act 1944 (1944) (London: HMSO).

The Labour Party (1980), 'Citizenship and Immigration: A Labour Party Discussion Document', *Socialism in the 80s* (London: The Labour Party/College Hill Press).

The Stephen Lawrence Inquiry: Report of an Inquiry by Sir William Macpherson of Cluny (1999), (London: HMSO).

Tower Hamlets Directorate of Education and Community Services (THECS) (1994), *Census 1991: Results for Wards in Tower Hamlets* (London: Tower Hamlets Council).

THECS (1995a), *Annual Report 1995* (London: Tower Hamlets Council).

THECS (1995b), *Ethnic Background of Pupils in Tower Hamlets 1996* (London: Tower Hamlets Council).

THECS (1996), *Tower Hamlets Language Census 1996* (London: Tower Hamlets Council).

United Nations (UN) Sub-commission on Prevention and Protection of Minorities (1952), *Yearbook of Human Rights for 1950* (New York: UN).

UN (1971), *UN Special Study on Racial Discrimination in the Political, Economic, Social and Cultural Spheres*, UN publication no. 71 XIV.2 (New York: UN).

UN Centre for Human Settlements (1987), *Global Report on Human Settlements 1986* (New York: Oxford University Press).

UN (1991), *World Population Prospects 1990* (New York: UN).

UN Department of International Economic and Social Affairs (1992a), *Long-range World Population Projections: Two Centuries of Population Growth, 1950–2150* (New York: UN).

UN Department of International Economic and Social Affairs (1992b), *Preparing Migration Data for Sub-national Population Projections* (New York: UN).

UN Economic Commission for Europe (UNECE) (1992c), *Changing Population Age Structures: Demographic and Economic Consequences and Implications* (Geneva: UN).

UN Department for Economic and Social Information and Policy Analysis (1995a), *World Population Prospects: the 1994 Revision* (New York: UN).

UN Department for Economic and Social Information and Policy Analysis (1995b), *Demographic Yearbook 1993* (New York: UN).

UN Department for Economic and Social Information and Policy Analysis (1995c), *World Economic and Social Survey 1995: Current Trends and Policies in the World Economy* (New York: UN).

UN Educational, Scientific and Cultural Organisation (UNESCO) (1995), *UNESCO Statistical Yearbook 1995* (Paris: UNESCO).

UN Population Division (1995), *World Urbanisation Prospects: the 1994 Revision, Estimates and Projections of Urban and Rural Populations and of Urban Agglomerations* (New York: UN).

UN Development Programme (UNDP) (1996), *The Human Report 1996* (New York: UN).

UNECE (1995), *Trends in Europe and North America 1995: the Statistical Yearbook of the Economic Commission for Europe* (New York: UN).

UNESCO (1995), *World Education Report 1995* (Oxford: UNESCO).

US Bureau of Census (1913), *Census 1913* (Washington, DC: US Bureau of Census).

US Bureau of Census (1991), *US INS (Immigration and Naturalisation Service) 1991* (Washington, DC: US Bureau of Census).

US Bureau of Census (1995a), *Statistical Abstract of the United States 1995: the National Data Book, and Country and City Data Book 1994 – A Statistical Abstract Supplement* (Washington, DC: US Bureau of Census).

US Bureau of Census (1995b), *USA Counties 1994* (Washington, DC: US Bureau of Census).

US Centre for Civic Education (CCE) (1993), *Standards for Civics and Government Grades 5–8 and 9–12* (Calabasas, CA: CCE).

United States Congress (U.S.C.) (1976), *United States Statues at Large 1974, containing the laws and concurrent resolutions enacted during the second session of the Ninety-third Congress of the United States of America 1974 and proclamations*, Vol. 88, part 1, Public Laws 93–246 through 93–446 (Washington, DC: US Government Printing Office).

U.S.C. (1968), *Bilingual Education Act Title VII, Elementary and Secondary Education Act of 1965*, as amended in 1967, Public Law 90–247, appx. A, sect. 702, stat. 816.

US Department for Education (US DfE) (1994), *Progress of Education in the United States of America: 1990 through 1994* (Washington, DC: US Department of Education).

US DfE (1997a), *America goes back to School: Partnership for Family Involvement in Education* (Washington DC: US Government Printing Office).

US DfE (1997b), *The Condition of Education 1997* (Washington, DC: US DfE).

US Department of Labour (1989), *The Effects of Immigration on the US Economy and Labour Market: Bureau of International Labour Affairs Research Report* (Washington, DC: US Government Printing Office).

US District Court, Southern District of New York (SDNY) (1974), *ASPIRA of New York Inc. vs. Board of Education of the City of New York,* 72 civ. 4002 SDNY (New York: SDNY).

US National Centre for Education Statistics (1997), *The Conditions of Education 1997* (Washington DC: US Department for Education).

US Supreme Court (1954), *Brown vs. Board of Education of Topeka* (Washington, D.C.: US Supreme Court).

Welsh Language Act 1993 (1993), (London: HMSO).

Welsh Office (1965), *Legal Status of the Welsh Language, Report of the Committee under the Chairmanship of Sir David Hughes Parry, 1963–1965* (London: HMSO).

Welsh Office (1993), *Welsh Social Survey 1992: Preliminary Results* (London: Government Statistical Service).

World Bank (1991), *World Development Report 1991* (New York: Oxford University Press).

Working Group on 14–19 Reform (2004), *14–19 Curriculum and Assessment Reform – Final Report of the Working Group on 14–19 Reform* (Nottinghamshire: DfES Publications).

Conference Proceedings

Bjurström, E. (2004), 'Multiculturalism and Youth Culture: The Construction of Ethnic Identity in Youth Styles', paper presented at the Youth, Ethnic Identity and the Future of Multiculturalism in Europe Seminar held at the Centre for Research on Nationalism, Ethnicity and Multiculturalism (CRONEM), University of Surrey, 21 July 2004 <http://www.surrey.ac.uk/Arts/CRONEM/seminar-04-07-21-CRONEM-BSA-abstracts.htm#Bjurström> (accessed 15 March 2007).

Creighton, M.D.D. (1896), The Right Rev., Lord Bishop of Peterborough and Honorary Fellow of Merton College, Oxford, 'The English National Character', The Romanes Lecture, delivered in the Sheldonian Theatre, 17 June 1896, (London: Henry Frowde, Amen Corner, E.C.), 8–9.

Cummins, J. (1993), 'Ideological Assumptions in the Teaching of English as a Second Language', paper presented at the 24 Annual Symposium of the Canadian Association of Applied Linguistics 'Teaching Minority Languages and Teaching Languages to Minorites', Otawa.

Husain, Hasanat M. (1996), 'Raising Our Educational Standards and Performance Levels', paper presented at the Greater Sylhet Development and Welfare Council Conference 1996, London.

International Organisation for Migration (IOM) (1990), 'Background Document', presented at the IOM Seminar on Migration, Geneva.

Julios, C. (1998), 'Bilingualism and the New British Identity', paper presented at the Political Studies Association's 49 Annual Conference at the University of Keele, in Dobson, A. and J. Stanyer (eds), *Contemporary Political Studies* 1, 92–107.

UN (1993), Report of the Department of International Economic and Social Affairs, Population and Development Planning, presented at the United Nations International Symposium on Population and Development Planning, New York.

UNECE (1994), *European Population Conference: Proceedings*, Vol. 1 (New York: UN).

Zill, N. (1992a), 'Trends in Family Life and School Performance', paper presented at the Annual Meeting of the American Sociological Association (ASA), Pittsburgh.

Zill, N. (1992b), 'What We Know About the School Readiness of Young Children in the United States', paper presented at the National Education Goals Panel Meeting.

Newspaper Articles

Ali, A.H. 'Muslim Women and the Key to Change', *Sunday Times*, 29 October 2006 <http://www.timesonline.co.uk/article/0,,2092-2426413,00.html> (accessed 1 March 2007).

Alibhai-Brown, J. 'I feel British, but I don't want Enforced Patriotism', *The Independent*, 29 January 2007 <http://comment.independent.co.uk/columnists_a_l/yasmin_alibhai_brown/article2193730.ece> (accessed 1 March 2007).

Akbar, A. 'Debate on the Veil shows how West is turning on Islam, Scholar Warns', *The Independent*, 27 October 2006 <http://news.independent.co.uk/uk/this_britain/article1932752.ece.> (accessed 1 March 2007).

'All Double Dutch?', *The Guardian*, 31 March 1998, 6.

'Anglican Leaders Support Right to keep Ban on Gay Adoptions', *Independent Catholic News*, 24 January 2007 <http://www.indcatholicnews.com/rightadopt329.html> (accessed 18 February 2007).

'Any one for Pernods?', *The Guardian Higher*, 31 March 1998, ii–iii.

'Banglatown Scheme gets Underway', *East End Life*, 15–21 September 1997, no. 179, 1.

Beard, M. 'Violence flares between Youths in Windsor over Plan to build Mosque', *The Independent*, 6 October 2006 <http://news.independent.co.uk/uk/this_britain/article1813595.ece> (accessed 1 March 2007).

Branigan, T. 'Racial Gap in Employment 'will take 45 Years to close'', *The Guardian*, 9 November 2006 <http://www.guardian.co.uk/print/0,,329622585–110414,00.html>. (accessed 27 February 2007).

Bright, M. and J. Kampfner 'Interview – Harriet Harman: the Constitutional Affairs Minister warns Colleagues that They can't be 'A Little Bit Against Discrimination'', *New Statesman*, 29 January 2007 <http://www.newstatesman.com/200701290028> (accessed 18 February 2007).

Brown, J. and R. Verkaik 'Shilpa tours the Media with Message of Peace, Love and Self-promotion', *The Independent*, 2 February 2007 <http://news.independent.co.uk/media/article2208276.ece> (accessed 1 March 2007).

Bunyan, N. and N. Sparrow 'Race Riot Town on a Knife-Edge', *Telegraph*, 5 June 2001 <http://www.telegraph.co.uk/news/main.jhtml?xml=/news/2001/05/28/noldh28.xml> (accessed 12 May 2007).

Byers, D. 'Ministers defy Downing Street in Gay Adoption Row', *The Times*, 25 January 2007 <http://www.timesonline.co.uk/tol/newspapers/sunday_times/britain/article1296042.ece> (accessed 15 February 2007).

Chapman, J. 'Blair caves in over Adoption Laws', *Daily Mail*, 25 January 2007 <http://www.dailymail.co.uk/pages/live/articles/news/news.html?in_article_id=431248&in_page_id=1770> (accessed 15 February 2007).

'Citizenship, Schools and the Imposition of National Values', *The Independent*, 26 January 2007 <http://coment.independent.co.uk/leading_articles/article2186492.ece> (accessed 1 March 2007).

Crawford, A. 'Crick hits out at Call for Britishness', *The Sunday Herald*, 31 July 2005 <http://findarticles.com/p/articles/mi_qn4156/is_20050731/ai_n14827389> (accessed 17 June 2007).

Crick, B. 'All this Talk of Britain is so … English', *The Guardian*, 12 April 2004 <http://society.guardian.co.uk/raceequality/comment/0,,1190252,00.html> (accessed 17 June 2007).

Cullinan, S. and K. Noble 'Sangatte', *Time*, 27 May 2002, 23.

'Dancing in the Streets as Shilpa wins Big Brother', *The Daily Mail*, 30 January 2007 <http://www.dailymail.co.uk/pages/live/articles/showbiz/bigbrother.html?in_page_id=1894&in_article_id=432147> (accessed 1 March 2007).

Elliot, F. 'Gay Adoption Row: Kelly puts Faith in Catholic Opt-out', *The Independent*, 28 January 2007 <http://news.independent.co.uk/uk/politics/article2192968.ece> (accessed 15 February 2007).

Frith, M. 'The World City: One in Three Londoners was born Overseas', *The Independent*, 14 November 2006.

Garner, R. 'Schools ditch Language Learning', *The Independent*, 25 May 2002, 1.

Giddens, A. 'Misunderstanding Multiculturalism', *The Guardian*, 16 October 2006 <http://commentisfree.guardian.co.uk/anthony_giddens/2006/10/tony_giddens.html> (accessed 1 March 2007).

Gillborn, D. 'Naïve Multiculturalism: Social Justice, "Race" and Education Policy under New Labour', *Times Education Supplement,* 4 September 1998, 26.

Gledhill, R. 'Bishop scorns "arrogance"', *The Times*, 30 January 2007 <http://www.timesonline.co.uk/tol/news/uk/article1299064.ece> (accessed 13 February 2007).

Gledhill, R. 'Bishop accuses Muslims of having Victim Complex', *The Times*, 6 November 2006 <http://www.timesonline.co.uk/tol/news/uk/article626214.ece> (accessed on 28 March 2007).

Graef, R. 'A Vote of No Confidence', *The Guardian*, 23 January 2007 <http://www.guardian.co.uk/comment/story/0,,1996482,00.html> (accessed 1 March 2007).

Hall, M. 'Lame Duck Blair caves in on Gay Adoptions', *Sunday Express*, 25 January 2007 <http://express.lineone.net/news_detail.html?sku=1106> (accessed 18 February 2007).

Hastings, C. and T. Harper 'Axe Big Brother, says Ex-Channel 4 Boss', *Telegraph*, 21 January 2007 <http://www.telegraph.co.uk/news/main.jhtml?xml=/news/2007/01/21/nbb21.xml> (accessed 1 March 2007).

Hattersley, G. 'Interview – You have to be Hard to be a Princess', *The Sunday Times*, 18 February 2007 <http://entertainment.timesonline.co.uk/tol/arts_and_entertainment/film/bollywood/article1400117.ece> (accessed 1 March 2007).

Henry, J. 'Britishness and the Class System', *Sunday Telegraph*, 22 January 2007 <http://www.telegraph.co.uk/news/main.jhtml?xml=/news/2007/01/21/nedu121.xml> (accessed 1 March 2007).

Henry, J. and M. Shaw 'Schools jump gun in ditching Languages', *The Times Education Supplement*, 24 May 2002, 1.

Hinsliff, G. 'Livingstone declares War on Race Equality Watchdog', *The Observer*, 26 November 2006 <http://observer.guardian.co.uk/print/0,,329643832-102279,00.html> (accessed 28 February 2007).

Hinsliff, G. and J. Doward 'Cameron blasts at Crude Bullying on 'British Values'', *The Observer*, 28 January 2007 <http://observer.guardian.co.uk/politics/story/0,,2000512,html> (accessed 1 March 2007).

Horwitz, T. and G. Forman 'Immigrants to Europe from the Third World Face Racial Animosity', *Wall Street Journal*, 14 August 1991, 1.

Hurst, G. 'Catholics get Time to adapt to Gay Rights', *The Times*, 25 January 2007<http://www.timesonline.co.uk/tol/newspapers/sunday_times/britain/article1295991.ece> (accessed 18 February 2007).

'Immigrants Main Election Issue at Smethwick – Labour Accusation of Exploitation', *The Times*, 9 March 1964, issue 55955, col. C, 6.

Johnston, P. 'Immigrants swell the Population at a Rate of 500 a Day', *Telegraph*, 3 November 2006 <http://www.telegraph.co.uk/news/main.jhtml?xml=/news/2006/11/03/nmigrant03.xml> (accessed 1 March 2007).

Kent, M. 'Shilpa wins the BB Crown', *The Sun*, 28 January 2007 <http://www.thesun.co.uk/article/0,,11049–2007040583,00.html> (accessed 1 March 2007).

'Labour loose Faith in Multiculturalism', *Telegraph*, 19 October 2006 <http://www.telegraph.co.uk/opinion/main.jhtml;jsessionid=BVMECJ0ZEEPRRQFIQMGSFGGAVCBQWIV0?xml=/opinion/2006/10/18/dl18101.xml> (accessed 1 March 2007).

Livingstone, K. 'To defend Multiculturalism is to defend Liberty', *The Independent*, 28 November 2006 <http://comment.independent.co.uk/commetators/article2021228.ece> (accessed 28 February 2007).

Maldonado, W. 'English Issue is Political Dynamite', *The San Juan Star*, 14 September 1995, 69.

Milne, S. and A. Travis 'Blair's Secret Plan to crack down on Asylum Seekers', *The Guardian*, 23 May 2002 <http://www.guardian.co.uk/uk_news/story/0,3604,720608,00.html> (accessed 9 June 2002).

Millward, D. 'Livingstone boycotts Phillips's Race Debate', *Telegraph*, 28 November 2006 <http://www.telegraph.co.uk/news/main.jhtml?xml=/news/2006/11/27/nslave127.xml> (accessed 15 March 2007).

'Mixed Responses', *The Guardian, Society Guardian*, 13 December 2006, 3.

'Mosley Speeches recalled – Powell figures "fantasy"', *The Times*, 22 April 1968, issue 57232, col. A, 2.

'Mr Wilson wants a Bigger Role for Navy – More Men Afloat: Helping to Keep Peace', *The Times*, 10 March 1964, issue 55956, col. A, 9.

Muir, H. 'Mayor's New onslaught on 'Alarmist' Race Watchdog', *The Guardian*, 27 November 2006 <http://www.guardian.co.uk/print/0,,329644262-103685,00.html> (accessed 28 February 2007).

Mulero, L. 'Dole pone por encima el Ingles' ('Dole puts English First'), *El Nuevo Dia ('The New Day')*, 13 October 1995, 7.

'Multiculturalism 'Drives Young Muslims to shun British Values', *The Daily Mail*, 28 January 2007 <http://wwww.dailymail.co.uk/pages/live/artilces/news/thml?in_article_id=432075&in_page_id=1770&ct=5> (accessed 1 March 2007).

Murphy-O'Connor, C., Cardinal 'Time to Stand Up for Our Beliefs', *The Times*, 26 November 2006 <http://www.timesonline.co.uk/tol/comment/faith/article649220.ece> (accessed 13 February 2007).

National Clearing House for Bilingual Education (NCBE) 'Passage of Proposition 227 in California', *Newsline*, 22 June 1998, 1.

Nash, I. 'The Kingman Report: laying the Foundation for a New Consensus', *The Times Education Supplement,* 6 May 1988, 11–14.

'No Race Problem in Leyton', *The Times*, 19 Dec 1964, issue 56199, col. F, 4.

'Panic and Prejudice', *The Times*, 27 February 1968, issue 57186, col. A, 9.

Pannick, D., QC 'A century ago immigration control was an alien concept – how it has changed', *The Times*, 28 June 2005 <http://www.timesonline.co.uk/tol/life_and_style/career_and_jobs/legal/article537244.ece> (accessed 29 June 2007).

Parekh, B. 'The Gifts of Diversity', *The Times Education Supplement,* 29 March 1985, 22–3.

'Parlez-vous Francais?' *The Guardian,* 15 July, 1998, 19.

'Peace and Prosperity: Regeneration to Breathe New Life into the Community', *East End Life,* no. 180, 22–28 September 1997, 6–7.

Phillips, T. 'Hooray for Shilpa, Hooray for Britain, Hooray for the Sun', Commission for Equality and Human Rights (CEHR), 30 January 2007 <http://www.cehr.org.uk/content/stories/sun20070130.rhtm> (accessed 1 March 2007).

Porter, A. 'Labour Gay Adoption Row', *The Sun*, 25 January 2007 <http://www.thesun.co.uk/article/0,,2-2007040156,00.html> (accessed 15 February 2007).

Robinson, J. and G. Hinsliff 'C4 Boss faces Big Brother Backlash', *The Observer*, 21 January 2007 <http://www.guardian.co.uk/race/story/0,,1995420,00.html> (accessed 1 March 2007).

Roman, N.E. 'Gingrich lays out Goals to reform Government', *The Washington Times*, 6 January 1998, A-1.

'Row erupts over Blunkett's 'swamped' Comment', *The Guardian*, 24 April 2002 <http://politics.guardian.co.uk/homeaffairs/story/0,11026,689919,00.html> (accessed 9 June 2002).

Russell, B. 'Schools told to promote Integration of Communities', *The Independent*, 31 October 2006 <http://education/independent.co.uk/news/article1943293> (accessed 1 March 2007).

'Skills Agency urges more Immigrants to learn English', *The Guardian*, 18 June, 1996, 16.

Specter, M. 'World, Wide, Web: Three English Words', *The New York Times*, April 1996.

'Surge in Racism in Schools blamed for 7/7 and Veil Row', *Daily Mail*, 20 November 2006 <http://www.dailymail.co.uk/pages/live/articles/news/news.html?in_article_id=417454&in_page_id=1770> (accessed 1 March 2007).

'The Immigration Problem', *The Times*, 5 March 1965, issue 56262, col. E, 13.

Travis, A. 'Charities and Union Leader attach Asylum Plans', *The Guardian*, 11 June 2002, 10.

Travis, A. ''Summer of Race Riots' feared after Clashes in 2001', *The Guardian*, 28 December 2006 <http://www.guardian.co.uk/guardianpolitics/story/0,,1979152,00.html> (accessed 12 May 2007).

Unz, R. K. 'Bilingualism vs. Bilingual Education', *Los Angeles Times,* 19 October 1997, M6.

Verkaik, R., B. Russell and J. Huggler 'Racism gets a Reality Check', *The Independent*, 18 January 2007 <http://news.independent.co.uk/media/article2162868.ece> (accessed 1 March 2007).

Wainwright, M. 'Another Country, Another World', *The Guardian*, 1 June 2000, 6.

Walsh, M. 'Microsoft set to wreck Language of Vikings', *The Guardian*, 1 July 1998, 15.

Wilson, G. and C. Davies 'BB's Goody evicted after Public Anger', *Telegraph*, 21 January 2007 <http://www.telegraph.co.uk/news/main.jhtml?xml=/news/2007/01/20/nbbro20.xml> (accessed 1 March 2007).

Wintour, P., W. Woodward and S. Bates 'Catholic Agencies given Deadline to comply on Same-sex Adoptions', *The Guardian*, 30 January 2007 <http://www.guardian.co.uk/frontpage/story/0,,2001834,00.html>(accessed 15 February 2007).

Woodward, C. 'Push for English-Only is on', *The San Juan Star,* 19 October 1995, 76.

Woodward, W. and S. Carrell 'Cabinet rejects Exceptions on Gay Adoptions', *The Guardian*, 25 January 2007 <http://www.guardian.co.uk/frontpage/story/0,,1998016,00.html> (accessed 15 February 2007).

Yeoman, F. 'Accept British Way of Life or Stay Away, Blair tells Immigrants', *The Times*, 11 December 2007 <http://www.timesonline.co.uk/article/0,,17129-2494782,00.html> (accessed 1 March 2007).

Zentella, A.C. 'English-Only Laws will foster Divisiveness, not Unity; they are Anti-Hispanic, Anti-Elderly and Anti-Female', *The Chronicle of Higher Education*, 23 November 1988, B1-B3.

Electronic Sources

Association of Local Government (ALG) (2001), 'Additional Educational Needs: The Impact of Ethnic Group and English as an Additional Language', Ref: EFSG–20, A Paper by the ALG Education Funding Strategy Group, ALG <http://www.alg.gov.uk/attachments/284/additional_educational_needs.pdf> (accessed 7 February 2003).

Association of Teachers and Lecturers (ATL) (2002), 'ATL urges the Home Secretary to withdraw Segregation Clause from the Immigration and Asylum Bill', ATL <http://www.askatl.org.uk/news/press_releases/pn100602.htm> (accessed 12 June 2002).

BBC News (2002), 'What is Britishness Anyway?' BBC News <http://news.bbc.co.uk/1/hi/uk_politics/1701843.stm> (accessed 17 June 2007).

BBC News (2006a), 'Muslims must feel British – Straw', BBC News <http://newsvote.bbc.co.uk/mpapps/pagetools/print/news.bbc.co.uk/1/hi/uk_politics/61>(accessed 28 February 2007).

BBC News (2006b), 'Top Racism Event faces Boycott', BBC News <http://newsvote.bbc.co.uk/mpapps/pagetools/print/news.bbc.co.uk/1/hi/uk_politics/61>(accessed 28 February 2007).

BBC News (2007a), 'Brown seeks to calm TV show row', BBC News <http://news.bbc.co.uk/1/hi/uk_politics/6273803.stm> (accessed 1 March 2007).

BBC News (2007b), '1968: Powell slates Immigration Policy, On This Day – 20 April 1968', BBC News <http://news.bbc.co.uk/onthisday/hi/dates/stories/april/20/newsid_2489000/2489357.stm> (accessed 19 June 2007).

Billig, M., D. Deacon, J. Downey, J. Richardson and P. Golding (2006), 'Chilly Britannia', *Catalyst* <http://www.catalystmagazine.org/Default.aspx.LocID-0hgnew0ed.RefLocID-0hg01b001006002.Lang-EN.htm> (accessed 23 June 2007).

British Educational Research Association (BERA) (1992), 'Ethical Guidelines for Educational Research' <http://www.bera.ac.uk/publications/guides.php> (accessed 11 February 2003).

Blair, T., PM (2006), Speech by the Prime Minister, 'The Duty to Integrate: Shared British Values', Number – 10 <http://www.number–10.gov.uk/output/Page10563.asp> (accessed 27 February 2007).

Brown, G., MP (2006), Speech by the Chancellor of the Exchequer, 'Stronger Together, Weaker Apart', Scottish Labour <http://www.scottishlabour.org.uk/brownspeechsept2006/?print=friendly&searchword=> (accessed 28 February 2007).

Cameron, D., MP (2007), Speech by the Leader of the Opposition, 'Bringing Down the Barriers to Cohesion', Conservatives <http://www.conservatives.com/tile.do?def=news.story.page&obj_id=134759> (accessed 19 March 2007).

Canadian Heritage (2007), 'Multiculturalism – Canadian Diversity, Respecting our Differences', Canadian Heritage <http://www.pch.gc.ca/progs/multi/respect_e.cfm> (accessed 14 March 2007).

Colley, L. (1999), 'Britishness in the 21st Century', Millennium Lectures Series, 10 Downing Street, 8 December 1999 <http://www.number-10.gov.uk/output/Page3049.asp> (accessed 19 June 2007).

Commission for Racial Equality (CRE) (2006), 'Race Convention 2006: Trevor Phillips' Opening Speech', CRE <http://www.cre.gov.uk/Default.aspx.LocID-0hgnew0nu.RefLocID-0hb00900c002.Lang-EN.htm> (accessed 1 March 2007).

Communities and Local Government (CLG) (2006), 'Launch of the Commission on Integration and Cohesion', Speech by Ruth Kelly MP at the launch on the new Commission on Integration and Cohesion on 24 August 2006, CLG <http://www.communities.gov.uk/index.asp?id=1502280> (accessed 16 June 2007).

Curriculumonline (2002), 'Citizenship – Overview', Curriculumonline <http://www.curriculumonline.gov.uk/Subjects/Ci/Resource.htm?oid=2947&taxonid=&hid=1002081&navid=&b=1&vl=1&SortPrice=3&page=&recreturned=> (accessed 13 February 2007).

Chavez, L. (1995), 'One Nation, One Common Language', Centre for Equal Opportunity (CEO) <http://www.ceousa.org/html/chavez.html> (accessed 12 June 2002).

Church of England (CoE) (2007), 'Letter from the Archbishops of Canterbury and York to the Prime Minister', CoE <http://www.cofe.anglican.org/news/pr0107lb.html> (accessed 18 February 2007).

DES (1988), *The Education Reform Act 1988* (London: HMSO) <http://www.hmso.gov.uk/acts/acts1988/Ukpga_19880040_en_2.htm#mdiv2> (accessed 9 June 2002).

DfES (1999), 'Guidance on Ethnic Minority Achievement Grant', DfES <http://www.dfee.gov.uk/ethnic/guide.htm> (accessed 9 June 2002).

DfES (2002a), *14–19: Extending the Opportunities, Raising Standards* (London: HMSO), DfES<http://www.dfes.gov.uk/14–19greenpaper/foreword.shtml> (accessed 9 June 2002).

DfES (2002b), *Removing the Barriers: Raising Achievement Levels of Minority Ethnic Pupils – Key Points for Schools*, DfES <http://www.standards.dfes.gov.uk/ethnicminorities> (accessed 9 June 2002).

DfES (2005), Press Release (Ref. 2005/0034), 'Major Investment for Foreign Language Learning – Kelly', 11 March 2005, DfES <http://www.gnn.gov.uk/Content/Detail.asp?ReleaseID=151443&NewsAreaID=2> (accessed 22 March 2005).

DfES (2006), 'Language Lessons', DfES <http://findoutmore.dfes.gov.uk/2006/10/language_lesson.html> (accessed 20 April 2007).

Equal Opportunities Commission (EOC) (2006), Press Release: Launch of Interim Report into BME Women in the Work Place, *Moving on Up? Bangladeshi, Pakistani and Black Caribbean Women and Work*, EOC <http://www.eoc.org.uk?Default.aspz?page=19443&theme=print> (accessed 26 February 2007).

EOC (2007), Press Release: Where are the Women missing from Scotland's Top Spots? EOC, 5 January 2007 <http://www.eoc.org.uk/Default.aspx?page=19843&theme=print> (accessed 28 February 2007).

ePolitix (2005), 'Davis warns on 'Outdated' Multiculturalism', ePolitix, <http://www.epolitix.com/EN/Bulletins/PressReview/Items/200508/604f7c4c-64f8-478> (accessed 28 February 2007).

EUROPA (1999), 'Languages' <http://www.europa.eu.int> (accessed 12 June 2002).

EUROPA (2007), 'Panorama of the European Union – United in Diversity', EUROPA <http://europa.eu/abc/panorama/index_en.htm> (accessed 12 June 2007).

John, C. (2002), 'Changing Face of Britain', BBC News <http://news.bbc.co.uk/hi/english/static/in_depth/uk/2002/race/changing_face_of_britain.stm> (accessed 22 May 2007).

Kirker, R., The Reverend (2007a), 'Equality (Sexual Orientation) Regulations Great Britain 2007 – Religious Adoption Agencies', Lesbian and Gay Christian Movement (LGCM) <http://www.lgcm.org.uk/> (accessed 17 February 2007).

Kirker, R., The Reverend (2007b), LGCM Press Release, 'Archbishops comment on Gay Adoption Debate', Lesbian and Gay Christian Movement (LGCM) < http://www.lgcm.org.uk/> (accessed 17 February 2007).

Mendoza, M. and H. Ayala (1999), *English Language Education for Children in Public Schools (Proposition 203)*, sec. 3, chp. 7, art. 3.1, 15–754, 6 January 1999, Onenation <http://www.onenation.org/fulltext/html> (accessed 20 February 1999).

Modood, T. (2005a), 'Multiculturalism or Britishness: A False Debate', *Connections*, Winter 2004/05, CRE <http://www.cre.gov.uk/publs/connections/articles/04wi_falsedebate.html> (accessed 28 February 2007).

Modood, T. (2005b), 'Remaking Multiculturalism after 7/7', Open Democracy, <http://www.opendemocracy.net/conflict-terrorism/multiculturalism_2879.jsp> (accessed 13 March 2007).

Murphy-O'Connor, C., Cardinal (2007), 'Cardinal asks Prime Minister and Cabinet to exempt Adoption Agencies from Equalities Act', Diocese of Westminster, <http://www.rcdow.org.uk/cardinal/default.asp?library_ref=&content_ref=1179> (accessed 17 February 2007).

National Archives (2007), 'Citizenship – Brave New World: Postwar Migration', National Archives <http://www.nationalarchives.gov.uk/pathways/citizenship/brave_new_world/immigration.htm> (accessed 29 June 2007).

Nuffield Foundation (2002), 'Nuffield Languages Team Responds to the 14–19 Green Paper', Nuffield Foundation <http://www.nuffieldfoundation.org/languages/news/nw0000000202.asp>(accessed 9 June 2002).

No. 10 Downing Street (1998), 'Speech by Prime Minister Tony Blair on education policy', 14 April 1998, No. 10 Downing Street <http://www.number–10.gov.uk/output/page1589.asp> (accessed 9 June 2002).

Unz, R.K. and G.M. Tuchman (1997), *English Language Education for Children in Public Schools (Proposition 227),* sec. 1, chp. 3, art. 2, 305, 3 July 1997, Onenation <http://www.onenation.org/fulltext/html> (accessed 9 September 1999).

Phillips, T. (2005), 'After 7/7: Sleepwalking to Segregation', Commission for Racial Equality (CRE), CRE <http://www.cre.gov.uk/Default.aspx?LocID=Ohgnew07s &RefLocID=0hg00900c002&Lang=EN&> (accessed 28 February 2007).

Populus (2006), 'Muslim 7/7 Poll', 4–5 July 2006, Populus <http://www.populuslimited.com/> (accessed 20 June 2007).

Refugee Council (2002), *Annual UK Asylum Statistics*, Refugee Council <http://www.refugeecouncil.org.uk/infocentre/stats/stats001.htm> (accessed 9 June 2002).

Social Research Association (SRA) (2002), 'SRA Ethical Guidelines 2002', SRA <http://www.the–sra.org.uk/index2.htm> (accessed 18 August 2002).

The Occidental Quarterly (2006), 'full text of Enoch Powell's famous speech to the Annual General Meeting of the West Midlands Area Conservative Political Centre, Birmingham, England, April 20, 1968', The Occidental Quarterly <http://theoccidentalquarterly.com/vol1no1/ep-rivers.html> (accessed 2 July 2007).

Index

Headings in italics indicate publications, legal cases or legislation. Numbers are filed as if spelled out.